ADVANCE READER'S COPY — UNCORRECTED PROOF

TEARS IN RAIN

TEARS IN RAIN

ROSA MONTERO

TRANSLATED BY LILIT ŽEKULIN THWAITES

Text copyright © 2011 by Rosa Montero
English translation copyright © 2012 by Lilit Žekulin Thwaites

Published by AmazonCrossing
P.O. Box 400818
Las Vegas, NV 89140

ISBN-13: 9781612184388
ISBN-10: 1612184383

In memory of Pablo Lizcano

Non ignoravi me mortalem genuisse.
[I have always known that I was mortal.]

—Marcus Tulius Cicero

Agg'ié nagné 'eggins anyg nein'yié.
[What I do shows me what I am seeking.]

—Sulagnés, artist from the planet Gnío

To every thing there is a season, and a time to every purpose
under the heaven:
A time to be born, and a time to die,
a time to plant and a time to pluck up that which is planted;
a time to kill and a time to heal,
a time to break down and a time to build up;
a time to weep and a time to laugh,
a time to mourn and a time to dance;
a time to cast away stones and a time to gather stones together,
a time to embrace and a time to refrain from embracing;
a time to get and a time to lose,
a time to keep and a time to cast away;
a time to rend and a time to sew,
a time to keep silence and a time to speak;
a time to love and a time to hate,
a time of war and a time of peace.

—Ecclesiastes 3: 1–8

CHAPTER ONE

B runa awoke with a start and remembered that she was
going to die.

But not right now.

A whiplash of pain shot between her temples. The apartment was in semidarkness and the afternoon light had faded
on the other side of the window. Dazed, she looked out over
the familiar urban landscape, the towers, the flat rooftops,
and the hundreds of windows over which shadows were
falling, as the pain inside her head continued to pound. It
took her a few moments to register that the thudding was
not just inside her skull. Someone was hammering on the
door. The clock showed 19:21. She caught her breath and sat
up with a grunt. Seated on the edge of the bed, her clothes
twisted and her bare feet on the ground, she waited a few
seconds while the liquid mess that was her brain stopped
sloshing around and stabilized. *Four years, three months, and
twenty-nine days*, she calculated rapidly. Even a hangover
couldn't prevent her from repeating the manic routine. If
there was anything that depressed her more than getting
drunk, it was doing so during the day. Alcohol seemed less
harmful, less despicable, at night. But starting to drink at
midday was pathetic.

The hammering at the door continued, chaotic, frenzied. Bruna tensed. It seemed more like an assault than an unexpected visitor. "Home, check the door," she whispered, and the face of the invader appeared on the main screen. A female intruder. It took her a few seconds to recognize the twisted and convulsed features, but that awful hair, dyed a shocking orange, was unmistakable. It was one of her neighbors, a replicant who lived in the east wing of the building. She'd barely exchanged a greeting with her in the last few months and didn't even know her name. Bruna was not particularly keen to have dealings with other reps. Although, if truth be told, she didn't mix much with humans either. *Stop and be done, damn it*, she moaned to herself, tortured by the noise. But the unbearable din forced her to get up and head for the door.

"What's up?" she mumbled.

The neighbor's fist stopped midblow and she jumped back, startled by Bruna's sudden appearance. She turned sideways, as if she were about to run off, and fixed Bruna with a distrustful look of her left eye—an opaque, yellowish eye split by the striking vertical pupil of the reps.

"You're Bruna Husky."

It didn't seem to be a question, but she answered anyway. "Yes."

"I have to speak to you about something very important."

Bruna looked her up and down. Her hair was tangled, her cheeks were smudged, and her clothes were dirty and wrinkled as if she'd been sleeping in them. Not unlike what Bruna herself had just been doing, to be fair.

"Is it a work-related matter?"

The question seemed to throw the woman off balance momentarily, but then she nodded her head in agreement and smiled. A half-smile, in profile.

"Yes. That's it. Work-related."

There was something disturbing, something not quite right, about this slovenly, trembling rep. Bruna weighed up the possibility of telling her to come back another day, but her hangover was killing her and she sensed that turning away a person so clearly full of nervous tension would prove much more difficult and tiring than listening to her. So she stepped back and let her in.

"Come in."

The android obeyed. She walked with short little hops, as if the floor were burning hot. Bruna shut the door and headed toward the kitchen area. She felt dehydrated and urgently in need of a drink.

"I've got purified water. Do you want a—?"

She didn't finish the sentence because she somehow sensed what was about to happen. She started to turn around, but it was already too late. A wire had been wrapped around her neck and was beginning to strangle her. She put her hands up to her throat where the wire was biting into her skin and tried to free herself, but the woman continued to tighten it more and more with an unexpected determination. Fatally attached to one another, assailant and victim moved around the room in a frenetic dance of violence, banging into walls and overturning chairs as the loop kept tightening and Bruna started to run out of oxygen. Until Bruna, desperately thrashing about, managed to sink an elbow into some sensitive part of her enemy's body, which caused the woman momentarily to relax her grip on her target. A second later, the woman was on the floor, and Bruna had immobilized her by falling on top of her. It was difficult to do, despite the fact that Bruna was a combat replicant, and hence bigger and more athletic than most. The neighbor seemed to possess an inhuman energy, the desperate strength of an animal.

"Cool it!" shouted Bruna, enraged.

And to her amazement, the woman obeyed and stopped writhing, as if she had been waiting for someone to tell her what she should do.

They eyed each other for a few seconds, gasping for air.

"Why did you do this to me?" asked Bruna.

"Why did *you* do this to *me*?" babbled the android.

There was a deluded and feverish look in her catlike eyes.

"What have you taken? You're high."

"You people drugged me; you've poisoned me," moaned the woman, and she started to cry with profound despair.

"*We* people? Who are *we*?"

"You…technohumans…reps. You kidnapped me; you infected me; you implanted your filthy things to turn me into one of you. Why have you done this to me? What had I ever done to you?"

Her moans had been increasing in volume and now she was shrieking like a woman possessed. *The neighbors are bound to complain again*, thought Bruna, irritated. She frowned with annoyance.

"What's behind all this idiocy? Are you mad, or just pretending to be? You're a replicant, too. Look in the mirror. Check out your eyes. You're a technohuman like me. And you've just tried to strangle me."

The woman had started to shake violently; she seemed to be suffering a panic attack.

"Don't hurt me! Please, don't hurt me! Help! Please!"

Her obvious terror was becoming unbearable. Bruna relaxed her hold a little.

"Calm down. I'm not going to do anything to you. See? I'm letting go. If you stay calm and still, I'll release you."

She let go of the woman little by little, as cautiously as she would a snake, and then jumped backward, beyond the reach of her hands. Whimpering, the android dragged herself away a foot or so and rested her back against the wall. Although the woman did seem to be somewhat calmer, Bruna regretted that she wasn't carrying her little plasma gun. It was hidden behind the stove, and to get it she would briefly have to take her eye off the android. It really was totally stupid to hide a weapon so well that there was no way of using it when it was needed. She glanced at the intruder, who was breathing with difficulty in the corner.

"What did you take? You're out of it."

"I'm a human…I'm a human and I have a son!"

"Sure. I'm going to call the police to come and get you. You tried to kill me."

"I'm a human!"

"What you are is a damned menace."

The android stared at Bruna in bewilderment. It was a wild and defiant stare.

"You people aren't going to succeed in confusing me. You won't trick me. I've exposed you. This is what I do with your wretched implants."

And with that, she twisted her head a little, sank her fingers quickly and violently into the socket of one of her eyes and gouged out the eyeball. There was a soft, squishy sound, a muffled gasp, a few trickles of blood. It was a moment of anguished, petrified madness. Then Bruna recovered her mobility and threw herself on the woman, who had collapsed in convulsions.

"By the great Morlay! What have you done, you wretched woman? A curse on all species! Emergency! Home, call Emergency!"

She was so stressed that the computer didn't recognize her voice. She had to take a deep breath, make a conscious effort to calm down and try again.

"Home, call Emergency. Call and be done with it, damn it!"

It was a high-speed connection, sound only. A male voice answered: "Emergency."

"A woman has just…A woman has just lost her eye."

"Insurance number, please."

Bruna pulled up the sleeves of her neighbor's dress and uncovered two bare, bony wrists. She wasn't wearing a mobile. She searched through the woman's pockets looking for her ID tag. She even checked around her neck in case she was wearing it on a chain, as many did. She didn't find a thing.

"I don't know. Can't we leave it till later? Her eye is on the floor. She's pulled it out."

"Most unfortunate, but if she's not insured and up to date with her payments, we can't do anything."

The man cut the connection. Bruna could feel something firing up inside her, a spasm of anger that she knew intimately and which functioned with the precision of a piece of machinery; in some hidden spot within her brain, the sluice gates of hatred opened and her veins flooded with its thick poison. *You're so full of fury that you end up cold as ice*, old Yiannis had once said to her. And it was true. The more irate she was, the more controlled she seemed—calmer and impassive, empty of emotions, save for that pure, sharp hatred that condensed in her chest like a black stone.

"Home, call Samaritans," she enunciated syllable by syllable.

"Samaritans at your service," replied a robotic voice immediately with its conventionally melodious voice. "Please forgive our delay in attending to you; we are the only civic association that offers health services to those who have no insurance. If you wish to make a financial contribution to our project, say *donations*. If this is a medical emergency, please hold the line."

The woman moaned softly in Bruna's arms, and the eye really was on the floor, round and much bigger than one could imagine, a greasy ball with a tuft of pale fibers, like a dead jellyfish or a sea polyp torn from its rock and thrown up on the beach by the tide.

"Samaritans at your service. Please forgive our delay in attending to you; we are..."

Bruna had seen worse things in her years in the military. Much worse. However, she found her neighbor's unexpected and ferocious action particularly disturbing. Pain and turmoil had erupted in her home in the middle of the afternoon.

"...say *donations*. If this is a medical emergency, please hold the line."

And that's what everyone did, wait and wait, because Samaritans couldn't cope with all the requests from the uninsured and was always overloaded. It was conceivable that the woman had insurance, but she was still unconscious or perhaps hopelessly deranged; either way, she wasn't responding to Bruna's shakes or calls, which in some ways was preferable, as her lack of consciousness was protecting her from the horror of what she had done. Maybe that was why she wasn't coming around. Bruna had seen it many times in the military: merciful loss of consciousness so as not to feel anything. Night had fallen, and the apartment was nearly dark, illuminated only by the glow of the city and the fleeting lights of the sky-trams.

"Home, lights."

The lamps obediently switched themselves on, wiping out the urban landscape on the other side of the window and adding a viscous, wet and bloody sheen to the eyeball on the floor. Bruna looked away from the extracted object, and her glance fell on the woman's face and the empty socket. A sinister hole. So in order to have something else to contemplate, she gazed at the main screen. She had the sound turned off, but the news was on and they were showing Myriam Chi, the leader of the RRM. They must have filmed her at a meeting, and she was speaking from the stage with her customary virulence. Bruna had no time for either Myriam or her Radical Replicant Movement. She had a deep mistrust of all political groups, and she was particularly repelled by the "we are victims" self-indulgence, the hysterical mythification of the rep identity. And where Myriam was concerned, Bruna knew her type well—people buried deep in their emotions like beetles in dung; junkies dependent on the most aggravating and deceitful sentimentality.

"Samaritans, how can I help you?"

Finally.

"There's been an incident in District Five, Dardenelles Avenue, apartment 2334. A woman has lost her eye. What I mean is, she's lost it completely; she plucked it out. The eyeball is on the floor."

"Victim's age?"

"Thirty."

All reps were around thirty. Between twenty-five and thirty, to be precise.

"Human or technohuman?"

Again the fury, again the rage.

"That question is anticonstitutional, as you well know."

There was a brief silence at the other end of the line. In any case, thought Bruna, her answer had already betrayed her.

"We'll be there as soon as we can," said the man. "Thank you for calling Samaritans."

Everyone knew that they prioritized humans, of course, a practice that wasn't legally acceptable, but it was what happened. And the worst bit, Bruna thought to herself, was that it made sense on one level. When a medical service was overloaded, maybe it was sensible to give priority to those who had a much longer life expectancy—to those who weren't condemned to a premature death, like the reps. Was it more beneficial to save a human who might still live another fifty years or a technohuman who might have only a few months to go? A cold, bitter taste of bile rose in her throat. She looked at the grotesquely incomplete face of her neighbor and felt a stab of resentment toward her. *Idiot, idiot, why have you done this? And why have you done it in my home?* Bruna had no idea what had motivated the woman, the reason for her strange behavior. She might be drugged, or perhaps unwell. But there was no doubting that the unfortunate, crazy woman hated herself—that much was clear—and hatred was an emotion that Bruna could well understand. Nothing better than cold hatred to combat burning anguish.

**Central Archive, the United States of the Earth.
Modifiable version**

ACCESS STRICTLY LIMITED
AUTHORIZED EDITORS ONLY

Madrid, January 14, 2109, 09:43
Good morning, Yiannis

IF YOU ARE NOT YIANNIS
LIBEROPOULOS,
CENTRAL ARCHIVIST FT711,
QUIT THESE PAGES IMMEDIATELY

ACCESS STRICTLY LIMITED
AUTHORIZED EDITORS ONLY

UNAUTHORIZED ACCESS IS A CRIMINAL
OFFENSE
PUNISHABLE BY IMPRISONMENT UP TO
A MAXIMUM OF TWENTY YEARS

Technohumans
Keywords: history, social conflict, Rep War, Moon Pact,
discrimination, biotechnology, civil movements, supremacism.
#376244
Entry being edited

Midway through the twenty-first century, projects connected with the geological exploitation of **Mars** and two of **Saturn**'s moons, **Titan** and **Enceladus**, led to the creation of an android that would be resistant to the harsh environmental conditions in the mining colonies. In 2053, the Brazilian bioengineering company **Vitae** used stem cells to generate an organism that was matured in a lab at an accelerated rate and was virtually identical to a human being. It was marketed under the name **Homolab** but quickly became known as a *replicant*, a term taken from a futuristic film very popular in the twentieth century.

Replicants were an instant success. They were used for mining exploration not only in outer space but also on Earth, as well as for deep-sea fish-farming. Specialist versions began to be developed, and by 2057 there were already four distinct types of androids available, for mining, computation, combat, and pleasure (this last specialization was banned years later). In those days it was inconceivable that Homolabs would have any control over their own lives. In reality, they were slave laborers with no rights. This abusive situation became less and less viable, and finally exploded in 2060 when a squad of combat replicants was sent to Enceladus to put down a revolt by miners who were also androids. The soldiers joined forces with the rebels and assassinated all the humans in the colony. The rebellion spread rapidly, giving rise to what became known as the **Rep War**.

Although the androids were at a clear disadvantage numerically, their endurance, strength, and intelligence were superior to those of the average human. During the sixteen months the war lasted, there were many losses, both human and technohuman. Fortunately, in ~~September~~ October 2061 **Gabriel**

Morlay, the famous android philosopher and social reformer, assumed leadership of the rebels and proposed a truce in order to negotiate peace with those countries that produced replicants. The difficult negotiations were on the point of failing countless times; among the humans there was a radical faction that rejected the granting of any concessions and advocated prolonging the war until such time as all the replicants started to die, given that in those days their life expectancy was only about five years. There were also humans, however, who condemned the use of slaves and defended the justice of the claims of the rebels. Referred to disparagingly by their adversaries as *replickers*, these android-supporting humans became very active in their pro-negotiation campaigns. This, together with the fact that the rebels had taken control of various production lines and were making more androids, finally resulted in the signing of the **Moon Pact** in February 2062, a peace agreement based on the concession of a series of rights to the insurgents. It should be noted that the android leader, Morlay, was unable to sign the treaty, which had been his great work, because just a few days beforehand he completed his life cycle and died; ~~thus ending his fleeting existence as a human butterfly~~.

As of that moment, civil rights were progressively won by the reps. These advances were not devoid of problems. The first years after the **Unification** were particularly fraught with conflict, and there were serious disturbances in various cities on Earth (Dublin, Chicago, Nairobi), with violent confrontations between **antisegregationist** pro-rep movements and human **supremacist** groups. Finally, the **Constitution of 2098**, the first Magna Carta of the **United States of the Earth** (**USE**) and still in force, recognized the same rights for technohumans as for humans.

It was also in this same constitution that the term *technohuman* was used for the first time, as the word *replicant* is loaded with insulting and offensive connotations. These days, *technohuman* (or *techno*, as it is used colloquially) is the sole official and acceptable term, although in this article the word *replicant* has also been used to ensure historical clarity. There are, however, groups of techno activists, such as the **Radical Replicant Movement** (RRM), who reclaim the ancient designation as a banner of their own identity: "I'm proud to be a rep. I'd rather be a rep than a human, never mind a technohuman" (**Myriam Chi**, leader of the RRM).

The existence and integration of technohumans has generated a fierce ethical and social debate that is far from being resolved. There are some who maintain that, since the original creation of replicants as slave labor was an erroneous and immoral act, their production should simply cease. This possibility is rejected outright by the technos, who view it as genocide: "What has once existed cannot return to the limbo of nonexistence. What has been invented cannot be uninvented. What we have learned cannot cease to be known. We are a new species, and like all living beings, we yearn to continue living" (Morlay). Currently, the management of the android production lines (these days referred to as *gestation plants*) is split fifty-fifty between technos and humans. An android takes fourteen months to be born, but once born it has the physical and mental development of a twenty-five-year-old. Despite technological advances, a life span of a decade is still all that has been achieved: at approximately the age of thirty-five, the cellular division of replicants' tissue accelerates dramatically and they undergo something like a massive carcinogenic process (known as **TTT, Total Techno**

Tumor), for which a cure has yet to be found, and which leads to their death within a few weeks.

Also controversial are the regulations specific to technohumans, especially those dealing with memory and with the period of time dedicated to civic work. A committee consisting of an equal number of humans and technos determines how many androids will be created each year, and with which specifications: computation, combat, exploration, mining, administration, or construction. As the gestation of these individuals is very costly, it has been agreed that all technohumans serve whichever company made them for a maximum period of two years, in work consistent with the area of specialization for which they were created. Thereafter they are granted a license, together with a moderate amount of money (the **settlement allowance**), to help them to set up their own lives. Finally, all androids are implanted with a complete memory set, together with sufficient actual documentary support (photos, holographs, and recordings of their imaginary past; old toys from their supposed childhood, etc.), since various scientific investigations have demonstrated that humans and technohumans coexist and integrate socially far better if the latter have a past, and that androids are more stable if they are furnished with mementos. The **Law of Artificial Memory** of 2101, currently in force, thoroughly regulates this sensitive area. Memories are unique and varied, but they all contain more or less the same version of the famous **Revelation Scene**, popularly known as the dance of the phantoms. This is an implanted memory of an event that supposedly took place when the individual androids were about fourteen years old, when their parents told them that they were technohumans and that they themselves lacked reality and were pure shadows, empty images, a firing of neurons. Once the memory has been installed, there can be no modification of any sort. The law prohibits and prosecutes vigorously any subsequent manipulation of, or illegal trafficking in, memories, a fact that neither stops the aforementioned trafficking nor prevents a lucrative underground market in memories. The existing regulations governing the lives of technos have been contested by diverse sectors, and both the RRM and various supremacist groups have several appeals lodged against the law. In the past decade, numerous university chairs in technohuman studies have been created (such as the one at the Complutense in Madrid) in an attempt to address the multiple ethical and social questions posed by this new species.

CHAPTER TWO

There was a time when sexual relations between humans and reps had been forbidden. Now they were simply frowned upon—except, of course, when it came to the ancient and venerable practice of prostitution. Pablo Nopal smiled sourly and contemplated the bare back of the girl warrior. A straight line of elastic skin, the perfect curve of the slim hip. Sitting up in bed, as he had just done, Nopal could also see one of her tiny breasts, which was gently rising and falling in time with her quiet breathing. Despite seeming to be asleep—and she surely was—she would leap up and, for all he knew, land him a forceful blow if he so much as brushed her waist with his finger. Nopal had slept with enough combat reps to be well aware of their habits and their disturbing defensive reflexes. It was safer not to kiss one on the neck in the middle of the night.

Indeed, the best thing to do in the middle of the night after having sex with such a girl was to leave.

The man slid out of the bed, picked up his clothes, which were scattered across the floor, and began to get dressed.

He was in a bad mood.

The hour when dawn was breaking, dirty and faded, with the night dying and the new day not yet arrived, always depressed him. That naked hour when there was no way to disguise the nonsensical nature of the world.

Nopal was rich and he was miserable. Misery was a basic component of his being, as cartilage is to bones. Misery was the cartilage of his mind. It was something he couldn't get rid of.

As an old writer whom he admired used to say, *Happiness is the same for everyone, but unhappiness is different for each person.* Nopal's misery manifested itself in a clear incapacity for life. He hated life. This was one of the reasons why he liked androids: they were all so eager, so desperate to keep living. He envied them, in a sense.

The only thing that had kept Nopal going in recent years—the only thing that really warmed his heart—was his search. Now, he tapped his mobile computer, brought up the list of androids onto the screen, and deleted the warrior girl with the thick, curly hair with whom he had just had sex. Obviously she was not the technohuman he was looking for. He gazed almost with affection at her flat profile. It had been an effort to gain her confidence, but now he hoped never to have to see her again. As was his habit, his basic misanthropy had triumphed again.

CHAPTER THREE

*T*he advantage of dealing with dead reps, thought Bruna as she entered the Forensic Anatomy Institute, *was that you didn't have to put up with tearful relatives: parents shattered by grief; off-spring stunned at suddenly becoming orphans; partners, siblings, and other whimpering family members.* Androids were solitary beings, islands inhabited by a single castaway in the midst of a motley sea of people. Or at least almost all reps were like that, although there were some who insisted in believing that they were fully human, and established stable, sentimental relationships despite death lurking at their heels, and who even managed to adopt a child—always a sick child or one with some problem—because the early use-by date of replicants prevented them from garnering the points necessary for a normal adoption. As for Bruna's own story, it had in fact been a mistake. Neither she nor Merlín had wanted to become a couple, but in the end they became trapped by their emotions. Until the inevitable heartbreak occurred. *Four years, three months, and twenty-seven days.*

It was three in the morning and the institute was deserted and ghostly, immersed in a bluish half-light. She had come at such a late hour with the intention of meeting up with Gándara, the veteran medical examiner who worked the night shift and was an old friend who owed her a few favors. But when she entered the office next door to Dissection Room 1, she found a young man with his eyes glued to a pornographic hologram. When he became aware of her presence, the guy switched off the scene with a flick of his hand and turned toward her.

"What...are you doing here?"

Bruna noted the hesitation, the start, the sudden suspicion in his eyes. She was used to her appearance making an impression, not just because she was a tall and athletic techno, but more than anything because of her shaved head and her tattoo—a fine black line that encircled her entire body vertically, running down the left side from her forehead, through the middle of her eyebrow, eyelid, and cheek, on to her neck, breast, stomach, and belly, her left leg, one of her toes, the sole of her foot and her heel, and then running up the back of the same leg, her buttock, waist, back, and the nape of her neck, completing the circle by traversing the shaved roundness of her head until it met up again with the descending line. Obviously, when she was dressed, you couldn't see that the tattoo formed a complete circle, but Bruna had verified that the line, which appeared to cut across a third of her head and then disappear down inside her clothes, had an undeniable impact on humans. Moreover, it showed that she was a combat rep: almost everyone in the military had elaborate tattoos.

"Gándara's not in?"

"He's on vacation."

The man seemed to relax a little when he saw that Bruna knew the chief medical examiner. He was a short, pudgy young man who had one of those standard, cheap plastic-surgery faces, a model picked from a catalog, the typical graduation present from parents with a modest income. It had suddenly become fashionable to have face jobs done, and there were half a dozen models that were repeated ad nauseam on thousands of people.

"Fine. Then I'll talk with you. I'm interested in one of the bodies. Cata Caín. She's a technohuman, and she's missing an eye. She died yesterday."

"Oh, yes. I did the autopsy a few hours ago. Was she a family member?"

Bruna looked at him for half a second, impassively. A rep related to another rep? This guy was an imbecile.

"No," she said eventually.

"Well, if she's not family and you don't have a court order, then you can't see her."

"I don't need to. I only wanted you to give me the results of the autopsy."

An exaggerated look of outrage appeared on his surgically modified face.

"That's even less likely! It's highly confidential information. Moreover, if you're not a family member, how were you able to get in here?"

Bruna took a deep breath and made an effort to appear friendly and reassuring—as friendly and reassuring as was possible given her shaved head, catlike pupils, and the tattooed line splitting her face. She felt it would be imprudent to reveal that old Gándara had provided her with a permanent entry pass to the institute, so she took out her private detective's ID and showed it to the guy.

"Look, the woman was my neighbor…and my client. She'd hired me to protect her because she suspected that someone wanted to kill her." Bruna was improvising on the spot. "I can't tell you any more, as I'm sure you'll understand; it's a matter of professional confidentiality. I was the one who contacted

Samaritans; she was with me when she yanked out her eye. If you've got the police report at hand, you'll see my name there, Husky. Caín went berserk, and I'm afraid she may have poisoned herself somehow. What I mean is, I'm afraid she may have been poisoned. I need to know as soon as possible. You see, I shouldn't be telling you this, but there might be more people who have been poisoned...and we might still be in time to save them. I'm not even asking you for the details; just give me the conclusions and we're done. Nobody will find out."

The doctor shook his head slowly and pompously. It was clear that he was making the most of his small degree of authority in order to be annoying.

Bruna furrowed her brow pensively. Then she hunted through her backpack and pulled out two one-hundred-gaia bills.

"Of course I'm more than happy to compensate you for your trouble."

"What do you take me for? I don't need your money."

"Take it. It will be helpful when you get your broken nose fixed."

The man touched his nasal appendage with a reflex reaction. He lovingly caressed the silicon nostrils, the bridge shaped by plastic cartilage. His emotions revealed themselves one by one in a clear succession on his face, like clouds scudding across a windy sky: first, relief upon realizing that his synthetic nose was still intact, then the gradual and overwhelming comprehension of the significance of her words. His eyes opened wide with concern.

"Is...is that a threat?"

Bruna leaned forward, placed her hands on the table, advanced her face toward that of the man until she was almost touching his forehead, and smiled.

"Of course not."

The medical examiner swallowed and mulled things over for a few moments. Then he turned toward the screen and muttered: "Open final reports, open Caín."

The computer obeyed and the screen began to fill with successive images of the one-eyed rep, an unfortunate naked, disemboweled corpse in various stages of dissection. In the last one, the laser scalpel cut the cranium as if it were slicing an orange in two, and a pair of robot tweezers delicately probed the gray matter, which was in fact quite pink. Bruna had never seen such a pink brain, and she had seen quite a few. The tweezers emerged from the greasy neuronal mass clutching a small item between the pincers: a tiny blue disc. *An artificial memory*, thought Bruna with a shiver, *and I'm sure it's not the original implant*. On the screen the voice of the medical examiner was running through the results: 'Given that the technohuman subject was 3/28 years old and still some time off her TTT, we can rule out a natural death. On the other hand, the memory implant that was found lacks a registration number and undoubtedly comes from the black market. This medical examiner is working on the hypothesis that the aforementioned implant was tampered with and caused the edemas and cerebral hemorrhages, provoking symptoms of emotional instability, delusions, convulsions, loss of consciousness, paralysis, and ultimately the death of the subject due to the complete breakdown of all neuronal functions. The implant has been sent to the bioengineering lab of the Judicial Police for analysis.'

Poor Caín. It was as if Bruna were again seeing her neighbor gouging out her eye with that horrible squishy sound like a suction cup being removed. As if she were hearing again her deluded words and experiencing her anguish. By the time the Samaritans arrived, Caín was already rigid, which was why Bruna wasn't surprised when they called her four hours later to tell her that Caín was dead. In the interim, Bruna had stopped by the caretaker's office and then gone into the woman's apartment with one of the janitors. That's how she found out that the woman's name was Cata Caín, that she was a clerk, and that this apartment was her first domicile after receiving the settlement allowance, since she was only three rep years—or twenty-eight virtual ones—old. Too young to die. According to the rental contract, she had been in the apartment eleven months, but the place looked empty and impersonal, as if no one was living there. Indeed, not one of those all-too-common, small, artificial mementos was to be seen: the customary photo of the parents; the childhood hologram; the grubby little candle from an old cake; the electronic poster with the dedications from university friends; the ring adolescents bought for themselves when they lost their virginity. There wasn't a replicant alive who didn't have such a collection of rubbishy trinkets; even though the reps knew that the objects were false, they continued to hold a sort of magic, to offer solace and companionship. Just as paraplegics dreamed about walking when they put on virtual eyeglasses, so reps dreamed about having roots when they looked at the artificially aged pieces in their glory box. And in both cases, despite knowing the truth, they were happy. Or less *unhappy*. Even Bruna herself, so resistant to emotional outbursts, had been incapable of ridding herself of all her prefabricated mementos. Yes, she had destroyed the family photos and the hologram of her grandmother's birthday party (she was turning 101, and she died a short time later; that is, she had supposedly died), but she couldn't throw out the collar belonging to her childhood dog Zarco, with the animal's name engraved on it, nor a photo of herself taken when she was about five years old—already perfectly recognizable, and with the same tired, sad eyes as she had now.

But Caín had not one single personal item in her apartment. What a profound level of despair and desolation she must have reached! Bruna pictured her walking through the night with an addict's anxiety, prying into the darkest corners of the city in search of relief, of a memory she could believe in, mementos that would allow her to rest for a time. She thought she could understand Caín, because she herself had felt like that often enough; she, too, had abandoned her home on occasion, as if to escape. She had burned up the night searching for the impossible. And on more than one occasion, as dawn was breaking, she had been tempted to inhale a shot of memory, a fake fix of artificial life. She hadn't done it, and she was glad that was the case. Cata Caín had exploded her brain with a dose of fictitious memories. Perhaps a batch of adulterated memories had arrived in the city. It had happened before, though never with such a lethal outcome. If that were the case, there would be more rep deaths over the next few days. But that wasn't Bruna's problem. The only thing she was after was to find out what had happened to her neighbor, and that had now been resolved.

She turned to look at the young medical examiner. He was sweating and very upset, probably because of the emotional conflict arising from being forced to obey someone out of fear—a situation that, in young men in particular, usually provoked a burst of repressed anger and humiliation, a hormonal jumble of testosterone and adrenalin. Right now he hated himself for having been a coward, and that would prevent him from reporting her. Anyway, what could he report? She hadn't done anything to him. Bruna shoved the two bills across the table and smiled.

"Thanks a lot; you're very kind. That's all I wanted to know. Give my regards to Gándara."

The doctor's flushed face accentuated the off-white color of the silicone implants. Bruna almost felt a twinge of compassion for him, a momentary weakness that was immediately overcome. She would never have broken his nose, of course, but the poor guy didn't need to know that. That was one of the few advantages of being different: she was despised because of it, but she was feared as well.

CHAPTER FOUR

Three days later, another rep died in similar circumstances, which were further complicated by the fact that he took two other technos with him. The assault took place on a sky-tram, so the incident was filmed by the transport company's security cameras. Bruna saw the video on the news. He was an exploration android, with a small, bony physique, but he easily overpowered the two more heavily built technos. The assailant was sitting in the rear of the tram; suddenly, he got up and walked quickly toward the front, grabbing the first rep by the hair. He pulled the head backward with one hand as he slit the throat cleanly with the other. The weapon he used had such a fine, narrow blade that it was almost invisible. So the effect is disconcerting, incomprehensible rather than violent: a stream of blood is suddenly spurting, and you can't understand why. The victim's body was still sitting upright in the seat, and the passengers next to him were still opening their mouths to scream when the murderer grabbed a woman on the other side of the aisle in the same manner and slit her throat, too. After which the little techno drove the point of the knife into one of his own eyes and collapsed.

The whole scene lasted barely a minute; it was an astonishingly rapid massacre, a spectacular slaughter, so much blood in so little time. *It's very hard to cut a throat with such speed and dexterity*, thought Bruna. Flesh is surprisingly tough, the muscles tense, the windpipe presents a tenacious obstacle. And yet, the two necks had almost been severed and the heads tipped backward grotesquely, displaying the obscene smile of the enormous cut. It wasn't easy to do, not even with a surgeon's scalpel; maybe with a laser knife, but the blade used seemed to be a normal blade. Her next thought was, *He wouldn't have been able to grab me by my hair*. That was why so many combat reps shaved their heads—they didn't want to give the enemy any advantage. The difference was that, unlike other combat reps, Bruna had continued to shave her head after she'd been granted her license from the military. After all, she was still doing risky work. Work that wasn't paying enough.

She had finished her last job almost two weeks earlier and had few savings to draw on. The USE had been in permanent financial crisis since Unification, but in recent times there seemed to be a crisis within the crisis and business everywhere was at a standstill. She desperately needed to find a client, so she decided to head out and do what she called an "information patrol": do a few circuits and try to catch up with her regulars, to find out what was going on out there and see if she could offer her services to anyone. She looked at her watch: 23:10. She could stop by Oli Oliar's joint and grab a bite to eat on her way through. Despite the frenzy of blood and killing, she was hungry. Or maybe she was hungry precisely for that reason. Nothing whet the appetite more than the sight of other people dying. *Four years, three months, and twenty-four days.*

It was January, the chilliest month of the short, mild winter, and it was a perfect night for walking. Using travelators in some stretches, Bruna took twenty minutes to get to Oli's bar.

It was a small, rectangular space, occupied almost entirely by the huge counter, which in turn was almost fully occupied by Oli's massive bulk. Because of her vast body and her equally enormous hospitality, Oli never turned up her nose at anyone: techno, alien—usually referred to as a *bicho*—or mutant. It was for this reason that her clientele was varied.

"Hi Husky, what brings you to this neck of the woods?"

"Hunger, Oli. Give me a beer and one of those algae and pine nut sandwiches you do so well."

The woman smiled at the compliment with the placidity of a whale and began preparing the order. Her movements were always astonishingly slow, but she organized things in such a way that she served all the customers efficiently on her own. Of course, it was a small space, with ten stools along the counter and another eight flush against the opposite wall, together with a small shelf for leaning on, which ran the length of the end wall, but the place was a hit, and at peak times up to thirty customers would squeeze themselves in. Now, however, it was half-empty. Bruna looked around; there was only one person she recognized, and she was seated at the other end of the counter. She was a billboard-lady for Texaco-Repsol and was wearing a horrible uniform in the corporate colors, crowned by a silly little hat. The screens on her chest and back played the company's damned commercials on a perpetual loop. Normally, because they were so irritating, billboard-people weren't allowed into bars, but Oli's heart was as big as her enormous breasts, so she allowed these walking electronic ads to hang out in the back of the bar as long as they turned the volume of the commercials down as low as possible. Which, unfortunately, wasn't usually all that low, as you couldn't mute the screens or turn them off. You either had to be a poor wretch or very unlucky in life to end up in that line of work: billboard-people were only allowed to take off their outfits for nine hours a day; the rest of the time they had to walk around public places, which meant that since they weren't allowed into most establishments, they would spend their day wandering the streets like lost souls, with the publicity slogans blaring in their ears nonstop. In return for such torture they were paid a scant few hundred gaias, although in this case, being Texaco-Repsol, the woman would undoubtedly get free air as well. And that was important, because each day there were more and more people unable to pay the cost of breathable air who would then have to move to one of the planet's contaminated zones. If truth be told, many would kill to have such a lousy job. Bruna remembered her meager bank account and turned to the owner of the bar.

"What's new?"

"Nothing. Apart from the rep deaths."

Another thing Bruna liked about fat Oli was that she wasn't given to prudish euphemisms. She always called reps, reps, but she was always much more friendly and respectful than those who never stopped talking about technohumans.

"And what are they saying about that, Oli? About the guy on the tram, I mean. Why do you think he did what he did?"

"They say he was on something. A drug. Dalamina, maybe. Or an artificial memory."

"There was a similar case last week, do you remember? The techno who yanked out her eye. And I know she had a memory implant."

Oli put a sandwich down in front of Bruna, then she leaned forward, her abundant breasts spilling over the counter, and lowered her voice.

"People are scared. I've heard there could be many more deaths."

"What's happening? Has there been a shipment of adulterated mems?"

"I have no idea. But they say this is just the beginning."

Bruna shivered. It was an unpleasant topic, something she found particularly unsettling. Not only because she still hadn't managed to rid herself of the alarming incident with her neighbor, but also because she had always found anything to do with memories repugnant. Talking about memories with a rep was like mentioning something dark and dirty, something unspeakable that, in the light of day, seemed almost pornographic.

"Do you know who's handing out the defective goods?" she asked, intrigued despite herself.

Oli shrugged her shoulders.

"No idea, Husky. Does it interest you? Maybe I could ask around."

Bruna thought about it for a moment. She didn't even have a client who might pay her bills, so she couldn't afford to waste time digging into something that wouldn't bring her any return.

"No, it doesn't really interest me at all."

"Well then, eat your sandwich. It's getting cold."

It was true. The sandwich tasted delicious, the algae perfectly fried and crunchy, not at all greasy. Merlín had loved algae and pine nut sandwiches. His face, a face distorted by illness, floated into her memory for an instant, and Bruna felt her stomach churn. She took a deep breath, trying to untie the knot in her gut and push her memories of Merlín down into the abyss again. If she could at least remember him happy and healthy rather than always trapped in pain. She bit angrily into her sandwich and returned to the problem of her lack of work. She decided to put her cards on the table.

"Oli, I'm out of work," she mumbled, her mouth full. "Have you heard of anything that might suit me?"

"Like what?"

"Well, you know, someone who wants to find something—or someone. Or vice versa. Someone who doesn't want to be found, or someone who wants to find out something, or who wants me to check out someone. Or someone who wants to put together evidence against someone, or wants to find out if there's any evidence against him."

Oli had interrupted her slow, majestic ministrations behind the counter and was looking fixedly at Bruna, her dark face impassive.

"If that's your line of work, it's a bloody mess."

Bruna smiled halfheartedly. She didn't smile too often, but she found fat Oli amusing.

"Messy or not, if you find me a client, I'll give you a commission."

"You don't say, Bruna," she heard from behind her. "It just so happens I have a job for you. And you don't have to pay me anything."

The android turned around to face the recent arrival. It was Yiannis. As almost always seemed to be the case where he was concerned, Bruna felt torn. Yiannis was the only friend she had, and she sometimes found the emotional weight somewhat asphyxiating.

"Hi, Yiannis, how's it going?"

"Old and tired."

He really meant it, and he looked it, too: old like before; old like always; old like the self-portraits of the elderly Rembrandt that Yiannis had taught her to appreciate in the marvelous holographs in the Museum of Art. There were not many people who, like Yiannis, entirely dispensed with the countless treatments for old age on the market, from plastic or bionic surgery, to gamma rays and cellular therapy. Some refused treatment out of sheer resistance to change because they were recalcitrant retrogrades, nostalgic for a golden age that had never existed. For the majority of those who didn't use these therapies, it was because they couldn't afford them. Given that people typically opted to pay for treatment rather than for clean air, having wrinkles had become a clear indication of extreme poverty. Yiannis's situation was somewhat different, however. He was neither poor nor a reactionary, although he might seem to be a somewhat old-fashioned and anachronistic gentleman in the twenty-second century. If he didn't make use of rejuvenating therapy, it was mainly for aesthetic reasons: he didn't like the havoc wreaked by old age, but he considered artificial alterations even worse, and Bruna understood him perfectly. She would have given anything to be able to age.

"You said you've got something for me?"

"Could be, but I'm not sure you deserve it."

Bruna furrowed her brow and looked at him, surprised.

"I don't know what you're talking about."

"Don't you have something to tell me?"

The rep felt little wheels of ill-humor—serrated cogs of irritation—starting to grind inside her. Yiannis always did the same thing to her: he interrogated and goaded her; he wanted to know everything about her. He was like her father. The nonexistent father whom a nonexistent murderer had killed when she was nine years old. Nine equally nonexistent years. She looked at her friend. He had a gentle face with indeterminate features. He had been quite handsome in his youth—Bruna had seen images of him—but not an overtly good-looking man, with small eyes, a small nose, and a small mouth. Time had left him looking as if someone had melted his face, and his white hair, pale skin, and gray eyes had fused into a faded monochrome. *Poor old man*, thought Bruna, noticing that her annoyance was dissipating. But in any case, there was no way she was going to tell him anything.

"Nothing in particular that I can recall."

"You don't say. You've already forgotten about Cata Caín?"

Bruna froze.

"How do you know about that? I haven't told a soul."

And as she was speaking, she thought, *But I gave my details to Samaritans, and I spoke to the police and with the caretaker of the building, and I had to identify myself to get into the Forensic Anatomy Institute; and we live in a damn society of gossips, with instantaneous and centralized information.* She began to sweat.

"Don't tell me I made it onto the news or the public screens."

The corners of Yiannis's mouth turned down. Bruna knew that that was his way of smiling.

"No, no. Someone who came looking for my help told me. Someone who has asked me to speak to you. She has work to offer you. I'll pass along her details."

Yiannis touched the mobile computer on his wrist, and Bruna's mobile computer beeped as it received the message. The android looked at the small screen: Myriam Chi, the leader of the RRM, was expecting Bruna in her office tomorrow morning at ten o'clock.

CHAPTER FIVE

Courage is a habit of the soul, Cicero used to say. Yiannis had grabbed hold of that thought by his favorite author like a person clutching at a dried branch when he's on the point of falling over a precipice. He had spent years trying to develop and maintain that habit and, in a way, that routine of courage had been hardening within him, forming a type of alternative skeleton that had managed to keep him upright.

Forty-nine years had passed. Almost half a century since the death of little Edú, and he was still carrying the scars. Of course, time had dimmed—or rather dulled—the unbearable intensity of his grief. That was normal; it would have been impossible to live constantly in that paroxysm of suffering. Yiannis understood this and forgave himself. He forgave himself for continuing to breathe, for continuing to enjoy food, music, or a good book while his son was turning to dust under the earth. Yet he sensed that in some way, a part of him was still in mourning. It was as if the disappearance of Edú had created a hole in his heart, so that he had only half-experienced everything since then. He could never totally concentrate on his reality because the pain buzzed nonstop in the background, like one of those maddening ringing sounds that some deaf people hear. Something inside him was definitely broken, and that seemed right to Yiannis. He found it necessary, because he would have been unable to bear his life continuing as usual after the death of his son.

Over time, however, something terrible had happened; something that Yiannis refused to believe could happen. First, his child's face began to fade in his memory; by resorting to that memory so much, he had worn it out. Now, he could only visualize Edú as he was in the photos and films he had kept of him; all the other images had been erased from his mind as if they had been wiped clean from a blackboard. The worst thing was that at some stage during the course of those forty-nine years, the internal thread that linked him with the father he had been had broken. When the old Yiannis of today remembered the young Yiannis, aged twenty, playing and laughing with his child, it was as if he were recalling an acquaintance from that long-distant era of his youth—a close friend perhaps but definitely someone else, and someone whom he had last seen a long time ago. The result was that he saw all those events from the outside: the pleasures of fatherhood and the horror of the unnecessary death; the slow death agony of the two-year-old child; the stupid illness that could not be treated because of shortages arising from the Rep War. It was a very sad story indeed, so tragic that he sometimes became teary when he recalled it. However, it was a story that he was no longer able to feel belonged to him; rather, it was a drama he had maybe once witnessed, or something someone had once told him.

And it was that remoteness that was so devastating, so unbearable.

The inner remoteness was the second, and definitive, death of his son. Because if *he* couldn't keep his little Edú alive in his memory, who else would?

How weak, how untruthful and unfaithful was human memory. Yiannis knew that during those forty-nine years that had gone by, each and every cell in his body had renewed itself. Not a single original organic particle remained of the Yiannis he had once been, nothing save that transcellular and transtemporal current of air that was his memory, that spiritual thread woven by his identity. But if that thread, too, were broken, if it were unable to remember itself continuously in time, how did his past differ from a dream? To stop remembering was to destroy his world.

It was for that reason—because he always felt that dizzy lack of trust in memory—that Yiannis decided to become a professional archivist. And for that same reason, from time to time he would really try to remember Edú from within. He would close his eyes and, with an enormous effort, endeavor to re-create some distant scene. Visualize again the old room, the outline of the furniture, the precise density of the shadow; feel the heat of the afternoon, the stillness of the air right against his skin; hear the silence barely broken by a calm, diminutive breath; smell the odor—so warm and so carnal—of that delightful little creature. Then and only then would he see again the child sleeping in his cot, and not even the whole child but maybe a reconstruction of his chubby little hand in all its purity and veracity, still baby soft; that perfect hand with its fingers curled, abandoned in repose and ignorant of its total vulnerability. With any luck, having reached this point, the memory would emerge from the past like a flash of light that pierced Yiannis, suddenly activating the suffering in all its intensity and making the old man cry. Cry from pain but also from gratitude, because somehow, and for just a moment, he had managed not simply to recall Edú, but to sense again that Edú had once been alive.

**Central Archive, the United States of the Earth.
Modifiable version**

ACCESS STRICTLY LIMITED
AUTHORIZED EDITORS ONLY

Madrid, January 19, 2109, 13:10
Good afternoon, Yiannis

IF YOU ARE NOT YIANNIS
LIBEROPOULOS,
CENTRAL ARCHIVIST FT711, QUIT
THESE PAGES IMMEDIATELY

ACCESS STRICTLY LIMITED
AUTHORIZED EDITORS ONLY

UNAUTHORIZED ACCESS IS A CRIMINAL
OFFENSE
PUNISHABLE BY IMPRISONMENT UP TO
A MAXIMUM OF TWENTY YEARS

Teleportation
Keywords: history of science, TP disorder, Cosmos Fever,
Robot Wars, Day One, Other Beings, Human Peace, Global
Agreements of Cassiopeia, sentient beings.
#422-222
Entry being edited

Teleportation or teletransportation (TP) is one of human-kind's oldest dreams. Although quantum teleportation had been attempted in the twentieth century, the first significant experiment took place in 2006, when Professor **Eugene Polzik,** of the Niels Bohr Institute at the University of Copenhagen, succeeded in teleporting a tiny, but macroscopic, object a distance of eighteen inches using light as the means of transmission of information about the object. It was not until 2067, however, with the discovery of the unsuspected light-boosting attributes of **astatine**—an extremely rare element on Earth but relatively abundant in the mines on Titan—that teleportation took a giant leap forward. In 2073, thanks to so-called **dense light**, capable of transporting 100,000 times more information in a manner that is 100,000 times more stable than **laser light**, Professor **Darling Oumou Koité** was teleported—or TP'd, as they say today—from Bamako (Mali) to Saturn's moon, Enceladus. It was the first time that a human had been TP'd across outer space.

As of that moment a genuine frenzy of exploration and conquest of the universe by the nations of Earth was unleashed. Given that teleportation eliminated distances and traveling a mile was thus no different from traveling a million miles, Earth's governing bodies became locked in a race to colonize remote planets and exploit their resources. This was referred to as **Cosmos Fever** and became one of the principal triggers for the **Robot Wars**, which devastated Earth from 2079 to 2090. Teleportation was always prohibitively expensive, and for this reason it was general practice to TP exploration teams of no more than two or three people. Given that credible information was available for scarcely a few hundred planets with colonizing potential, it was not unknown for envoys from various countries to coincide at a particular target, either by chance or as a result of espionage, often resulting in violence. Numerous explorers died in combat or were assassinated, and the ongoing recurrence of diplomatic incidents heightened tensions worldwide. As the better-known destinations were seized or converted into bitterly disputed territories, the powers of Earth began to take more and more risks and to send their explorers to ever more remote and obscure places, which increased exponentially the already high loss of life among those being teleported. In 2080, the last year of Cosmos Fever, 98 percent of the explorers from Earth died (about 8,200 individuals, almost all of them technohumans). The majority of them simply disappeared during the transfer, ~~perhaps disintegrating through error in deep intergalactic space, perhaps instantly volatilized while being TP'd to an unexpectedly fiery planet~~.

By that stage, something that the scientists and governments had known since the earliest days of this technology had become public knowledge: teletransportation is an atomically imperfect process that can have grave side effects. This is a consequence of the **Heisenberg Uncertainty Principle**, according to which not all the characteristics of a particle can be measured accurately. The very act of teleportation subjects particles to infinitesimal but essential changes. This means that any teleported organism experiences microscopic alterations; thus, what is reconstructed at its destination is not exactly the same as the original subject. Normally these alterations are minimal, subatomic, and imperceptible, but in a significant number of cases, the changes are important and dangerous: eyes moved to cheeks, defective lungs, hands without fingers, and even skulls lacking brains. This destructive effect of teleportation is referred to as **TP disorder**, and those individuals afflicted by visible deformities are colloquially known as

mutants. It has, moreover, been established that repeated instances of teletransportation inevitably lead to organic harm. The likelihood of suffering a serious TP disorder increases exponentially with each transfer, reaching 100 percent as of the eleventh TP. The **Global Agreements of Cassiopeia** (2096) are currently in force, and these restrict to six the number of times living things (humans, technohumans, **Other Beings**, and animals) can be TP'd during their life span.

The risks involved in transfers, the deaths and numerous disappearances of explorers, the prohibitive costs, and the beginning of the Robot Wars all combined to put an end to Cosmos Fever and to the enthusiasm for teleportation. As of 2081, TP was used solely to support the exploitation of the distant planet Potosí, the only heavenly body beyond the solar system discovered during Cosmos Fever whose resources proved sufficiently profitable to develop a mining industry. In the early years, ownership of Potosí was shared by the European Union, China, and the American Federation. Post-Unification, it belongs to the United States of the Earth, although the most productive mines have been sold to the **Kingdom of Labari** and the **Democratic State of Cosmos**.

The first documented encounter between human beings from Earth and Other Beings, or ETBs (extraterrestrial beings), took place on May 3, 2090, a date thereafter known as **Day One**. On that day an alien spaceship landed on the Chinese sector of the mining colony of Potosí. Inside it were **Gnés** explorers, a people from the planet **Gnío**, close to Potosí; both planets circle the star Fomalhaut. Their ship was very fast and very advanced, technically, although their displacement method was conventional and they traveled at well below the speed of light. They knew nothing of physical teleportation but had developed an ultrasonic means of communication supported by light beams, and capable of reaching phenomenal distances in record time. Thanks to such messages, or **telegnés**, the Gnés had established nonvisual contact with two other remote extraterrestrial civilizations, the **Omaás** and the **Balabís**. We humans had ceased to be alone in the universe.

The impact of such a remarkable discovery was absolute. Three days later **Human Peace** was signed, thereby ending the Robot Wars. Though the accord was undoubtedly deemed to have been driven by the fear the extraterrestrials inspired in the inhabitants of our planet ~~(the very name—Human Peace—almost suggests a desire to highlight the unity of this species against the aliens)~~, a positive feeling of community began to develop over the few short years leading into the Unification process and the creation of the United States of the Earth in 2098. At the same time, contact was established with the three ETB civilizations, and there is no doubt that the existence of teleportation was the most significant factor enabling a genuine political and cultural exchange among the four worlds: for the first time, everyone could meet face-to-face. There were studies, reports, the intensive training of translators, negotiations, preagreements, emissaries being TP'd, myriad telegnés crisscrossing the galaxies, and frantic diplomatic activity across/throughout the universe. It soon became clear that the four species were in no way competing against one another and posed no threat to one another. Their home planets were vast distances from one another, and teletransportation was equally harmful to all of them. The grandeur of the cosmos seemed somehow to encourage human nobility, and the talks advanced rapidly and harmoniously, culminating in the Global Agreements of Cassiopeia in 2096, the first interstellar treaty in history. The agreements regulate the patenting and use of technologies ~~(for example, we buy the Gnés' telegnés, and they buy teleportation from us, but both the intellectual property and the rights to exploitation belong exclusively to the civilization that developed the particular invention)~~, the exchange of goods, the type of currency, the use of teletransportation, terms of migration, etc. Faced with the need to coin a word that would define our new partners in the universe and identify us with them, the term **sentient beings**, an expression borrowed from the Buddhist tradition, was agreed to. The sentients (**G'nayam** in Gnés, **Laluala** in Balabí, **Amoa** in Omaánese) constitute a new level in the taxonomy of living things. If, up to that point, human beings had belonged to the kingdom *Animalia*, the phylum *Cordata*, the class *Mammalia*, the order *Primates*, the family *Hominidae*, the genus *Homo* and the species *Homo sapiens*, after the agreements a new rank was added—the line *Sintiente*, located between class and order—because, curiously, all extraterrestrials appear to be mammals and to have hair of one sort or another.

Although teleportation has enabled the four civilizations to exchange ambassadors, it is not very common to see an alien in person. In total, there are fewer than twenty thousand aliens on our planet, a tiny number compared with the four billion citizens of Earth, known as Earthlings. Each diplomatic delegation consists of three thousand individuals, spread across the most important cities in the USE. There are also about ten thousand Omaás, who TP'd to Earth fleeing from a religious war on their own planet. That said, their unusual looks are extremely well known to all, thanks to the images screened on the news. The official name for extraterrestrials is **Other Beings**, ~~but they are commonly referred to as *bichos*, or creeps.~~

CHAPTER SIX

"I found this on my desk two days ago," said Myriam Chi. She leaned forward and handed Bruna a small holograph ball. Bruna held it in her palm and pressed the button. Immediately, a three-dimensional image of the RRM leader formed on her hand. It was no more than four inches tall, but it clearly showed Myriam in her entirety, smiling and waving. Suddenly, from nowhere, a minuscule hand appeared holding a knife, and the blade, enormous by comparison, slit the rep's belly from top to bottom and, using the tip of the weapon as a lever, skillfully extracted her intestines. Her guts spilled out and the hologram switched off. That was it, but it was more than enough.

"Shit," murmured Bruna despite herself.

She had felt the impact of the scene in her stomach, but a millisecond later she had managed to recover her aplomb. She pressed the button again and this time paid closer attention.

"You're smiling the whole time. It must be an image from a news bulletin, or—"

"It's from the end of one of last year's rallies. We holographed the whole thing and sell it in our souvenir shop. Our sympathizers buy it. It's a way of raising funds for the movement."

"So anyone can get hold of it."

"We have many supporters, and that hologram is one of our most popular items."

Bruna picked up a particular timbre in Myriam's words, an ironically sarcastic tone, and glanced up. The other woman gazed back at her with an impenetrable look. Long, wavy, chestnut-brown hair, a tailored suit, makeup on her face. For the leader of a radical movement, she had an oddly conventional look. Bruna pressed the ball again. The superimposed image of the disembowelment seemed to be real, not virtual. Maybe it was of an animal in some slaughterhouse.

"It's in fact a fairly clumsy piece of work, Chi. I'd say it's a homemade job. But it's very effective, because that wholly unexpected and horrific butchery prevents you from noticing the defects. Can I hang on to it?"

"Of course."

"I'll return it as soon as I've analyzed it."

"As you can understand, there's no way I want it. But yes, I suppose it's evidence that has to be kept."

Hah, thought Bruna, *I've got you.* Myriam had accompanied the sentence with a small sigh, and her strong and somewhat arrogant pose of the world-leader-who-is-above-such-trifles had cracked a little, showing a flash of fear. Yes, of course she was frightened, and rightly so. Husky vaguely recalled other, earlier incidents during Chi's rallies that were violent and disruptive, even some supremacists who had tried to shoot her—or was it blow her up with a bomb? When Bruna had arrived at the RRM headquarters, she'd had to go through various security checks, including a full body scan.

"And you say that, apart from you, there are only two other people authorized to enter this office?"

"That's right. My personal assistant and the head of security. And neither of them opened the door. The register that records lock activity shows no one entering here from the time I left the previous night until when I returned the following morning. And by then the holograph ball was already on my desk."

"Which means that someone has manipulated the register. Maybe someone internal. The head of security?"

"Impossible."

"You'd be amazed at the infinite possibilities of the impossible."

Myriam cleared her throat.

"She's my partner. We've been together for three years. I know her. And we love each other."

Bruna had a fleeting vision of Myriam as a potential lover. That cold self-assurance punctuated by the fragility of fear; that loud, intrusive activism linked with her old-fashioned appearance. Why, she even had fingernails painted in the retro style! All those contradictions magnified her attractiveness. For a moment Bruna convinced herself that she could understand why the head of security had fallen for her. But finding Myriam sexy put Bruna in a bad mood.

"And what can you tell me about your personal assistant? Do you love him enough to exonerate him, too?" she asked, with uncalled-for rudeness.

Myriam Chi didn't react.

"He's also beyond suspicion. We've worked together for too many years. Don't make a mistake. Don't waste your time looking where you shouldn't. I repeat that this is linked to trafficking in adulterated memories. I'm certain of it. That's what you have to investigate and that's precisely why I've called you: because you saw one of the victims."

Indeed, Myriam had told her all this in a commanding tone as soon as Bruna had arrived. The RRM leader had explained to her that before Cata Caín, there had already been four other reps who had died in similar circumstances. And that when she became interested in the matter and went to talk with friends and colleagues of the victims, she began to receive strange threats: anonymous, untraceable phone calls; increasingly threatening messages on her computer; and finally the holograph ball, more intimidating because of its appearance in her office than because of its gruesome content. Bruna wasn't used to having her clients tell her what she had to do; usually, it was the opposite. People hired private detectives when they felt at a loss, when they felt threatened but weren't sure by what, or when they needed to prove some suspicion so dark that they didn't even know where to begin to look. A private detective's clients were generally lost in confusion. Otherwise they would have gone to the police or the courts. And Bruna knew from experience that the more confused the person hiring her was the better their working relationship would be, because then the client would give the sleuth greater freedom and be more grateful for the smallest fact the detective might find. If truth be told, a private detective was a finder of certainties.

"Why haven't you been to the police?"

Chi smiled sardonically.

"You mean, to the *human* police? You want me to go and ask them why there's someone out there killing reps? Do you think they're going to be very interested?"

"There are technohuman cops as well."

"Oh, right. Four wretched imbeciles playing the part for the sake of appearances. Come on, Husky, you know we're totally discriminated against. We're a secondary species and third-class citizens."

Yes, Bruna knew it. But she felt that the discrimination against reps encompassed a greater discrimination—that of the powerful against the wretched. Like that poor human in Oli's bar, the Texaco-Repsol billboard-lady. The world was basically unjust. Perhaps reps had to put up with worse conditions than humans, but for some reason, feeling that she was part of a victims' collective made the detective feel ill. She preferred to think that injustice was democratic and rained its formidable blows on everybody.

"Moreover, I don't trust the police, because it's likely the enemy has infiltrators on the inside. I'm convinced there's something much bigger behind this business of adulterated memories. Something political."

Come on, thought Bruna, irritated. *Next she'll say there's a plot.* They were entering the paranoid zone typical of these radical movements.

"Something that might even be a conspiracy."

"Well, Chi, allow me to question that. I don't usually support conspiracy theories," Bruna couldn't avoid answering.

"That's fine by me, but conspiracies exist. Look at the recent revelations about the assassination of President John F. Kennedy. We've finally managed to find out what happened."

"But at this stage, a century and a half after the assassination, the truth is of no interest to anyone. I'm not saying that conspiracies don't exist; what I am saying is that there are far fewer than people imagine, and they tend to be improvised, one-off jobs rather than perfect Machiavellian constructions. People believe in conspiracies because it's a way of believing that deep down, horror has some order and meaning, even if that meaning is evil. We don't support chaos, but there's no question that life is totally senseless. Pure sound and fury."

Myriam looked at her with some surprise.

"Shakespeare...what an educated quotation for someone like you."

"And what am I like?"

"A detective, a combat rep, a woman with a shaved head and a tattoo that splits her face."

"Right. Well, I'm equally surprised that a political leader would recognize Shakespeare's words. I thought activists like you dedicated your lives to the cause, not to reading and painting your fingernails."

Myriam smiled crookedly and briefly lowered her head, pensive. When she raised it once more, her face again showed that unexpected fragility that the detective thought she'd seen moments earlier.

"Why don't you like me, Husky?"

The detective shifted uncomfortably in her seat. In reality, she was sorry she had said so much. She didn't know why she was behaving in such an unusual way. Discussing chaos in life with a client? She must have lost her mind.

"It's not that. Let's just say I find people with a victim mentality annoying."

She'd done it again! Bruna was astonished. She was continuing to argue with Chi, totally out of control.

"You think, for example, that denouncing labs that don't look for a cure for TTT is feeling victimized? I have the data: only zero-point-two percent of the budget for medical research is spent on the search for a cure for Total Techno Tumor, even though we reps make up fifteen percent of the population and we all die of the same thing."

Four years, three months, and twenty-three days, thought Bruna, without being able to do anything about it. She was just as unable to do anything about the awful impulse to keep arguing.

"Believing that the entire universe is conspiring against you seems like a victim mentality to me. As if you were at the center of everything. The feeling of superiority is a defect that tends to accompany a victim mentality...as if you deserved any merit for being a product of fate."

"Fate and human genetic engineering in our case," whispered Myriam.

The two women stopped talking and the seconds passed with embarrassing slowness.

"I know you, Bruna," the RRM leader finally said in a soft voice—so soft that the sudden use of her first name seemed both necessary and natural. "I know people like you. You're so full of anger and hurt that you can't put words to what you feel. If you admit your pain, you're scared that you'll end up being nothing more than a victim, and if you acknowledge your anger, you're scared you'll end up being a tyrant. The point is that you hate being a rep but you don't want to admit it."

"Don't tell me—"

"That's why I disturb and intrigue you so much," continued Myriam, unperturbed. "Because I represent everything you fear. That rep nature that you hate. Relax. In reality, it's a very common problem. Look at the people on the Trans Platform—you know, the association that encompasses all those people who want to be what they're not: women who want to be men; men who want to be women; humans who want to be reps; reps who want to be humans; blacks who want to be white; whites who want to be black. At this stage, we don't seem to have aliens who want to be Earthlings, or vice versa, but it will happen; we haven't spent enough time in contact with the extraterrestrials yet. I think we reps and humans are sick beings; we always feel our reality isn't enough. So we consume drugs and give ourselves artificial memories; we want to escape from the confinement of our lives. But I assure you that the only way to resolve the conflict is to learn to accept it and find your own place in the world. And that's what we do in the RRM. That's why our movement is so important, because—"

Despite herself, Bruna had listened to Chi's argument with a degree of attention, but when the woman cited the RRM, a stream of uncontrollable and liberating sarcasm popped out of the detective's mouth.

"An eloquent homily, Chi. A fantastic speech. You should turn it into a holograph and sell it in your shop. But how about we get back to the matter in hand?"

Myriam smiled. A small grimace, tight and cold.

"Of course, Husky. I don't know what I was thinking. I'd forgotten that I've just hired you, and you charge by the hour. My assistant will give you all the information we've gathered on the earlier cases, and will deal with you regarding your professional fees. You can ask him to add a few gaias for the time you spent listening to the speech."

Bruna felt the sting of the small slight. It was as if she'd been slapped. And in a way, deservedly so.

"I'm sorry if I seemed rude earlier on, but—"

Myriam completely ignored her and continued to speak. Or rather, to give orders.

"Just one more thing: I want you to go and see Pablo Nopal."

"Who?"

"Nopal. The memory writer. You don't know who he is? Well, you should. Unfortunately for him, he's quite well known."

In fact, Pablo Nopal's name did ring a vague bell with Bruna. Wasn't he the one who'd been accused of murder?

"He had problems with the law, didn't he?"

"Exactly so."

"I don't remember much. I don't like memorists."

"All the worse for you, because I think that in this instance you'll have to talk with a few. Go and see Nopal right away. He might know who wrote the adulterated memories. And then come and tell me. I want you to give your reports to me alone. That's all for now, Bruna Husky. I hope to have some news from you soon."

"Just a minute. We haven't talked about your personal security. I think you should change your habits and take certain additional measures. Maybe we should—"

"It's not the first time I've been threatened with death, and I know perfectly well how to defend myself. Moreover, I have an excellent head of security, as I've told you. And now, if you don't mind, I have a complicated morning in front of me."

Bruna stood up and shook the woman's hand. A hard, rough hand despite the fingernails painted a delicate shade of pastel blue. On the wall behind Myriam's chair there was the inevitable framed picture of Gabriel Morlay, the mythical rep reformer. How young he looked. Too young, given his fame. Chi, on the other hand, had little wrinkles at the corners of her mouth and lacked a certain freshness overall. She must already be close to her TTT, although she was still a beautiful woman. Myriam's attractiveness hit Bruna again like a burst of air. The private detective felt dissatisfied and uncomfortable.

She suspected she'd behaved like an idiot. She expelled that irritating thought from her head and tried to concentrate on her new assignment. She'd have to speak with that excellent head of security, she said to herself. The fact that she was Myriam Chi's life partner not only didn't exonerate her but turned her into a suspect as well. It was statistically proven that money and love were the main causes of violent crimes.

CHAPTER SEVEN

After her interview with Chi, Bruna went back home on the sky-tram and, before heading up to her apartment, stopped off at the supermarket on the corner to stock up on provisions and buy a new card for purified water. During those periods when she didn't have work, the android never found a moment to attend to her daily needs, despite supposedly having all the time in the world. Her pantry emptied, surfaces became covered with layers of dust, and the sheets stayed on her bed so long that they acquired an almost solid smell. Whenever she picked up a job, however, Bruna needed to organize her surroundings in order to feel that her head was in shape. Having a sharp mind was an essential requirement of her profession. The mark of a great detective wasn't her investigative skills but her ability to think on her toes. So, after putting the shopping away in the kitchen and inserting the water card in the meter, Bruna spent a few hours cleaning and tidying her apartment, washing her dirty clothes, and throwing out the empty bottles that were lined up like tenpins by the door.

Then she served herself a glass of white wine, sat down in front of the main screen, and for a few minutes enjoyed the neat calmness of her apartment. She set herself to thinking about her new case and how to approach it. The first steps in an investigation were important; if you made a mistake, you could sometimes end up wasting a lot of time and adding confusion to what was already confused. She grabbed her electronic tablet—since taking notes by hand seemed to help her think—and started to jot down the ideas that were buzzing around in her head. Though she wasn't creating a list of priorities, a rebellious streak made her leave the memorist for later, disregarding the words of the rep leader, who had insisted that she start with him. But she did write on the tablet, *Why is Chi interested in Nopal?* Underneath, she added other phrases using the stylus: *Hologram, Threats against Chi, Lock register, Traffickers, Document four other cases, Victims—chance or choice?* After hesitating for a moment, she added *Pablo Nopal.* She told herself that putting him in eighth place was rebellious enough.

She opened the holograph, took out the chip, put it in her computer and began to examine the image minutely using an analysis program. It was the same program the police used, a powerful tool that immediately deconstructed the original fragment of Myriam and showed the image's ID properties, which, understandably, corresponded to those of the RRM. As for the additional footage, the program couldn't find the original sequence on the web, so it performed a hypothetical reconstruction. It was the gutting of a pig and might have originated in a legitimate slaughterhouse, because the animal seemed to have been killed first in the regulation manner, using anesthesia and a stun gun. The image's ID properties had been carefully erased, together with all its electronic tags, making it almost impossible to track down. Although there were now fewer and fewer slaughterhouses—in part due to a growing sensitivity toward animals, and in part because in order to reduce CO_2 emissions, the government required meat

eaters to acquire an expensive license—hundreds of them were
still in operation across the planet. Moreover, the recording could have been made at any stage during the last three
years, this being the software's maximum life span, according
to the program. As to the chip itself and the holograph ball,
they were basic, everyday products, the sort any kid could
buy in the local corner store to make a hologram to take to
school. It would be very difficult to extract useful data from
them. Nevertheless, Bruna started an exhaustive analysis of the
sequence with the pig and left it running in the background.
The analysis program would take hours to complete its task.

She decided to take a break and eat something. She put
an individual serving of compressed fish cakes into the Chef
Express, and in one minute it was ready. She removed the lid,
poured herself another glass of wine, and returned to sit in
front of the main screen, eating straight from the container.

"Find Pablo Nopal," she said out loud.

Various possibilities came up, and Bruna touched one,
leaving a faint, greasy food stain on the screen. The man's
image came up instantly, a life-size 3-D head shot on the
right-hand side of the screen, with various film clips on the
left. Dark hair, slim, with a long, narrow nose, thin lips, big
black eyes. An attractive guy. He was thirty-five: TTT age,
had he been a rep. But he wasn't. According to the records,
Nopal was a playwright and novelist, as well as a memorist.
And he did indeed enjoy a certain celebrity—not just for his
books, which were well received, but also for a couple of
scandals in his past. Seven years earlier, he had been accused of
the murder of his elderly uncle, a patrician millionaire. Nopal
just happened to be the sole beneficiary. He even spent a few
months in custody, but in the end, there was some murky

business about contaminated evidence, and Nopal was cleared due to lack of evidence.

His reputation was tarnished, however, and many people continued to believe that he was guilty; in fact, the government stopped commissioning memories from him because of it all, so he hadn't gone back to being a practicing memorist. *At least not officially*, Bruna thought to herself, because black market memories also needed memorists to write them. Three years after his acquittal, Nopal was implicated in another violent death—this time, of his private secretary. He had been the last to see the victim alive, and for a time he was targeted by the police, although in the end he was never even accused. Naturally, both incidents increased the sales of his books. There was nothing like a really bad reputation to make you famous in this world.

Bruna studied Nopal's face. Yes, it was attractive, but it was also disturbing. An easygoing smile but too sardonic, too tough. An indecipherable expression in his eyes. He had published three novels, the first a few months after his uncle's death. The title was *The Violent Ones*, and the book's publication had been celebrated with a small cultural event. Bruna typed in her password and credit account number, paid five gaias for the book, and downloaded the text onto her electronic tablet. She planned to just glance through it, but she began to read and couldn't stop. It was a short, unsettling novel, the story of a boy who lived in one of the Zero Air Zones. Bruna had been in one of those supercontaminated, marginal sectors during her time in the military, and she had to admit that the author knew how to convey the desperate and poisonous atmosphere of those wretched holes. What happened was that the boy became friends with the recently arrived adolescent daughter of a judge. Magistrates, like doctors, police, and other socially necessary professionals, were posted to the Dirty Air Sectors on double salary, and for no longer than a year, to prevent any health repercussions. Bruna knew that even under those conditions, many refused to go. The novel told the story of the relationship between the two youths during those twelve months. At the end of that time, the night before the judge and her family were to leave, the two adolescents killed her with a hammer. The scene was brutal, but the novel was written in a way that was so convincing, so true to life, and so distressing that Bruna experienced a genuine complicity with the killers and wanted them to escape justice. Which they didn't, so the end of the story was depressing.

Bruna switched off the tablet. She was numb from having spent several hours in the same position and had the strangest feeling of grief. There was something in that damn novel that seemed to have spoken directly to her. Something strangely close to home, recognizable. Something bordering on the unbearable. *Four years, three months, and twenty-three days.*

She leapt up and paced back and forth feverishly. The apartment had only two rooms: a lounge-kitchen, and a bedroom. Neither of them was very big, so two strides took her to a wall, and she had to turn around. She looked through the picture-window; the city shimmered and hummed in the dark. She approached the large jigsaw puzzle board: she'd been doing the puzzle on it for more than two months, but there was still a central hole of about a hundred pieces to be filled. It was one of the hardest puzzles she'd ever undertaken: an image of the universe, with a great deal of blackness, and few celestial bodies from which to get her bearings. She looked at the jagged edges of the hole for a moment and fiddled with the loose pieces, trying to find one that would fit. Hidden order within chaos. Usually when she was solving jigsaw puzzles, she felt closer to serenity than at any other moment in her edgy life, but right now she couldn't concentrate, and she ended up abandoning the puzzle without having managed to place a single piece. It was Nopal's fault, she thought, and the fault of that revolting novel that had hit so close to home. Those damn memorists were all equally perverse, equally repugnant. And then, as on so many other occasions when anxiety was exploding inside her body, Bruna decided to go for a run—physical tiredness was the best tranquilizer. She put on an old pair of track pants and sneakers, and left the apartment. When she hit the street, it was midnight on the dot.

She shot off so fast in the direction of the park that she quickly ran out of breath. She reduced her pace and tried to find a well-balanced rhythm, breathing easily, accommodating her body. Little by little she got into the relaxed and hypnotic rhythm of a good run, her feet almost weightless, hitting the sidewalk in time to her heartbeat. Above her head, the public screens spilled out the usual stupid messages, juvenile little quips, music clips, personal images from someone's last holiday, or news items covered by amateur journalists. In one news item, she saw an Instant Terrorist blowing himself up on Gran Vía, fortunately causing only his own death. Just as well that at this stage, Ins were so incompetent and clumsy that they rarely managed to do much damage, thought the android; but once those antisystem crazies learned to organize themselves and make good homemade bombs, the Ins would turn into a nightmare. Every week, someone in Madrid set themselves on fire, for who knew what reason.

Bruna entered the park through the corner gate and crossed it on the diagonal. It was a lung park rather than a park with vegetation. The rep liked running between the rows of artificial trees because it was easier for her to breathe: they absorbed much more carbon dioxide than genuine trees and you could really notice the higher concentration of oxygen. Yiannis had told her that decades earlier artificial trees were built so that they more or less simulated real ones, but those absurdly mimetic creations had long been abandoned in the search for a more efficient design. The android was aware of at least half a dozen tree models, but the ones in this lung park, which belonged to Texaco-Repsol, were like enormous banners made from an almost transparent, and extremely fine, red metallic thread, floating strips three feet wide and about thirty-three feet long that swayed with the wind and produced small, chirruping, cricketlike noises. Crossing the park was like passing through the baleen filter of an enormous whale.

When she came out on the other side of the park, Bruna caught herself turning right rather than taking a left and heading for home along Reina Victoria Avenue, as she had intended. She jogged for a minute without really knowing where she was going, until she realized that she was heading for Nuevos Ministerios, one of the city's deprived neighborhoods, a prostitution and drug-dealing district. Maybe she could find a memory trafficker there. It was not the ideal spot to be walking around unarmed at night, but on the other hand, a combat rep out exercising was unlikely to be the most desirable target for criminals.

Despite its name, Nuevos Ministerios was very old. It had been built two centuries earlier as a government hub, and it consisted of a collection of interconnected buildings that formed a gigantic, zigzagging mass. It must have been an ugly and inhospitable cement monstrosity from its inception. During the Robot Wars, Nuevos Ministerios was used to house displaced people, and afterward there was no way of getting them out of there. The original refugees sublet rooms to other tenants illegally, and the area rapidly deteriorated. The windows were broken, the doors burned, and the former gardens had become filthy, empty esplanades. But there were also noisy bars, squalid Dalamina-smoking dens, wretched cabarets. An entire world of illegal pleasures overseen by the local gangs, who paid the clean air fees. Bruna reached the outer perimeter of Nuevos Ministerios and walked past Comet, the area's best-known hangout, a dive on the outer boundary frequented by some well-to-do customers keen to dip their toes into the dark side of life. The music was deafening, and there were quite a few people hanging around the door. The majority of them were bodies for hire, figured the detective after giving them a quick glance. Just then, an adolescent-looking boy caught up with her and started to jog along beside her.

"Hi, tough girl. I see you enjoy sport. How about doing some exercise inside with me? I work wonders..."

Bruna looked him over; he had the typical, telltale eyes with the vertical pupils, but he was too young to be an android. True, he could have had plastic surgery, but most likely he was wearing contact lenses that made him look like a rep. Many humans had a morbid sexual curiosity with androids, and the male prostitutes took advantage of it.

"Are you a human or a techno?"

The boy looked at her, uncertain, weighing up which answer would better suit his purpose.

"Which do you prefer?"

"Frankly, I don't give a damn. It was a matter of curiosity, not business."

"Come on, cheer up. I've got candy. Top quality."

Candy. Meaning oxytocin, the love drug. As a legal substance, it was bought in drugstores by couples in a stable relationship to improve or reawaken their relationship. The candy he was referring to, however, was an explosive cocktail of a massive dose of oxytocin combined with other synthetic neuropeptides. A veritable bomb—banned, of course—that Bruna had taken on occasion with sizzling effect. But this was neither the time nor the place.

"Don't waste your time. I'm serious. I don't want anything you have to offer."

The young man frowned briefly, somewhat upset, but was sufficiently professional to continue being charming. As he was always telling himself, an out-and-out *no* today might be a *sure—give me a hit* tomorrow.

"Okay, stripy-face, some other time. But if I were you, gorgeous, I wouldn't keep running in that direction. It's a bad area, even for tough girls."

They had reached the first building, the point where the dark esplanades of the Inner Zone began. The youth turned around and began to jog toward the distant lights of Comet. Then Bruna had an idea.

"Hang on!"

The kid returned, smiling and hopeful.

"No, it's not that," the rep said quickly. "It's just a question. You must buy the candy from someone, right?"

"Do you want me to turn someone in to you?"

"No, it's not that either. But I am interested in the people who sell drugs. Do you know the local traffickers?"

The smile disappeared from the boy's face.

"Hey, don't make trouble for me. I'm off."

Bruna grabbed him by the arm.

"Cool it. I'm not the police, I'm not a dealer, so don't be scared. I'll give you a hundred Gs if you answer a few simple questions."

The prostitute thought about it.

"First give me the money and then I'll give you the answers."

"Fine. I don't have any cash, so put yourself in receiver mode."

They activated their mobiles, and Bruna keyed in one hundred gaias on hers and sent through the transaction. A beep signaled the successful transfer of funds.

"Okay. Go ahead."

"I'm interested in artificial memories. Do you know of anyone around here who sells them?"

"Mems? No idea. I don't use them. But way over on the other side of that half-ruined stall where that red light is, there's a smoke den. And I've heard that on the other side of the smoke den, in among the arches, is where the traffickers hang out."

"You've *heard*? Come off it. Then where do you get your candy from?"

"Listen, I'm a professional. I have a personal supplier who brings it to my place; a real gentleman, nothing to do with this—he only sells oxytocin. Over there's the hard stuff, like strawberry and other flavored cocaine, mems, ice…But I know nothing about that. I don't do drugs. Just candy, which goes with my line of work. I'm sorry, but that's all I know. Head for the red light and look under the arches on the left."

The android sighed. "That information isn't worth the money I gave you."

"What do you expect? I'm a good boy!" he replied, with a charming smile.

And, giving a half-turn, he started to run toward the bar.

Bruna began to cross the filthy esplanade. Half the lights were broken, and the shadows formed irregular pools and dark patches in the shadows. Luckily, she could see quite well in the dark, thanks to the improved eyesight of reps. It was assumed that vertical pupils were good for that, although Myriam Chi and other extremists would say that feline eyes were nothing more than a segregationist's trick to make reps more easily recognizable. Either way, night vision enabled Bruna to distinguish several dozen people wandering around the place, alone or in groups. She passed three or four of them, elusive beings who moved out of her way. There were also some characters sleeping on the ground, or perhaps they'd passed out, or maybe they were even dead—junkies with their brains fried by drugs. They were mere dark shapes, barely distinguishable from the rubble and other waste that littered the zone. Near the entry to the smoking den, Bruna saw a couple of combat replicants, no doubt hired gorillas. They watched her go by with furious expressions on their faces, like guard dogs in a frenzy because they couldn't leave their posts to go and bite the intruder. Bruna walked under the arches, leaving the smoking den behind her. The red street light bathed the shadows with a ghostly, bloodlike sheen. She walked slowly through the arcade; in front of her the darkness was thickening. A few columns farther along she thought she detected the outline of a person. She was focusing on making out what it was when someone suddenly landed hard on top of her. With an automatic defensive reflex, the rep grabbed the aggressor's arms, and was already on the point of smashing his head against the wall when she registered that he wasn't an assailant but a poor idiot who had unintentionally bumped into her. Worse still, he was a child. A genuine child. The boy was looking at her, terrified. Bruna realized that she had almost lifted him off the ground, and gently let him go. For heaven's sake, he didn't even seem to have reached the legal age!

"How old are you?"

"Four...fourteen," jabbered the child, rubbing his forearms painfully.

Fourteen! What the heck was he doing on the street? He was breaking the adolescent curfew.

"What are you doing here?"

"I...I'd arranged to meet a friend."

The android noticed the shake in his hands, the splotches on his face, his grayish teeth. They were the effects of strawberry, and of Dalamina, the synthetic drug in vogue. So young, and he was already a wreck. The shadow Bruna had seen a few arches farther down was walking quietly toward them now. As the woman reached them, she smiled in a soothing manner. She was about fifty, with one ear much higher than the other. She had to be a mutant deformed by teleportation. The misplaced ear, located almost on top of her head, poked out from her sparse hair, like the ear on a dog.

'Hi. What are you looking for, techno friend?"

Her voice was surprisingly beautiful, modulated, and as smooth as silk.

"I want some strawberry...I want strawberry..." interrupted the boy, agitated by his need.

"Shut up, kid. Who do you take me for?"

"Sarabi, give me a fix, please," he moaned.

The mutant looked Bruna up and down, trying to work out if the rep posed any kind of risk.

"Give the boy the damn drug. It's all the same to me," said the detective.

And it was true, because the boy was already an addict and needed the fix not just to relieve his withdrawal symptoms but also because the puny-bodied creature had undoubtedly stolen and bashed and maybe even killed someone in order to put together the money for his fix. Gangs of feral kids were terrorizing the city, and not even the curfew was able to curb them effectively. Whenever Bruna thought about those wild adolescents, she felt less saddened by her inability to have children.

"But I don't know you," grunted the woman.

"And I don't know you either," Bruna replied.

"Can I use a lie detector?"

"That ridiculous gadget? Sure, why not?"

The woman took out something like a small magnifying glass and held it in front of one of Bruna's eyes.

"Do you have any intention of causing me harm?" she asked emphatically.

"Of course not," answered the detective.

Satisfied, the mutant put away the gadget. Lie detectors were supposed to capture certain movements of the iris if a person wasn't telling the truth. They were sold in catalogs for ten gaias, and they were a real rip-off.

"Please, Sarabi, please give me the strawberry."

"Calm down, kid. I may have something for you, but first you've got to give me something, too."

"Yes, yes, of course. Here."

The boy took various crumpled bills out of his pockets, which the mutant smoothed out and counted. Then she hunted in her brown, fake-leather backpack and took out a see-through blister pack with a small, fuchsia-colored tablet. The boy grabbed it from her hand and ran off. The mutant turned toward Bruna.

"You still haven't told me what you're after."

Her beautiful voice seemed an anomaly in such a sinister character.

"I want a mem. Do you sell them?"

The woman looked annoyed.

"Hmmm, an artificial memory. Those are huge words. In the first place, mems are very expensive."

"That's not an issue."

"And besides, I don't traffic in that stuff."

"You don't say. So where can I find someone who does?"

The woman looked around as if she were searching for someone, and Bruna followed her eyes. It looked like there was no one in the arcade although, despite her sharp eyesight, even the detective couldn't see clearly more than a few yards farther along, as the place was buried in shadows.

"Honestly, I couldn't say. A few mem sellers used to come by here before, but I haven't seen them for a few weeks. It seems things are getting ugly in the memory market—you know, because of the dead reps. Sorry, *technos*."

"Yes, those two recent victims," said Bruna, testing the waters.

"Hmmm, more than two, more than two. There were others before them."

"How do you know?"

"Well, I have ears, as you can no doubt see," said the mutant with a burst of laughter.

Then she suddenly became serious.

"How much are you willing to pay for the mem? For one that's top quality, written by a true memory artist."

"How much would it cost?"

"Three thousand gaias."

Bruna was shocked but tried to keep her expression impassive. Anyway, she hoped the RRM wouldn't raise objections about her expenses.

"Fine."

"Well then, you really are in luck. Because, while I don't traffic in them, it just so happens I've got a really good mem right here that a colleague gave me to pay off a debt. Have you got the three thousand Gs?"

"Not in cash. I can transfer it to you."

The woman waved her hands in front of her as if she were wiping steam from a mirror.

"I don't like to use mobiles. They leave a trail."

"Well, that's all I've got. It's that, or nothing."

The mutant thought it over for half a minute, grumbling. Then she took a long narrow tube out of her bag and showed it to Bruna. She might just as well have been showing her a thermometer for animals, since the rep had never seen a memory applicator like this one. The woman manipulated her wrist computer.

"Okay. I'm ready. Put through the transaction."

When she heard the beep, the mutant checked the information and then handed the tube over to the detective. It was less than a quarter of an inch wide and about eight inches long, and perhaps made of titanium, since it weighed nothing. Bruna turned it around in her fingers a few times.

"As you know, the mem's inside. There. Have a look. And this is the insertion gun. Do you know how it works?"

"I guess so, though the applicators I know are different. Bigger, and more like a real gun."

"Then it's been a while since you saw a mem. You have to insert the thinner end into your nose, put it in as far as you can, and press these two buttons at the same time. Then the injector will take its measurements and set up the memory so that it is on the right trajectory. And when it's done that, it'll emit a warning sound and then fire. It takes about a minute. You have to keep as still as you can during the whole process. Rest your head against something. And be very careful which end you put in your nose, or you'll end up firing the mem into your hand. Enjoy!"

She provided the instructions with a hint of mockery in her silky voice, as if she found Bruna's ignorance amusing. Or maybe she was delighted that she'd charged her more than the going rate. *Laugh while you can*, Bruna thought vindictively, as she watched the woman disappear among the arches. If she found out that the mutant was in any way involved in the deaths, her fun times would be over. The android took a deep breath, trying to dispel a certain tightness in her chest, and headed back home. About halfway along the esplanade she started to run, and didn't ease up until she reached home. When she walked into her apartment, she was clutching the metal tube so tightly that her nails had left their imprint on her palms.

She was drenched in sweat and her stomach was churning. She looked at the mem and thought, *It's like having a corpse in my hand. Even worse than that. Like having a living being shut away inside it. An entire existence anxiously waiting to be liberated, like the genie in the bottle in* A Thousand and One Nights. She recalled a couple of combat reps whom she'd seen some time back, in the military, injecting memories. Watching them hadn't been pleasant, at least initially—the guys threw up. But there must be something good about mems if so many people did them. Bruna inserted the tube into her nose. She was standing in the middle of the room with no support. She wasn't going to fire the insertion gun; she just wanted to see how it felt. The tube's metal was cold and she felt a bit suffocated having it in her nose. Would it hurt? Just by pressing two buttons she could have another life, be another person. She felt slightly nauseous. She removed the tube and threw it onto the table. She needed to find someone to analyze the mem. Maybe it was one of the adulterated implants.

CHAPTER EIGHT

B oth the subway and the sky-trams were on strike, which meant the travelators were so crammed with people that the excessive weight slowed their speed and, in some cases, even managed to stop them. There was no hope of finding an available cab, so some desperate people were trying to hitch a ride in private vehicles. But it was already well known that those few individuals authorized to own their own vehicles were not usually the most sympathetic.

Bruna had left home in good time, anticipating the long walk and the confusion typical of strike days, but even so she was having a hard time forcing her way through the hundreds of cyclists and pedestrians. It was 17:10, rush hour, and she was already ten minutes late for her appointment with Pablo Nopal. The memorist had suggested they meet in the Museum of Modern Art, an uncomfortable and unsuitable place for a conversation. But Bruna couldn't impose her own conditions; she was the one who'd asked for the meeting. Taking them two at a time, she went up the hundreds of little steps that seemed to cascade around the enormous, luminous cube of the museum like a concrete waterfall. She held her wrist mobile up against the electronic ticket machine at the entrance and once in, she crossed the lobby at top speed, heading for the temporary exhibition hall. And there, at the entrance to the hall, she spotted the memorist: white, collarless shirt; wide black pants; lank, dark hair falling over his forehead. The very picture of casual elegance. Such lustrous hair. Was it the result of expensive capillary treatment or his genetic inheritance from generations of rich ancestors? The writer was leaning against the wall with graceful indolence. When he noticed the detective approaching, he half-smiled and stood upright. They had only seen each other on the screen when they set up the meeting, but there was no question the android was easy to spot.

"You're late, Husky."

"The strike. My apologies."

Bruna took a quick look around her. In the main hall she'd just crossed there were some armchairs and at the far end, a cafeteria.

"Where shall we talk? Shall we sit over there? Or maybe you'd prefer to have something in the café?"

"Hold on! Are you in a hurry? We could have a look at the exhibition first."

The rep looked at Nopal uneasily. She had no idea what he had in mind; she didn't have a good sense of what his game was, and that always made her anxious. The man was about her height and his eyes were right in line with hers. Too close, too inquisitive. By the great Morlay, how she hated memorists! The detective couldn't help but look away, and faked interest in a poster promoting the exhibition. She read it three times before becoming conscious of what he was saying.

"*The History of Fakes: Fraud as Revolutionary Art*," Nopal read out loud. "Interesting, isn't it?"

The android looked at him. What was he going on about? Was there a hidden message in his comment? A double meaning?

The detective had already heard people talking about this exhibition and she would never have come to see it of her own accord. She was irritated by the fakes phenomenon—the latest thing in the plastic arts. Pedantic critics and delirious aesthetes had decreed that imposture was the purest and most radical artistic manifestation of modernity, the vanguard of the twenty-second century. The most sought-after artists of the moment were all successful forgers whose fakes had been thought authentic for some period of time. Because, as Yiannis—who always knew about everything—had told her, to be a true fake you not only had to imitate to perfection the picture or the sculpture of a famous artist, but you also had to get someone to believe it: a buyer, the owner of a gallery, a museum, the critics, the media. The bigger the deception, the greater the prestige of the fake work once the forgery had been uncovered. And if nobody noticed the artifice and it was the artist himself who had to reveal it after some time had passed, then the work was considered a real masterpiece. This fashion had changed the art world. Now, at auctions, many people bid madly for a Goya or a Bacon or a Gabriela Lambretta secretly hoping that in a few months' time it would be found to be a fake and its value would triple.

"To be honest, it's a topic that's of no interest to me at all," growled Bruna.

No? How strange; I thought you'd like it."

"Why? Because I'm a copy, too, an imitation, a fake human being?"

Pablo Nopal gave a charming smile. Charming and totally untrustworthy. He started to walk around the exhibition and Bruna found herself compelled to follow him. He was a slim man, and he moved lightly inside his roomy, floating garments, as if he had no bones.

"Not at all. I didn't say that. I thought you'd like it because you're an intelligent person. I've learned a bit about you. And intelligent people know that, one way or another, we're all frauds. That's why I find the fakes to be the most perfect representation of our times. They're not art; they're sociology. We're all fakes. But, I find you extraordinarily hypersensitive—wouldn't you agree, Husky? If I were you, I'd try to analyze the reason behind such an exaggerated susceptibility."

Because you're a damn memorist, condescending and pedantic, Bruna would have liked to have replied. She chewed over her words for a few seconds, trying to tone them down a little.

"Well, I don't think I'm hypersensitive. It's more a weariness in the face of prejudice. It's as if people assumed you'd be interested in forgery because of your past. What I mean is, you ought to be used to people looking at you and asking themselves who you really are. Are you Pablo Nopal, the memorist and the writer? Or an individual who killed his uncle and got out of jail because the evidence was tainted?"

She looked at him out of the corner of her eye, a little frightened by her own words. Maybe she'd gone too far and the interview would be over then and there. But that air of bored superiority seemed to be asking to be goaded. Bruna knew the type: they liked to be challenged, even humiliated. At least a little.

"Bad example, Husky. I haven't assumed anything about you. You're the one who's imagined an insult and then felt offended. That's another thing they say about you. They say you are easily stirred up and quite intractable. By the way, my uncle was an evil man and I'm innocent. The tainted evidence had to do with another matter."

They viewed the exhibition in silence for a few minutes. *The fakes recover the historical, artistic legacy and transmute it into a social intervention, simultaneously reaffirming and negating its meaning. There is no greater act of cultural subversion*, read the text written on the wall in 3-D letters. *The usual nonsense*, thought Bruna. There were works from various periods, from a twentieth-century painting by Elmyr D'Ory, to two pieces by the famous Mary Kings, the most acclaimed artist of the moment, who had invented another persona, a painter called Zapulek, and then dedicated herself to forging Zapuleks—in other words, to forging herself.

"Right, let's start again," said Nopal. "What did you want to see me about? Let's sit down over there."

On the other side of the room there was a skylight, and beneath it, two soft armchairs. It was actually a good place to talk, isolated and yet so visible that it seemed to convert the meeting into something accidental and innocent. The perfect spot for a difficult rendezvous, Bruna said to herself, mentally taking note of the fact, in case she should ever have need of such a space. But why had Nopal chosen it? It was obvious that they hadn't ended up there by chance.

"Why did you have me come to the museum?" she asked.

"I don't like people coming to my home. And this is a comfortable place. So talk to me."

Clearly, he was an extremely private person. Somehow he had managed to remove part of his biography on the web. No matter how hard she searched, the android could not find a single detail about his childhood. Nopal seemed to appear from nowhere at the age of ten when he was officially adopted by his uncle. So much mystery was a feat of disinformation in this hyperinformed society.

"My client—I didn't tell you her name before—is Myriam Chi…"

Bruna paused briefly to see if the information was producing any sort of reaction, but the man remained impassive. "She thinks you might be able to help us with our investigation."

"What investigation?"

"Those reps who suddenly seem to go mad, kill other reps, and commit suicide."

"The tram case?"

"Not just that one. There are, in fact, at least four other similar cases."

"And where do I fit in?"

"It's not public knowledge, but they go out of their minds because they inject themselves with adulterated artificial memories. Someone has started selling deadly mems."

Nopal's thin lips curved in an acid smile; he leaned forward until he was a few inches from Bruna's face, and repeated slowly and sarcastically: "And where do I fit in?"

What an annoying character, thought Bruna. This was one of those moments when the detective wished that the formal way of addressing people was still in use—a usage that was originally courteous in intent but in the end, before it became obsolete, had enabled you to distance yourself disdainfully from the person to whom you were speaking, as Bruna had observed so many times in old movies. Yes, an icy *sir* would have suited her very well right now. *Sir is a revolting memorist,* she would have said to him. *You, sir, might well be the bastard who wrote the lethal mems. If it would please you, sir, sit back in your chair and stop trying to impress me.*

"Well, you are a memorist."

The writer sprawled in his chair and sighed.

"I gave that up—or rather, they fired me some years ago, as you no doubt know. And before you foolishly make another rude remark, I'll tell you that, no, I don't write illegal memories. I have no need to. My novels sell very well, in case you didn't know. And I have the money I inherited from my dear uncle."

"But you might know of other memorists. There aren't many. Do you know anyone who might be involved in that business?"

"I cut all ties with that world when they sacked me. Let's just say I didn't particularly enjoy continuing my association with them."

"Well, Myriam Chi thinks you might know something."

Nopal smiled again. This time almost fondly, much to Bruna's surprise.

"Myriam has always believed me to be more powerful than I am."

His brow furrowed in thought. Bruna waited in silence, sensing that the man was about to say something, but she wasn't expecting to hear what he finally came out with.

"How old are you, Husky?"

"What does that have to do with anything?"

"I'd say you're about 5/30 years...Maybe 6/31. Which would make it possible."

"Make *what* possible?"

"That I wrote your memory."

Bruna gasped. Sweat drenched the back of her neck.

"That's a revolting idea," she whispered.

She clenched her teeth to hold back the nausea.

"You know what, Husky? There's another reason I decided to meet you here rather than at home. I've had problems with some reps. On the whole, you technohumans aren't too fond of memorists, and on one level, I can understand why."

"You're not allowed to identify yourself as the author of a memory. It's forbidden. You can't do that."

"I know, I know. Calm down, Bruna. Forgive my earlier comment. Honestly, I'd never tell you. Even if it weren't banned, I wouldn't tell you. Even if I knew. I promise."

The slight feeling of relief she felt at Nopal's words made her realize how terrified she was. She also felt something akin to gratitude. It was a stupid emotion, unjustified and too close to Stockholm Syndrome, but she couldn't avoid it. *Four years, three months, and twenty-two days.*

"Nevertheless, we memorists not only feel no antipathy toward reps, but we also have a special fondness for you. Or at least I do. To be able to construct a person's memory is a privilege beyond description. Can you imagine? Memory is at the root of our identity, so in a way I'm the father of hundreds of beings. More than the father. I'm their personal little god."

Bruna shivered. "I'm not my memory. Which, moreover, I know is fake. I am my actions and my days."

"Well, now, that's debatable. And in any case, it doesn't alter what I was saying to you, because I was talking about my feelings, about how I see things. And I was telling you that I love reps. You inspire a special feeling in me. A deep complicity."

"Right. Well, forgive me for not feeling the same way. Forgive me for not thanking my little personal god, whoever that might be, for that entire arbitrary fake garbage."

"Arbitrary garbage? It's real life that's arbitrary. Much more arbitrary than we memorists are. I've always tried to do the best possible job; I thought about and wrote every one of those five hundred scenes so carefully."

"Five hundred?"

"You didn't know? A life consists of five hundred memories, five hundred scenes. That's enough. I always tried to balance some things with others, offer a certain illusion of meaning, a sense—in the end—of a harmonious whole. My speciality was the revelation scenes."

"The damned dance of the phantoms."

"My revelation scenes were...*compassionate*—that would be the word. Enlightening and compassionate. They encouraged maturity in the rep."

"My memorist killed my father when I was nine. I adored him, and a criminal stupidly killed him in the street one night."

"Those things do happen, unfortunately."

"I was nine years old! And I spent five years suffering like hell until I turned fourteen and experienced my dance of the phantoms. Until I found out that my father didn't really exist, which meant that he hadn't been killed, either."

"It's not like that, Bruna. As you know, those five years you refer to didn't exist. It's nothing more than a false memory. All the scenes were inserted at the same time into your brain."

A knot of angry, burning tears squeezed the detective's throat. She had to make an effort to speak, and her voice came out hoarse.

"And the grief? All that pain I have inside? All that suffering in my memory?"

Nopal looked at her gravely. "That's life, Bruna. That's how it is. Life hurts."

There was a brief silence and then the man stood up.

"I'll make a few phone calls and try to find out what's going on among the memorists. I'll get in touch with you if I find anything."

Nopal leaned over and brushed Bruna's tattooed cheek with a finger. Such a light touch that the rep almost thought she had imagined it. Then the memorist smoothed his hair, regained his charming and barely trustworthy smile and, giving a half-turn, walked away. The android—still seated, still stunned—watched him as he left, her thoughts buzzing around in her head like a swarm of bees. Five hundred scenes. That miserable pittance was her entire life? She was trying to gather the strength to stand up when she heard the sound of an incoming call. She looked at her wrist mobile: it was Myriam Chi.

"We have to talk," said the leader without even bothering to greet her.

"What's up?"

"I'll tell you in person. Come and see me tomorrow morning at nine."

And she cut the connection. Bruna was left staring at a blank screen, filled with self-loathing. She was bitter about having to obey a client like Myriam Chi, who trumpeted her orders as if Bruna were her slave; and losing her self-control with the memorist made her feel literally ill. The armchair in which the detective was sitting was at the back of the exhibition space, and a slow stream of visitors was passing by in front of her, crossing from the one side of the gallery to the other, and beginning the return walk to the entrance. But strangely, no one was looking at her. No one appeared to notice the tall, striking technohuman; too much invisibility for it to be normal. Yes indeed, Nopal had gotten it right when he arranged to meet her here. Illuminated by the skylight as if by a spotlight, Bruna felt like one more fake. Without a doubt, the least valuable one in the entire collection.

CHAPTER NINE

"**B**runa! Bruna! Get up! Wake up!"
The rep opened one eye and saw a human figure rushing toward her. She sat bolt upright in her bed, yelled, and chopped defensively with her hand. Her arm passed cleanly through the colored air without meeting any resistance. She refocused her vision and recognized old Yiannis.

"Dammit, Yiannis, I've told you a million times not to do this!" she growled, her tongue numb and her mouth dry.

The full-length holograph figure of the archivist was floating around the room. He was the only person whom Bruna had authorized to make holo-calls.

"I will not have you entering my home like this! I'm going to put you on the prohibited list!"

"Sorry, but there was no way of waking you, and Myriam Chi—"

"Oh, shit—Chi!"

Before the old man had even mentioned the rep leader, Bruna had already seen the time on her ceiling, 10:20, and her neurons, abused by her hangover, had painfully begun to fire up, reminding her of a missed appointment. The previous day began to reconstruct itself hazily in her memory: the meeting with Nopal, Chi's phone call, the excessive glasses of wine when she got home. Drinking by herself—or rather, getting drunk by herself—was the penultimate stage of alcoholism. There was no question that she had a problem with alcohol, and now she also had a problem with her sole client, whom she had stood up. Bruna leapt out of bed so quickly that her jellylike brain seemed to bang against her skull and she had to hold her head between her hands and close her eyes for a few moments. That was it. She would never ever have another drink.

"I know I'm going to be late for my appointment with Chi. I know I've fucked up," she groaned, her eyelids still tightly shut.

"No. It's not that, Bruna. You won't be late."

The rep lifted her head and saw that Yiannis had turned his back to her. *Of course, I'm naked. My poor old gentleman*, she thought to herself, feeling a sort of irritated affection toward him. Her Chinese bathrobe was lying on the floor. Bruna picked it up and put it on.

"You can look now. What do you mean I'm not going to be late?"

Yiannis—or rather his holograph—turned around. His face was strained and pale; there was no doubting that he was the bearer of bad news. A burst of adrenaline ran up Bruna's spine and her headache magically improved.

"What's going on?"

"Chi is dead."

"What?"

"Early this morning in the subway, she attacked a secretary from the Department of Labor. She gouged out the woman's eyes and smashed her windpipe. It goes without saying that the woman was a techno. Then Chi threw herself onto the tracks in front of a train. She died instantly."

"How do you know?"

"It's on the news."

Bruna ordered the home system to turn on the screen and found herself face to face with images of the android leader: Myriam at a rally; Myriam on the street; Myriam smiling, arguing, doing an interview. Beautiful and full of life. On the news there was no talk of her having an adulterated memory, but that didn't mean anything because, as far as Bruna knew, the information about the illegal memories had not been made public yet for any of the deaths. Was Myriam's behavior due to the havoc wreaked by a lethal implant as well? And if so—as was most likely—who had injected it through her nose? Because it was unthinkable that the RRM leader would have done it voluntarily. Myriam's death was murder. And it was also the biggest failure of Bruna's professional career. She hadn't even been able to keep her client alive for two days.

"I told her. I told her she had to be careful; I told her we should—"

"Be quiet, Bruna, be quiet and listen."

The hologram of Yiannis now appeared to be seated in the air and staring fixedly not at Husky's screen but at another point more to the right, probably the screen in his own house. But they were both seeing the same thing. A journalist, a famous but unpleasant individual with shiny blond hair called Enrique Ovejero, was discussing the event with an avid, sensational emphasis.

"And what people are asking themselves is, what's happening with the technos? Are they ill, perhaps? Is it an epidemic? Could humans become infected? Why are they so violent? So far they've only attacked other androids, but could they pose a threat to normal people? We have with us José Hericio, a controversial figure whom many of you will know, a lawyer, and secretary-general of the HSP, the Human Supremacist Party. Good morning, Hericio, how are you? First of all, from your perspective, the death of one of your greatest enemies, the leader of the RRM—is it good news?"

"No, Ovejero, for heaven's sake, I don't delight in the death of anyone. Moreover, not only is it not good news but I think it's also cause for great concern. Did you know there were other, earlier cases of violence?"

"Yes, of course. There was the one in the sky-tram last Thursday, and the one with the woman who gouged out her eye. With Chi, that makes three very similar cases in less than a week."

"No, no, I'm talking about before those. There were four other such cases earlier on. In other words, seven in total. It's just that the earlier cases went unnoticed because they were further apart. But they were all in the last six months. The seven cases are clearly interconnected, and not just because of that obsession with gouging out their own—or someone else's—eyes. They have other elements in common as well."

"What other elements?"

"My dear Ovejero, please allow me to keep that information to myself."

It was true. There had been four suicides who hadn't attacked anyone other than themselves. Three of them had gouged out their eyes, and all four had injected an adulterated memory. Or that was what Bruna had read in the documents Chi had given her. Hericio must have been referring to the mems when he was talking about what they had in common. Where could he have gotten a hold of those facts? The supremacist leader was a repulsive character with silicon cheeks, grafted hair, and a weak, slobbery mouth—one of those mouths that are permanently moist. Bruna had always felt that his fanatical extremism turned him into a clown of sorts, and that no one could take his awful nonsense seriously, but in the most recent regional elections, the HSP had won an astonishing 3 percent of the vote.

"Come on, Hericio. So how is it that the ordinary citizen knows nothing about these other incidents?" the slimy Ovejero asked, feigning outrage.

"Because, once again, our government—and I'm speaking not just of the regional government, but of the planetary one as well—is concealing information. Concealing it, or what would be even worse, it's not aware of it, because we're in the hands of the most incompetent politicians humanity has ever had in its history. And that's extremely serious, because we in the HSP have reliable information that suggests that a rep conspiracy is underway, a secret plan to seize power from humans."

"Hold on; wait a minute. What are you saying? That the technohumans are preparing a coup d'état? But so far, the victims have only been technos."

"Of course, because this is just the beginning. All this is part of a Machiavellian plan that I can't reveal right now. But I assure you—and listen carefully to what I'm saying—I assure you that before long, the victims will start to be humans."

"Look, Hericio, those are very dangerous, and very extremist, assertions, and I don't—"

"Unfortunately, it will happen. It will happen very soon! Because this government of mental weaklings and replickers is incapable of doing anything to prevent it."

"So, what should we be doing, according to you?"

"Look, the reps are our mistake. In fact, I even pity them—I feel sorry for them— because they're monsters that we humans created. They are the children of our arrogance and greed, but that doesn't stop them from being monsters. We have to put an end to this aberration as soon as possible, and in our party's platform we spell out clearly how to do this. In the first place, shut down forever all the production plants; and then, given that their lives are so short, it will be enough to intern all the reps until they die."

"Sure. The famous concentration camps of the sixties. I remind you that the horrendous Rep War was unleashed for far less than that."

"That's why we have to act quickly, without warning, and with a firm hand. There's a lot more of us than them. We can't allow them to attack first."

"Assuming that they do attack at some point, Hericio. In conclusion, on this program we don't always share the opinions of our guests, but we are strong supporters of freedom of expression. So we leave you with the categorical views of the leader of the Human Supremacist Party. Many thanks."

Bruna was stunned. It was a long time since she had heard anything so violent. And Ovejero seemed the more guilty to her for having invited such a cretin on to a live show, and for allowing him to unleash his paranoid propaganda without contradicting him or cutting him off, barely simulating a show of dissent. But then, what could you expect from a nasty character who referred to humans as "normal people"?

"This is unheard of. I think they should be reported for incitement to violence between the species," spluttered Yiannis.

Maybe Hericio had paid Ovejero, thought Bruna. Or perhaps antirep fanaticism was growing far more quickly than she had believed. She shivered. *Come on, Husky, you know we're totally discriminated against*, Myriam had said. And she had spoken of plots and conspiracies too—from the human side. It couldn't be; they were all crazy. It had to be something simpler and more idiotic than a conspiracy: a consignment of damaged mems. She noticed a light tingling sensation in her head, a tiny idea struggling to emerge. She decided to ignore it; normally, her ideas came to the surface of their own accord if she ignored them.

"I have to go to the RRM, Yiannis."

"Yes. And I have to go to work."

The hologram of the old man disappeared. Bruna had a quick vapor shower, put on a purple metallic skirt and blue T-shirt, and took a double serving of coffee out of the fridge to drink on the way. She caught a cab and didn't take long to get to her destination. In fact, she hardly had time to shake the container to heat up the coffee and then drink it before they pulled up in front of the headquarters of the Radical Replicant Movement.

"You've left my cab stinking of coffee," the driver grumbled.

"Well, it's a very pleasant aroma. You should charge me less for the ride," replied Bruna calmly.

But when she got out of the cab, a disturbing thought crossed her mind: *that cabdriver was unpleasant to me because I'm a rep.* Bruna shook her head, irritated with herself. She hated having any thoughts that smacked of a persecution complex. And it was a well-known fact that cabdrivers generally loathed people eating or drinking in their vehicles. *Four years, three months, and twenty-one days.*

At the entrance to the RRM there were two police cars, as well as the usual security guards. Bruna had to identify herself several times and pass through the scanner before they would allow her to go upstairs. She asked for Valo Nabokov, the head of security and Chi's lover, and to her surprise, the woman received her immediately. When Bruna walked into her office, Valo was standing with her back to Bruna, looking out the window. She was as tall as Bruna and probably also a combat rep, but she was dressed in a much more feminine and sophisticated manner: tight-fitting pants under a full, diaphanous skirt with 3-D spots depicting rosebuds on it, and huge platform shoes. She wore her hair—deep black and thick—in an intricate bun on top of her head.

"Sit down, Husky," she commanded without turning around.

There was a fake-leather armchair and a red acrylic chair. The detective chose the plastic chair. A few interminable moments passed without anything happening, and then Valo turned around. It was a given that she wasn't ugly. All technos had regular, even features (sometimes Bruna felt that this was one of the reasons why humans didn't like them), but they weren't all equally attractive. The head of security, for example, was rather unattractive. Combat replicants were flat-chested, because it worked out better when they had to fight, but Nabokov had enormous implants in her breasts, which she carried very high and barely covered, making them look like a large tray of meat underneath her square, pale face.

"Tell me something," she shot out.

"About what?"

"You've been working for us for two days. Tell me what you've discovered. Tell me who did this to her."

"I don't know anything yet."

The woman fixed her blazing eyes on Bruna. Huge bags under her eyes darkened her face.

"You've lost her. It's your fault. She was your responsibility and you've done nothing."

"Chi didn't hire me to protect her but to investigate the deaths of the reps. Her security was your responsibility."

Valo closed her eyes with an almost imperceptible expression of pain. Then she looked at Bruna again, with the face of a madwoman. Her bun was half-undone, and she looked like one of the furies on the ancient medallions that Yiannis had once shown her.

"Get out."

"Hold on a minute, Nabokov. I'm sorry about your loss, but it's important that we talk—"

"Get out!"

"Myriam called me yesterday. I think she had something to tell me; maybe she'd discovered something. She told me to come and see her this morning at nine o'clock."

Valo stared at her and Bruna ended up lowering her gaze. She noticed the android's hands: big, bony, trembling. Twitching hands that, remarkably, seemed to be covered with dark, regular freckles. No, they weren't freckles; they were tiny, half-healed wounds, perhaps burns.

"But you didn't make it," Valo whispered.

"What?"

"To the appointment at nine. You didn't make it."

Bruna became embarrassed.

"True. I...was held up. And then I saw the news."

And at this totally inappropriate moment, the little thought that had been eluding her earlier popped up inside the detective's head. It wasn't just strange that Hericio would have so much information, it was also odd that Chi would have it. How had the rep leader come to know so much? And how was it that each of them knew that all the individuals concerned had inserted adulterated memories? Who would have provided them with information that only the police knew? When all was said and done, maybe the conspiracy theories were based on something real. Moreover, the victims' obsession with eyes couldn't be the result of a chance deterioration in the mems.

All these thoughts went through Bruna's mind in an instant as Valo walked around the table and dropped wearily into the chair next to the screen. Then she raised her head and looked fiercely at Bruna.

"You're fired."

"Fired?"

"Get out of here. Right now."

Damn, I'm going to be stuck with the 3,000 Gs the artificial memory cost me, Bruna thought initially in a twinge of financial anxiety. And immediately afterward, she thought, *But it can't be. I don't want to drop this matter. I've got to clear up what's happened. I have to keep investigating.*

"Fine, I'm going, but before I go, please answer one question. How did Chi find out about—?"

"There's nothing more to discuss. You don't work for us any longer. You're off the case. Keep the advance. That way we're even. And now get out of here!"

No, they weren't quits, because Bruna had been crazy enough to buy a mem on the black market, but this wasn't the best moment to talk about expenses. Valo seemed to be beside herself. The detective got up and left the room, more irritated by all the questions she hadn't been able to ask than by the harshness of her sudden dismissal. She was heading quickly down the corridor toward the exit, lost in thought and chewing over her doubts, when she bumped into Habib, the rep leader's personal assistant. She had met him two days ago. He was the one who had provided her with the information about the first deaths and about how she would be paid. He was a brilliant and charming exploration techno. It would have been easy to flirt with him were it not for the fact that Bruna had no wish to be on close terms with any android again.

"Well, well, Husky, where are you off to in such a hurry? I was on my way to find you."

"I've just been fired. If that's what you were on your way to do, it's already done."

Habib opened his eyes wide in surprise. "What are you saying? Was it Valo? Don't pay any attention to her. She's gone mad, and I can understand why. We're all a bit unhinged. It's been a terrible blow."

His voice shook a little, perhaps on the verge of breaking.

"Yes, it's affected me too," responded Bruna.

"Don't go, Bruna. We need you more than ever now. Come on, let's go to my office."

All the RRM rooms were the same austere, monastic, militant cells, as if ornamentations were ideologically forbidden. But at least there was a small spray of mimosa in a vase on Habib's table.

"Is it real?"

The man gave a half-smile.

"It's a holograph. Speaking of which, I believe you still have Myriam's holograph ball, the one with the threat."

Bruna remembered that she had left a detailed analysis program of the images running. It should be just about done by now, and she hadn't seen the results yet.

"Yes. I was running the last few tests. I'll return it this afternoon. So, am I still on the case or not?"

"Of course you're still on it. I'll speak with Valo. Anyway, she doesn't have the authority to fire you."

"Do *you*?"

"I do, but I'm not going to. If what you're asking about is the power structure within the RRM now that Myriam is dead, I can tell you that I'm her successor until we hold an extraordinary meeting, which I've just called. It will be in two weeks' time."

"And then what will happen?"

"Most likely, they'll ratify me in the position. But that doesn't mean I murdered Myriam so that I could take her place," he added with a dry laugh devoid of any joy.

"Murdered?"

"I'm convinced she would never have injected herself with a mem."

"So am I. By the way, speaking of adulterated memories, how did you find out about the earlier cases?"

"That was Myriam's doing. She came in one day with the information. She was very worried."

"But who provided it?"

"I don't know. All she told me was that someone reliable had given it to her."

"Weren't you surprised she knew about the mems? They're something you can only know about if you have access to the official autopsy reports."

"Well, no, it didn't surprise me at all. Myriam always was extremely well informed. She had confidants and contacts everywhere. She even had the odd memorist friend. She was an extraordinary woman."

In fact, it wasn't all that difficult, reflected Bruna; she herself had accessed the report on Cata Caín. As to the memorist, she couldn't help but think about Pablo Nopal.

"When was the last time you saw her, Habib?"

"She came to my office yesterday afternoon. There were things we had to decide about the RRM, work-related matters. But I found her very nervous, very distracted. I asked her if she was okay, and we began talking about the deaths. Then she got up and left. She said she was very tired and she was thinking about going home soon to sleep. But she didn't leave, or at least not by the main entrance. Her bodyguards hung around waiting until midnight, and when they went upstairs to get her, they couldn't find her anywhere."

"How come they waited so long?"

"She often stayed late working on her own."

"And they weren't concerned when they didn't find her?"

"Yes, they were worried, and they called me. I got onto Nabokov, who knew nothing either, because Chi hadn't come home. That was when we got really frightened. And rightly so."

They stopped talking for a few seconds while violent images of Myriam's death flashed blindingly inside their heads and the space between them seemed to acquire a blood-red brilliance.

"At what time was your conversation with Chi?"

"Between about 18:00 and 19:00. I was the last person to see her alive."

Bruna tried to hold back a small start. Myriam's call had been at 18:30.

"Are you sure?"

Habib smiled. He, too, had huge bags under his eyes and looked haggard.

"Absolutely. And you don't have to hide your surprise. I was there when she rang you, Husky. Moreover, I know what she wanted to tell you."

He paused dramatically, something Bruna found difficult to endure.

"It's possible…You have to promise to keep all this a complete secret, Husky; there's too much at stake. So, there is unfortunately a possibility that some reps may be implicated in the deaths. It's not exactly the best news for our movement, but I'm afraid there's considerable evidence."

"What are you saying? Implicated how? What evidence are you talking about?"

"There have always been violent reps, as you know. And if you want me to be honest, I understand it perfectly, because the marginalization and disdain that humans subject us to are hard to bear. But in the RRM we're not in favor of violence, either ethically or strategically. The intention of our movement is precisely to provide a democratic stage for the battle, for the dignity and equality of our species."

Bruna suppressed a gesture of impatience. "Sure, sure, I know. But we were talking about proof."

"The lock on Myriam's office was manipulated by a rep from Complet, our maintenance company. The door register was altered so that it wouldn't record the code of the person who put the holograph ball on the table."

"Have you spoken with the company?"

"Our technicians discovered the lock manipulation yesterday morning, and we immediately went to the Complet head office. We got there just minutes too late. They'd obviously fled in a real hurry after they'd wiped their databases."

"A most opportune escape."

Habib sighed.

"Yes, I thought so, too. I find it very hard to believe, but it's possible that someone from the RRM warned them of our visit. The problem is that it could have been just about anyone, because lots of people knew about it: the technicians, some members of the council, Valo's crew..."

"Valo's crew?"

"The combat reps who make up our security team. You already know we've had numerous assaults. Yesterday, we took ten of our team to the Complet head office, just in case."

"How long have you been working with Complet?"

"Four or five months. I can get you the exact date. But, in any case, the company's involvement seems to suggest it's not just a question of an isolated act of violence against an individual but something much more complex, sophisticated, and meticulously organized. And there's something else. Did you see that fanatic, Hericio, on the news?"

"Yes."

"Isn't it strange that he would be talking about all those things right now? And doesn't it seem odd to you that's he's so well informed? We know Hericio has been meeting with a rep."

"How do you know?"

The corners of Habib's mouth twitched wryly and he waved his hand gently in the air.

"Well, let's just say that we try to be fully abreast of our enemy's activities. And one of our people saw Hericio meeting the rep in a public, if discrete, place."

The armchairs under the skylight in the Museum of Modern Art flashed into Bruna's mind.

"Where did they meet?"

"A sky-tram stop. Is that particularly important?"

The detective shook her head, feeling a little foolish.

"The fact is that we believe it may have been one of the Complet employees. It's a company composed exclusively of androids. We always try to work with our own. Anyway, Myriam thought that the HSP had somehow managed to buy off that miserable lot. And that it's all a scheme to discredit our movement, to create an antitechno climate of opinion that would favor their party."

Bruna thought this over for a moment.

"Sounds plausible. The trouble is, Habib, that we can't rule out that it might be a new group of terrorist reps."

"But why would they attack other technohumans?"

"To frighten the androids and make them think that we're dealing with a supremacist conspiracy, as you said yourself. To radicalize the reps and unleash violence between the species."

"Hmmm, yes. Maybe...In any event, it's critical that we clarify what's happening as quickly as possible. Because there's no question that social tension is growing all the time. Myriam was well aware of the urgency, and that's why she rang you yesterday. I know what she wanted to ask you: that you investigate the HSP, and Hericio in particular. By the way, I think the sight of Hericio on the news this morning adds weight to Chi's theory."

Bruna agreed, slowly. "Okay. I'll see what I can do."

They stood up, and Habib escorted her to the door of the office. Barely two steps, in such a small room. Before she left, Bruna turned to him.

"Just one more question. What's the matter with Nabokov's hands?"

The man frowned and stood looking at her as if weighing up his answer.

"Valo's unwell," he said, finally. "She's…she's beginning
to show the signs of TTT. Or that's what we think, because
she's refused to see a doctor. She's going to a healer instead.
Those marks are the bites of a viper. An African viper whose
venom is said to cure rep cancer. Well, you know how these
things are."

Yes, Bruna knew. The inevitability and ferocity of TTT
meant that many androids looked for miracle cures, and a dis-
ordered and motley market of alternative treatments and shady
therapists flourished around the technos. Like all reps, she too
was sent unsolicited publicity from a horde of charlatans who
promised to get rid of tumors via magnetism, gamma rays,
chromatic therapies, or animal toxins, as in Nabokov's case.
But as far as she was aware, to date no one had been able to
save themselves from the early death.

The detective returned home overwhelmed by a deep
depression. She had days that seemed warped from the start,
and life, like a soaking-wet blanket, began to weigh heavily
on her shoulders. The viper bites scam reminded her that she
hadn't checked her mail for days, so she opened her lobby
mailbox and came across a cacophony of 3-D and holograph
flyers. They were programmed to switch on as soon as they
were exposed to light, and now, newly activated, they filled
the small box with a hectic confusion of colors and shapes,
tiny voices, and shrill music. That's why she hated to pick up
her mail, she remembered with irritation, and she began to
remove the advertisements by the handful, throwing them into
the yellow container under the mailboxes: flyers for vacations
by the beach; for Torres solar bicycles; gyms; lipo-laser beauty
treatments; and the timeworn, cursed miracle cures for techno
cancer. The promotional material landed, shrieking, inside the

container and once there, back in darkness, fell silent again. *What a relief,* thought Bruna. In her frenzy of cleaning, she was on the point of throwing out a small message container as well. Fortunately, she spotted it in time and opened it. Inside was the mem she had bought from the trafficker. She had sent the mem to a lab for analysis, and now the results had arrived. She was impatient to discover what they were, and started to read the report right there, leaning up against the mailboxes. It said that the mem was illegal but not adulterated and so would neither incite someone to violence nor be lethal. The report was followed by a detailed description of the scenes in the memory: five hundred, just as Nopal had in fact suggested. She gave them a cursory glance, with the same repugnance she would feel if she were looking at the squashed innards of a cockroach. The bill for the lab's work was attached at the bottom: 300 gaias. Just what she needed. The only plus was that she wouldn't have to go back and see the unpleasant dog-eared mutant. That was now a trail going nowhere.

The first thing she did when she got inside her apartment was go to the fridge, pour herself a glass of white wine, and drink it in one gulp. She ordered the house to raise the blinds and open the windows wide. She needed light and air. She was obsessed by her memory of Myriam: the thought of her sudden fit of madness, the violence of the attack on that woman, the wheels of the subway train crushing her body. And then she saw Nabokov's hands again, with their small, regular, violet wounds. She poured another glass of wine, warmed up a couple of soy and algae burgers, and ate them, chewing each mouthful deliberately, slowly and rhythmically, concentrating on the business of eating so as to empty her head of the oppressive images that were persecuting her. By the time the plate was empty, she had calmed down enough to get to work. She poured herself another glass of wine, sat down in front of the screen and confirmed that Habib had already sent her the documents from the maintenance company. She spent a fair bit of time tracking its business details through the various sections of the regional administration. In the end, it turned out that Complet had emerged from nowhere a week before the RRM had contracted the company, that there were only two permanent employees—both androids—and that the Radical Replicant Movement was its sole client. All quite odd.

Lost in thought, Bruna checked her computer for the analysis of the film clip of the disembowelment. The analysis had been completed hours earlier and the results were indeed there. The program had been unable to identify the location, to reconstruct the deleted ID, or to provide any other evidence connected with the recording, although an analysis of the background suggested a 51 percent probability that the evisceration of the animal had been performed privately rather than in a slaughterhouse. There was nothing new except for one image. At one particular moment, the blade of the knife fleetingly reflected part of the face of the person recording the hologram: half an eyebrow; a fragment of a cheek; half an eye; and the vertical pupil—of a rep. The detective's mood darkened; the guilt—or at least the collaboration—of technohumans was becoming more and more evident. She made a copy of the images, removed the chip from her computer, put it back inside the holograph ball and called an instant courier service. When the small robot beeped at her door twenty minutes later, she placed the sphere, the mem, and her astronomical bill for expenses in the drawer of the automated courier, and sent the whole lot to Habib.

That accomplished, she spent the rest of the afternoon wasting time.

She tried to review the documentation regarding the first four deaths that Habib had given her, but she was too tired, and the wine induced a mellow, irresistible sleepiness. She tried lying on the bed and taking a nap, but she found she was too tense to be able to rest. She thought about doing some exercise, but just the thought of the effort made her feel exhausted. She sprawled on the sofa with another glass of wine in her hand, almost catatonic, but minutes later an inner itch made her stand up and wander erratically around the room. She managed to place one more piece into her jigsaw puzzle, but that took such an effort that she then gave up. She read a few pages of Malencia Piñeiro's latest novel without managing to make sense of any of it. She put on a pair of 3-D glasses and began to play some virtual games: the archery competition, the rocket race, and the giant slalom. This was dizzying and obsessive entertainment that usually cleared her head and managed to stupefy her, but on this occasion the repetitive games got on her nerves.

Then she looked at the clock—21:30—and realized that she had in fact been whiling away time until just this moment, until night fell and Gándara started his likely shift, until she could go to the Forensic Anatomy Institute to see Myriam Chi's body.

It was quite cool, so Bruna pulled on a thermal jacket over her T-shirt and short metallic skirt, and headed outside. She was feeling a little nauseous: too many glasses of wine for the two soy burgers in her stomach. But half an hour later, as she was walking down the somber corridors of the institute, her steps resonating on the worn stone floors, she worried that she was still too sober and regretted not having had a few more glasses of wine.

Luckily, Gándara was on duty that evening. She could see him through the large window that separated the office from Dissection Room 1 personally rummaging around inside a cadaver. Although it wasn't necessary to touch the bodies these days, thanks to robots and telesurgery, Gándara continued to put his hands inside almost all of his corpses; he maintained that no technology could replace the complexity and subtlety of firsthand observation. There he was now, leaning over something that had once been someone and looking—so appropriately—like a tawny vulture: his face relatively free of wrinkles thanks to routine beauty treatments; his nose sharp and prominent; his eyebrows bushy; a bristling head of hair; a long, skinny neck; and round, intense black eyes. Gándara looked up, saw the detective and waved with his gloved and very bloody hand for her to come in. Bruna hesitated for a moment, and the medical examiner waved his dripping hand again, the blood clots shining like red lacquer under the powerful spotlight. Then the rep glimpsed a dark, chubby face on the dissected corpse on the table; it was the body of an unknown male. She breathed a sigh of relief and opened the door to the dissection room. She didn't know if she would have been able to cope had Gándara been dissecting Chi's remains.

"Hi, Husky, how's life? I believe you came by here the other day."

"Yes."

"You terrified my assistant."

"He frightens easily."

"He's a cretin. Are you here about Chi?"

"Spot on. Always so perceptive."

"It was obvious. That cretin Kurt told me you were interested in the Caín case."

"Right again."

Gándara continued to examine the dissected body as he spoke. A body that Bruna forced herself to look at because it wasn't anything anymore. That spent flesh, that ever-so-dark blood, those kilos of organic material were nothing. It had once been a human, but death made everything equal.

"And Chi's case is effectively the same. She had a lethal memory implant too, exactly like Caín. Do you want to have a look?"

"At the memory?"

"No. At Chi. I've sent the mem to the bioengineering lab."

No, thought Bruna, *I'm going to say no. I don't want him to show me the rep leader.* But she couldn't form the word.

"Morgue, take out Myriam Chi," the medical examiner ordered the central system. Then, turning to Bruna, he added, "Wait a minute while I clean myself up a bit."

Gándara washed his gloved hands under a vapor jet as the cold room opened and a robot-cart wheeled in the body of a woman. *I don't want to see her*, Bruna reiterated to herself. But she approached the capsule, walking slowly and automatically.

"She's a bit the worse for wear. She threw herself in front of a train, as you know. But on the other hand, for someone who's been run over, she's more or less intact, apart from the loss of one leg. The blow damaged her internally. Capsule, open!"

The transparent metal cylinder opened its lid with a pneumatic hiss. Inside, surrounded by a thin cloud of liquid nitrogen, lay Myriam Chi's body. Bluish, naked, with a shaved head, and scars from the autopsy marking her skull and chest. But with her face untouched. And without makeup. Childlike and defenseless. Lower down, the grotesque mess that was her legs.

The severed member, in bits, carefully reassembled like the pieces of a puzzle. The menacing image in the holograph ball flashed across Bruna's mind like a spasm: Chi's body, sliced open and abused. When she had seen the image the first time, it was still a lie. She closed her eyes and expelled the memory from her mind. *I don't feel anything*, she thought. *This is nothing more than a piece of frozen meat.*

"She's quite beautiful despite everything, don't you think? Tomorrow, I'll return the body to the people at the RRM, and they'll be able to stage a lovely protest show with her funeral."

"Gándara, I need you to give me the lab reports on the mems. I have to find out what those damn implants contain."

"I'd love to know that, too, but the bioengineering people haven't given me anything. Not for this one, not for Caín, not for the people on the sky-tram. Oddly enough, the Judicial Police have decided that those reports are secret."

"The appropriate decision, it seems to me," said a voice behind them.

Bruna and the medical examiner turned around. He was a huge man, taller than Husky, and twice as wide. His massive body blocked the door.

"Because I'm afraid that if you had the reports, you—who I assume to be Gándara, the medical examiner—would have passed them on to this android. Whom I don't know," continued the man.

He spoke slowly, spacing out his words as if he were half-asleep. There was something lethargic about him—about his green eyes, partly veiled by heavy eyelids that seemed incapable of opening completely, and about his solid body and the way it planted itself vertically on the floor as if it wanted to screw itself into the stone.

"We don't know who the hell you are, either," Bruna replied with studied rudeness.

But she was lying, because the cheap, conventional three-piece suit—gray shirt and pants, and a slightly darker thermal jacket—were a civil servant giveaway. He was undoubtedly a policeman.

"Inspector Paul Lizard, from the Judiciary," said the huge man, showing his ID. "And you are?"

"I'm the victim's sister," said Bruna, sarcastically.

"You must be the detective hired by the RRM, right? Bruna...Bruna Husky," said Lizard, impassive, consulting the notes on his mobile.

"A clairvoyant."

"Well, I'm delighted to meet you. I specifically wanted to talk to you."

"About what? About why you're hiding the matter of the adulterated memories from everyone?"

"Maybe. Could you drop by the Judiciary tomorrow? I assume you know where we are. At 13:00?"

"And why should I do that?"

"Because it would be good for you. Because we could help each other. Because you're an inquisitive woman. Because if you don't come, I'll have you arrested and brought in."

As he was speaking, the man was approaching them. And now he was standing next to the cylinder and contemplating Chi's body with surprisingly watchful eyes under the sleepy eyelids. *It's a look that hides his tenacity*, thought Bruna.

"If no one explains that there are adulterated mems out there that are driving reps mad, then it just looks as if we technos are dangerous murderers. It's clumsy, but it works."

The words had come out of Husky's mouth of their own accord, as if someone else had dictated them to her. But as soon as she said them she realized that they were true, that Myriam Chi was right—there was a conspiracy—and that maybe this devious, granite-like inspector was also part of the plot. The RRM leader had said so already: you can't trust the police.

"And why does it work? Well, because deep down, all you humans are afraid of us…You despise us and, at the same time, you fear us. You too, Inspector? Do I scare you? Do I disgust you?"

"Husky, you do say some silly things," muttered Gándara, clearly displeased.

Ah, thought Bruna, *you too*. The old medical examiner was aligning himself with the recent arrival, a fellow human. Birds of a feather always ended up sticking together. *But no, that wasn't it*, the rep thought again, making an effort to be rational; it was hardly surprising that her words would make Gándara feel uncomfortable, because she rarely let loose with such fiery speeches. It was as if she felt obliged to speak for Myriam Chi—as if she had to say what Myriam would have said.

"The only thing that frightens me is stupidity," said Lizard.

"How many rep inspectors are there in the Judicial Police Force?"

The man gave a weary sigh.

"Answer! How many technohuman inspectors are there?" repeated Bruna, almost shouting.

Lizard looked at her with an easygoing calmness.

"None," he replied.

Husky was stunned. She wasn't expecting that reply. To tell the truth, before that moment, it would never have occurred to her to ask such a question. Something hurt inside her head. A thought that was burning like an emotion. A rational recognition of marginalization. She noted the mindless defense mechanism of anger taking hold inside her. She did an about-face and, without any farewell, left the room. She could just hear Paul's thick voice behind her.

"Remember, tomorrow at 13:00 in the Judiciary."

Bruna charged down the dark corridors, crossed the lobby without greeting the guards and left the institute as if she were running away. But her flight lost its momentum as soon as she abandoned the building. She stopped a few yards from the entrance, in the middle of the night and the middle of the empty street, not knowing what to do or where to go. She was too upset to go home; too angry to go to one of her usual hang-outs, such as Oli's bar, and put up with the banal chitchat of some acquaintance; too full of death to remain on her own. *Four years, three months, and twenty-one days.*

The cold air was a relief to her burning cheeks. She was standing on the sidewalk, feet slightly apart, feeling all the weight of her body, her neck sweaty, her arms relaxed, her stomach smooth and taut, her legs agile. Flesh alert, eager. A body raging with life. An acute unease began to take shape inside her, like a storm cloud in a late summer sky. Suddenly she remembered something and started to rummage through all her pockets. Finally, wrapped up in a crumpled piece of paper inside a box of painkillers in her backpack, she found what she was looking for—a candy. An oxytocin cocktail. The tiny pill must have been lying forgotten in its hiding place for months, and it was a bit sticky. Bruna gave the pill a superficial clean, rubbing it between two fingers, and then she placed it under her tongue to speed up the impact of the drug. And for a few minutes, she focused on breathing and waiting. On relishing the cold night air. On emptying her mind and becoming all body.

There was a car parked in front of the entrance to the Forensic Anatomy Institute. It wasn't a regulation police vehicle, but the gray license plates indicated that it was an official car. Without doubt the car belonged to Inspector Paul Lizard—the Reptile, the Caiman, that barely trustworthy hulk. Bruna inhaled deeply. Her skin was burning, but from within now. In a few moments, the rep would do something about that. About all that energy and fire. Shortly, Bruna would begin to cruise the city; she would surf the night in search of sex—of a carnal explosion capable of defeating death. The only possible eternity was between her legs. Like most humans and technohumans, Bruna was more or less bisexual; only a few individuals were exclusively heterosexual or homosexual. But on the whole, she preferred men, and in any case, tonight she wanted a man. Maybe someone as big as the reptile Lizard, a gigantic human whom she'd have begging for her android vagina. Bruna let loose a brief laugh. Her heart was beating faster, her body seemed to be boiling; the air was charged with pheromones. The rapture of the night. She was a star on the verge of bursting, a pulsating quasar. She walked a few steps, relishing her vigor and her agility, her hunger and her health. Relishing a ferocious happiness. She put her hand under her short metallic skirt and, leaning against the parked car, she took off her panties. Tonight she wanted to roam the city without any underwear. It wasn't the first time she had done so, and it wouldn't be the last. What pleasure to feel herself completely open, rid of hindrances, available. Before she headed off, she left her panties on the windscreen of the policeman's car. The world buzzed around her and the beat of life throbbed in her veins, her heart and, in particular, at the center of her naked flower, right down there.

**Central Archive, the United States of the Earth.
Modifiable version**

ACCESS STRICTLY LIMITED
AUTHORIZED EDITORS ONLY

**Madrid, January 22, 2109, 11:06
Good morning, Yiannis**

IF YOU ARE NOT YIANNIS
LIBEROPOULOS,
CENTRAL ARCHIVIST FT711, QUIT
THESE PAGES IMMEDIATELY

ACCESS STRICTLY LIMITED
AUTHORIZED EDITORS ONLY

UNAUTHORIZED ACCESS IS A CRIMINAL
OFFENSE
PUNISHABLE BY IMPRISONMENT UP TO
A MAXIMUM OF TWENTY YEARS

Floating Worlds
Keywords: History of Science, Labaric Cult, aristopopulism,
Plagues, Robot Wars, bilateral agreements, Second Cold War.
#63-025
<u>Entry being edited</u>

The **Floating Worlds** in existence at present are the **Democratic State of Cosmos** and the **Kingdom of Labari**. These two gigantic artificial structures maintain fixed orbits with respect to Earth, and are authentic worlds with complete autonomy. Although, for strategic reasons, Cosmos and Labari both adhere to a cryptic policy of data concealment, it is assumed that there are between five and six hundred million inhabitants on each of the Floating Worlds. They are all humans, as neither world allows technos or aliens to live there, a fact which converts these Worlds into zones that are undoubtedly more secure for our species.

The first references to the eventual need for the construction of an artificial world in the stratosphere to provide accommodation for at least a portion of humanity in the event of a catastrophe surfaced in the so-called **Atomic Era**—the decades in the mid-twentieth century that followed the explosion of the first nuclear fission bombs among civilian populations (**Hiroshima** and **Nagasaki**). But the idea of building alternative worlds in space became a social necessity and a real possibility during the twenty-first century, following the havoc wreaked by **global warming**, which raised the level of the oceans by six feet and inundated some 18 percent of the Earth's surface and, even more critically, following the high loss of life, despair, and insecurity caused by the **Plagues**, the **Rep War**, and the **Robot Wars**.

The Kingdom of Labari is named after the founder of the **Church of the One Creed**, the Argentinian **Heriberto Labari** (2001–2071). A podiatrist by profession, Labari was born on September 11, 2001, the day of the well-known attack on the World Trade Center in New York, a coincidence he would subsequently use as evidence of his predestination. When he turned thirty, Labari pronounced that he had received a divine message. He gave up his work, founded the Church of the One Creed, and dedicated himself to preaching about the **Labaric Cult**, which, according to him, was the original and primordial religion brought to Earth by extraterrestrials in remote times and subsequently perverted and broken up through ignorance and greed into the planet's various beliefs. The cult offered a syncretic mix of the best-known religions, especially Christianity and Islam, together with ingredients from role-play and fantasy, with overtones reminiscent of a medieval, hierarchical, sexist, subservient, and highly ritualistic world. In order to disseminate his teachings, Heriberto Labari wrote some twenty science fiction novels that quickly became very popular. "My fantastic tales are the Christian parables of the twenty-first century," he once declared. It must be remembered that the founding of the Church of the One Creed coincided with the terrible years of the Plagues, one of the most violent and tragic periods in the history of humanity, and Labari's message seemed to offer security and the possibility of salvation. When the prophet died in 2071, killed by a fanatical Shi'ite assassin, there were already hundreds of millions of **Ones** throughout Earth. Some of them, ranging from Arab sheiks from the Persian Gulf region to important Western entrepreneurs, were hugely wealthy.

A few years before his death, Labari had begun to speak about the construction of a stratospheric world, not only in order to flee from an ever more convulsed Earth, but also to create a perfect society based on the rigid parameters of the Labaric Cult. His posthumous novel, *The Kingdom of the Pure*, specified in great detail what such a place would be like. Labari is shaped like a thick ring or, rather, an enormous pneumatic tire. By all accounts, it was generated by semiartificial bacteria capable of reproducing themselves in space at dizzying speed and forming a light, semiorganic, porous, and practically indestructible material that does not lose its shape. The details of this highly innovative technology remain a secret. It is striking that a society that is officially antitechnology has been capable of a scientific discovery of this caliber, even if the processes employed are either natural or seem to imitate nature in some way. The Kingdom's inhabitants live inside the walls of the outer ring; and, in the interior, an immense reservoir of water and hydrogen-releasing algae supplies the Kingdom's energy needs.

While Labari is the result of a new religion, Cosmos is the product of an ideology. ~~Although perhaps both end up being the same.~~ When the Moon Pact, which ended the Rep War, was signed in 2062, there was only one state that did not sign it: Russia. At that time, the old Russian empire was going through the worst moment in its history. It was a bankrupt nation, devastated by gangs and drastically reduced in size thanks to successive wars and bitter conflicts with its neighbors, who had been shrinking its borders. Since the Russians were so poor and backward that they did not even have technohuman production plants, the fact that they had not signed the Moon Pact did not alter in any way the effectiveness of the agreement. But the refusal to sign made **Amaia Elescanova**—who had just been elected president of that nation in ruins—famous overnight.

Elescanova (2013–2104) was the founder and leader of the **Regeneration** (or   u) **Party**. She argued that all the evils of the world were the result of the abandonment of utopias and of surrender to the abuses of capitalism. While she maintained that both Marxism and the Soviet model were obsolete, she nevertheless demanded the creation of a common revolutionary front to end the world's inequalities. In her essay *Responsible Minorities and Contented Masses*, the cornerstone of her ideology, Elescanova proposed a society governed by the wisest and the fittest, along the lines of Plato's republic but strengthened by scientific advances: "The same zygote could even be employed to boost the best qualities of the new ruling class, by employing eugenic techniques (...) Science and Social Conscience United to Create the Supermen and Superwomen of the Future (~~capital letters in the original text~~)."

Regenerationism, or **aristopopulism** as it rapidly came to be called, spread like wildfire throughout the world, especially after the mid-2070s, when various nations began to impose a charge for clean air, and citizens with fewer resources were forced to emigrate en masse to the more polluted zones. But it was not just the financially weak sectors that adopted Elescanova's doctrine. Powerful parties from various countries and differing ideologies—from the extreme left to the extreme right—joined forces with the Russian leader in 2077 to form the **International Aristopopular Movement (IAM)**, an antibourgeois, antireligion, and anticapitalist organization although, paradoxically, one that had considerable capital at its disposal.

A movement such as this naturally aspires to world domination, but perhaps Earth did not appear to the IAM to have much of a future. Whether it was for this reason or the news that the Labarians were going to build a floating kingdom, what is certain is that the IAM's first decision was to build its own extraterrestrial platform. In fact, a fierce competition of sorts arose between the Ones and the Aristopopulists to see who could finish their project first, as if the remarkable achievement of an artificial world might serve as an advertising ploy for their respective, if opposing, life visions. Despite starting the race later, the IAM won; the Democratic State of Cosmos was inaugurated in 2087, while the first subjects of the Kingdom of Labari did not arrive until 2088.

Although the plans and details are also unknown in this instance, there is no question that Cosmos is a dazzling construction. A multitude of pyramids made out of carbon nanofibers are linked to one another to form a megapyramid. The result is a sort of tubular net, a framework from which the buildings or living modules are hung, interconnected by "streets" that run through the interiors of the tubes.

The construction of these artificial worlds was observed on Earth with growing distrust and apprehension. However, any effective opposition to the creation of these floating nations was prevented by the fact that the two projects were being driven by multinational social movements and, more important, by the chaos and loss of life provoked by the **Robot Wars**. And when they were finally inaugurated, millions of desperate residents of Earth attempted to gain admission to either of the worlds in order to escape the tremendous desolation caused by the wars. Cosmos and Labari did not participate in the **Global Agreements of Cassiopeia,** because they refused to grant technohumans and aliens the same rights as humans. Nevertheless, both the Ones and the Aristopopulists subsequently signed bilateral agreements with the United States of the Earth, although relations have never been easy. This coexistence, full of suspicion, secrets and tension, has been dubbed the **Second Cold War** by analysts. That said, given that the two worlds continue to be mortal enemies and have no diplomatic relations whatsoever, the USE has on occasion found itself obliged to carry out the role of unofficial intermediary.

Finally, some sources speak of the existence of a third Floating World, a much smaller structure, possibly even self-propelled—more a megaspaceship than an orbital platform—inhabited by a democratic, tolerant, and free society that enjoys a reasonably just and happy life. This community would have begun its clandestine existence during the turbulent years of the Robot Wars, and since then would have managed to hide itself in space. It is known as **Avalon**, but everything points to its existence being an urban myth.

CHAPTER TEN

The first thing Bruna was conscious of, as always, was the stabbing throb in her temples. The hangover drilling through her head like a fiery screw.

Next, she sensed a reddish light through the membrane of her eyelids—eyelids that were still too heavy to feel like opening. But the light suggested that it was very bright. Maybe it was daytime.

Whiplashes of pain shot across her forehead. Thinking was torture.

Bruna nevertheless forced herself to think. And to remember. A black hole seemed to have swallowed up her most recent past, but on the other side of that enormous void the rep began to recover broken images of the previous night, landscapes glimpsed through the fog. Noisy venues full of people. Packed dance floors. Before that, the Forensic Anatomy Institute. Chi's corpse. The street, the moon. And Bruna putting a candy under her tongue. Again, she glimpsed a confusion of venues. A faceless character inviting her to have a drink. The public screens chattering against a black sky. A group of musicians playing. A hand making its way up her back. She shivered, and that forced her to become aware of the rest of her body apart from her ever-present, pounding head. She was facedown on what seemed to be a bed, arms bent on either side of her body, her face resting on her left cheek.

Bruna breathed slowly so as not to arouse the monstrous headache further. She had no recollection of how the night had ended, and she had absolutely no idea where she might be. She loathed waking up in a strange house. She hated greeting a new day in a neighborhood she didn't know, and having to check location coordinates on her mobile in order to find out where she was. She felt the sheet with her right hand, but it was impossible to determine by touch alone if it was her own bed. She had no alternative but to open her eyes. *Four years, three months, and twenty days.*

She raised her eyelids very slowly, afraid to look. Sure enough, there was a lot of light; a merciless daylight that beat down on her retinas. It took her a few seconds to overcome the dazzle, then she recognized the small fake-leather armchair half-covered by the messy pile of her clothes—the metallic skirt, the thermal jacket. And the T-shirt tossed on the familiar synthetic wood floor. She was in her own apartment. That was a start.

The good news encouraged her and, supporting herself on her hands, she managed to raise her trunk. As she was doing so, she noticed out of the corner of her eye that beside her the bedspread was bulging over what appeared to be another person. She wasn't alone. Not everything was going to be so simple, of course.

Being totally nude wasn't the best way to introduce herself to a stranger, so she grabbed the jacket from the nearby armchair and clumsily put it on, still sitting on the bed. Then she took a deep breath, summoned all her energy and stood up. Standing next to the bed, her temples throbbing, she looked at her visitor, who, judging by the lump, was very big. A bulky body lying on its side with its back to her, completely covered by the sheet. Well, not entirely. Up top some hair was visible—coarse—and the nape of a neck, a green neck.

Bruna gasped for air.

It couldn't be.

It *couldn't* be.

She put a hand up to her head to relieve her headache and contain the riot of horrific thoughts. Stealthily, she made her way around the bed until she was close to the face of the sleeping occupant—a wide, flat nose; bushy eyebrows; greenish skin.

She had slept with a *bicho*.

She felt like throwing up.

But had she really slept with a *bicho*? What she meant was, had she…? Merely exploring the idea in her head turned her legs to jelly. She had to sit down on the bed so that she wouldn't fall. And that movement woke the alien.

The alien opened his eyes and looked at her. His eyes were honey colored, with a melancholy expression. He was an Omaá. Frantic, Bruna tried to remember what she knew about Omaás. They were the most numerous Others on Earth because, apart from the diplomatic delegation, there were the thousands of refugees who had fled from the religious wars on their world. Those refugees were the poorest aliens precisely because they were stateless, and that meant they were the most despised of the *bichos*. They were…hermaphrodites? Or was that the Balabís? *Hell's bells!* Bruna was terrified at the thought of having to see her bedmate in his entirety.

Moving slowly, meticulously and with infinite calm—the same way that a human would move in the face of a small animal he didn't want to frighten—the *bicho* sat up in the bed, naked from the waist up, and with the rest of him covered by the sheet. *Oh, yes,* thought Bruna with faint disgust, *and these are also the translucent ones.* What was most disturbing about extraterrestrials was their appearance, at the same time so human and so alien. The impossible similarity of their biology. The Omaá was tall and muscular, a robust version of a man with arms and hands and nails on the ends of his—Bruna stopped to count them—six fingers. But the head—with its bristly hair and bushy eyebrows, its wide nose that resembled a snout, and its sad eyes—was too much like that of a dog. And then there was the worst part, the skin: semibluish; greenish in the wrinkles; and worst of all, semitransparent, which meant that, depending on the activity and the light, you could make out bits of the internal organs, pink suggestions of pulsating viscera. Hell, what would it feel like to touch that wretched thing? She had no memory of having touched that skin, and if truth be told, she didn't want to remember either. So *now* what were they going to do? Ask each other their names?

The *bicho* smiled timidly.

"Hi. I'm Maio."

His voice had the husky roar of the sea crashing against rocks, but you could understand him all right, and his accent was more than acceptable.

"I...I'm Bruna."

"Pleased to meet you."

A silence bristling with unasked questions sprang up between them. *And now what?* the rep asked herself.

"Do you remember...Do you recall when we got home last night?" Bruna asked, finally.

"Yes."

"In other words, you...ahem...I mean, do you remember everything?"

"Yes."

Damn, thought Bruna, *I'd rather not go on checking.*

"Well, Maio, I've got to go. Sorry. I mean, *we* have to leave. Right now."

"Okay," said the *bicho* with a friendliness bordering on gentleness.

But he didn't move.

"Come on, we're going."

"Yes, but I have to get up and get dressed. I'm naked."

Oh, yes. Of course! Were Omaás that modest? Though it went without saying that she wasn't ready to look at him either.

"I'll get dressed, too. In the bathroom. And in the meantime, you..."

Bruna left her sentence hanging in the air, grabbed her clothes from the previous night so that she wouldn't have to waste time looking for something else, and locked herself in the bathroom. Dazed, her head still splitting with pain, she had a short vapor shower and then put on the metallic skirt and T-shirt again. She grunted with displeasure when she realized that she didn't have any underwear at hand and remembered what she'd done with her panties the night before. Not having the garment now really annoyed her. She wet her face with a tiny jet of her really expensive water in an attempt to clear her head and then stealthily opened the door. In front of her, the alien stood waiting for her beside the bed like a well-behaved dog anxious to please. He had to be about six and a half feet tall. He was wearing a sort of tubular skirt that hung from his waist down to the middle of his calves. That was when Bruna remembered that that was how the Omaás dressed, with those skirts made from material that resembled fluffy wool in warm, earthy colors—ochre, burgundy, mustard yellow. Elegant attire, although the skirt that Maio was wearing was quite threadbare. The worst thing was that on top he was wearing a horrendous Earthling T-shirt, one of those promotional freebies, with a garish image of a frothy beer. It was two sizes too small and was stretched to bursting point across his strong chest.

"It's to cover me up. The T-shirt. I've noticed that you Earthlings don't like to look at bodies with transparent skin," said the alien in his oceanic voice.

Yes, of course, thought Bruna. Omaás usually went about with their chests bare, apart from some wraparound belts whose usefulness was totally unknown to the rep. Maybe they were just for decoration. Anyway, the T-shirt was awful. He was an astral beggar.

"Right. Good. Okay. Well then, let's go," spluttered the detective.

They left the apartment and on the way down they came across a couple of neighbors. Bruna could see the amazement in their eyes, and the fear, repugnance, and curiosity. *Just what I needed*, she thought. *Apart from being a rep, now I'm with a* bicho*, and on top of that, a* bicho *with the grubby looks of a vagrant.* When they reached the street, they stopped, facing one another. *Should I have offered to let him use the bathroom?* wondered Bruna, feeling slightly guilty. *And shouldn't I have offered him some breakfast?* If he was a refugee, as seemed likely, maybe he was hungry. And what did these creatures eat? The problem was the alien's sad dog look, those ever-so-human eyes that you only ever found on strays, that wretched appearance of an abandoned little animal, despite the size of his bulky body. *For heaven's sake*, thought Bruna. She'd slept with some dreadful people during her craziest nights, but waking up with a *bicho* was going too far.

"Well, good-bye, then," said the rep.

And she headed off without waiting for a reply, hopping onto the first travelator she came across. A few yards farther on, just before the travelator took a wide curve around a corner, she couldn't resist the urge to look back. The alien was still standing by the entrance to her building, looking at her helplessly. *Get lost*, thought Bruna. And she let herself be carried on her way until she had lost sight of the *bicho*. Finished. Never again.

And now where am I going? she asked herself. At that very moment, an incoming call sounded on her mobile. It was Inspector Paul Lizard. Oddly enough, thought Bruna, she could still remember the Caiman's name.

"We have a date in twenty minutes, Husky."

"Uh-huh. I haven't forgotten," she lied. "I'm on my way over there."

"So why are you on a travelator going in the opposite direction?"

The rep became irritated.

"You're not allowed to locate anyone by satellite without their permission to do so."

"Indeed, Husky, you're quite right, unless you're a judicial inspector like me. I can locate anyone I please. Incidentally, you're going to arrive late. And if you keep going in the opposite direction, you'll be even later."

Bruna cut off her mobile with a smack of her hand. She'd have to go and see Lizard, although she wasn't at all happy about it: maintaining her private detective's license was always a question of how well she got on with the police. She jumped over the handrail of the travelator onto the sidewalk and started to hunt for a cab. It was Saturday and a beautiful day, and Reina Victoria Avenue, with its central, tree-lined little park, was full of children. They were rich children, who were taking their plush, animal-shaped robots for a walk: tigers, wolves, small dinosaurs. One little girl was even flying a few handspans above the ground with a toy reactor strapped to her back, despite the prohibitive price with which the waste of fuel and resultant excess pollution were penalized. For what it cost the child to fly for an hour, a human adult could pay for two years of clean air. Bruna was used to putting up with life's inequities, especially when they didn't impact on her personally, but that day she felt particularly irascible, and the sight of the child made her even more bad-tempered. She sat back in the cab and closed her eyes, trying to relax. Her head was still aching and she hadn't had breakfast. When she arrived at the headquarters of the Judicial Police half an hour later, she was beginning to feel really hungry.

"Hi, Husky. Twenty minutes late."

Paul Lizard was wearing a pink tracksuit. *A pink tracksuit! It must be his idea of casual weekend attire.*

"I'm hungry," said the rep by way of a greeting.

"You are? Me too. Hold on."

He connected with the canteen in the building and ordered pizzas, chicken-flavored sausages, fried eggs, hot rolls, fruit, cheese with toasted sunflower seeds, and lots of coffee.

"They'll bring it to the evidence room. Come with me."

They went into the room, which was empty, and sat down at the large holograph table. Paul ordered the lights to dim.

Across the table, lit solely by the milky brightness coming from its top, the man's face looked like stone.

"Listen, Husky, let's play a game. A game of collaboration and exchange. You tell me something and I tell you something. Turn and turn about. And no tricks."

Even you *don't believe that*, thought Bruna, and then she also recognized that she didn't have much to tell. Not many cards to play.

"Oh yes, Lizard? Well, then, I want you to explain to me why nobody's talking about the adulterated memories. And what's on those memories."

The man smiled. A nice smile. A surprisingly charming smile that, just for a moment, seemed to change him into a different person. Younger. Less dangerous.

"You go first, of course. Tell me, how do you think your client died?"

Bruna frowned.

"Clearly, she was murdered. I mean, they implanted the adulterated memory against her will."

"How can you be so sure that she didn't do it voluntarily?"

"She didn't strike me as a woman who would take drugs. Moreover, she knew about the lethal mems; she wouldn't have risked it. Especially after being threatened."

"Ah, yes. The famous ball that appeared in her office. What was on the ball?"

"You don't know?" Bruna asked, surprised. "Haven't the RRM made it available to you?"

"Habib says he hasn't got it, that you have it."

"I returned it to him by courier yesterday."

"Well, I've just spoken to him and he hasn't received it. The robot must have disappeared mysteriously along the way. But you analyzed the message."

Bruna thought for a moment. The ball had been lost? It was all a bit strange.

"Hmmm, one second, Lizard. Hold on a bit. It's your turn to give me information, now."

Paul agreed.

"Fine. Have a look at these people."

The holograph images of three individuals began to form on the tabletop—three corpses: a man with a perfectly round and neat hole in his forehead, definitely a laser shot; another man with his throat cut, covered in blood; and a woman with half her face blown off, maybe by a conventional explosive bullet or by a plasma shot. Bruna gave a slight start; the half-face of the victim that remained was vaguely familiar. Yes, that misplaced ear was unmistakable.

"Do you recognize them?" asked the policeman.

"Only the last one. I think she's a drug trafficker from Nuevos Ministerios. I bought a mem from her three days ago."

"And what did you do with it? Have you used it?"

"Who are the others?"

"They're all illicit traffickers. Known dealers. Someone has started to murder them. Could it be to take revenge for the lethal memories?"

"Or to get rid of the competition and be able to sell the adulterated merchandise? I sent the mem off for analysis. It was normal. Pirated, but harmless."

Paul nodded in agreement again. Just then the canteen robot arrived with their lunch. The quality of the dishes probably wasn't all that good, but they were hot and turned out to be reasonably tasty. They placed the trays on the table and, for several minutes, dedicated themselves to eating with silent relish, while the images of the three corpses continued to float around in the air. It seemed like a lot of food, but after a few minutes Bruna confirmed with some astonishment that, between the two of them, they had managed to eat all of it. The rep poured herself another coffee and looked at Lizard with a benevolence produced by her full stomach. Sharing a meal with someone when you're hungry predisposes you to complicity and coexistence.

"Okay. I think you were going to talk to me about the content of the holograph ball Chi received," said Lizard, pushing aside the plates.

Bruna sighed. Her hangover was much improved.

"No, no. It's your turn. I've told you about the illegal mem."

Lizard smiled and manipulated the table again. Two new corpses appeared in front of them, floating like ghosts. Two reps. Strangers.

"I don't know who they are," said Bruna.

"Well, as you'll see, they're two odd corpses. They worked for the RRM. That's to say, they worked for an outside maintenance company whose sole client was the RRM. Does this sound familiar to you?"

The private detective maintained an impassive expression on her face.

"How did they die?" she asked, stalling for time.

"Two shots to the back of the head. Executed."

Should she tell him or not? But she didn't want to reveal any details Habib had given her without the android's permission. After all, he was her client. She decided to give Lizard a different piece of information instead of that one.

"No idea. I don't know anything about that. As far as the holograph ball is concerned, you could see Chi giving a speech at—"

"No, don't worry about that bit; I know what the message was about. Habib told me. What I want to know is the outcome of your analysis."

"The disembowelment images are of a pig, and there's a fifty-one percent probability that they're not from a legal slaughterhouse but produced domestically. And I couldn't find a single trace, fact, clue, or ID. Just..."

"Just...?"

"Can I use your holograph table?"

"Of course."

Bruna used her mobile computer to request access and Lizard approved it. Within seconds the menacing message took shape in front of them. The table provided magnificent resolution and the image was life size; it was quite unpleasant. When the film had finished, the detective touched her wrist screen and transferred the original video of the pig, cleaned up and reconstructed. She focused on the knife, blowing up and sharpening the image until they could see the eye of the rep.

"Hmmm. So the sequence was recorded by a technohuman," murmured Lizard thoughtfully. "Interesting."

"You can keep a copy of the analysis."

"Thanks. So the two androids who worked for the RRM don't ring a bell?"

"I'd never seen them before in my life," Bruna replied with the calm aplomb of someone telling the truth. "But it occurs to me that you could run them through an anatomical recognition program to check if the eye you can see on the knife belongs to either of them. Speaking of which, where did you find the bodies?"

Lizard gathered up the last bits of the soft cheese on the plate with his fingers and ate them with delight. A look of concern preceded the rest of his words.

"That's the strangest part. We found all the bodies in the same place, in Biocompost C."

In other words, in one of Madrid's four main garbage recycling centers.

"In the garbage dump?"

"The two technos were lying on top of the most recent mountain of waste. As if they'd been carefully placed there. The garbage robots are programmed to detect any sentient waste products and raise the alarm, so they stopped work and did so. And the other, earlier bodies were partially buried in that same mountain of waste, in varying stages of decomposition. The two males must have been dead for at least a month, but the bodies were reconstructed in the holograms you've just seen."

"In other words they were somewhere else and were brought to Biocompost C."

"Exactly so. As if someone had wanted us to find all of them together so that we'd link the cases. Obvious criminal clues for idiot detectives."

Bruna smiled. This big man with the lazy voice had a certain charm, though it wouldn't do to trust him.

"Lizard, I know there've been other, earlier, similar cases of rep deaths. Earlier than the ones that came to light this week. Four others. That fascist Hericio said so on the news. And Chi was investigating them."

Lizard raised his eyebrows, genuinely surprised for the first time.

"Chi knew about them too? Well, well…Then it was the region's worst-kept secret. And what exactly was it that she knew?"

"That they were three men and one woman, all technohumans, all suicides, and none of them killed anyone else before killing themselves. They took their own lives in different ways, all of them quite ordinary: cutting their veins, drug overdose, throwing themselves off something. The last three—I mean, the last in time, the most recent ones—gouged out one of their eyes. And they all had adulterated mems."

"Nothing else? She knew of no other detail that linked the dead people?"

"Chi hadn't found anything that would link them. They seem to be victims chosen at random."

"Could be, Bruna. But, in addition, they all had the word *revenge* tattooed on their bodies."

"All of them?"

"All seven."

"Chi as well?"

"Yes."

"I didn't see it."

"It was on her back."

"Gándara didn't say anything about it."

"You left in a hurry last night. Look."

The close-up of a back floated in the air. Long, undulating, white. But marked by the purple outline of some bruises. Near the smooth start of the buttocks was the word *revenge*, written in ink in very distinctive, cramped, and rounded letters. The word was just over an inch long and about half an inch tall. It had that purplish grape color of tattoos done with a cold laser gun, like the tattoo Bruna had. They healed themselves as they were being done.

"That's Chi," Lizard explained. "But all the tattoos are the same, and they're in the same spot."

He switched off the table and looked at Bruna with a slight smile.

"I think I'm telling you too much, Husky."

And it was true. He was telling her too much.

"Tell me just one more thing, Lizard: what do the lethal mems contain?"

"Rather than mems, they're induced-behavior programs, outstanding pieces of bioengineering. And the implants evolved from one victim to the next. That is, their programs were becoming more sophisticated."

"As if the first deaths were prototypes."

"Or test runs, yes. The implants have a very short memory load. Thirty or forty scenes instead of the usual thousands."

"The normal number is five hundred."

"So few? Well, in these mems there are only a few scenes that make the victims believe they're human and have been the object of persecution by reps…or technos. And then there are other scenes that are like premonitions; compulsive acts that the victims feel obliged to carry out. Something like psychotic delusions. The implants induce a kind of programmed and extremely violent psychosis. The impact is so strong that it destroys the brain in a couple of hours, though we don't know if that subsequent organic degeneration is intentional or a secondary and unwanted consequence of the implant."

"And the obsession with eyes?"

"Blinding themselves or blinding someone else is something that started with the second victim. It's one of the delusional scenes. Something voluntarily induced, without a doubt."

"The criminal's signature. Like the tattoo."

"Perhaps. Or a message."

Someone really sick has to be behind all this, thought Bruna. *A perverse mind that takes delight in the removal of an eyeball. Of a rep eye. Revenge and hatred, sadism and death.* The detective felt a vague discomfort in her stomach. She must have eaten too much.

"And why has nothing been said publicly about this? Why is the business of the implants being kept secret?"

Lizard stared at Bruna.

"It's always useful to hold back some detail that only the criminal would know," he said finally with his lethargic voice, after a somewhat overlong silence.

"You had the tattoos for that. Why keep something quiet that proves that the reps are victims as well, and not just frenzied killers?"

Another silence.

"You're right. There are orders from above to say nothing. Orders that make me uncomfortable. There are things happening in this case that I don't understand. That's why I've contacted you. I think we can help each other out."

Bruna discreetly rubbed her stomach. The nausea had increased. Something wasn't right. Something *really* was not right. Why was Lizard telling her all this? Why had he been so generous with his tip-offs? And what on earth had made him openly say that he distrusted his bosses? Here? In the Judiciary Police headquarters. In a place where all conversations were probably monitored. She took note of the fact that the blonde fuzz that grew along her spinal column was standing on end. It was like a faint electric current running up her back and it always happened to her before she went into combat. Or when she found herself in a dangerous situation. And right now she was in danger. This was a trick. She looked at Lizard's heavy, fleshy face and found it revolting.

"I have to go," she said abruptly as she stood up.

The man raised his eyebrows.

"Why the hurry?"

Bruna contained herself and faked an almost amiable calmness.

"We've told each other everything, haven't we? I don't know anything more. And you're not going to tell me anything else. I have an appointment and I'm late. We'll be in touch."

"Wait."

The android felt the inspector's hot, rough hand on her skin and she had to call on all her self-control to stop herself from elbowing him in the face and breaking free. She gave him a haughty, questioning look.

"You certainly do have something to tell me. You were attacked by Cata Caín."

Bruna took a deep breath and turned back round to face him. Lizard let her go.

"Yes. It's in the police report. So?"

"You were in one of the induced scenes in Caín's mem. According to the program, your neighbor had to spy on you, go to your apartment, strangle you with a cable until you were unconscious, tie you up, gouge out your eyes and then kill you."

Despite herself, Bruna was deeply affected by this information. She opened her mouth but had no idea what to say.

"Isn't that interesting? There's your name, Bruna Husky, in the scene in the mem. Your name, your image, and your address. Why do you think you've been included in a killer implant?"

"So, you've brought me in to interrogate me?"

"I'm not interrogating you. Officially, I mean. I'm just asking you."

"Well, I'm answering you that I have no idea."

"It's odd. You should have been a victim, but you weren't. A matter of chance? Or of prior knowledge?"

"What are you insinuating?"

"Maybe you knew what was on the mem. Maybe you even collaborated in the making of the implant."

"Why would I include the scene of my murder?"

Lizard gave a lovely smile.

"To have a superb alibi."

Bruna felt relieved. Oh, she preferred him like this, openly taking her on, clearly hostile. She returned his smile.

"I'm afraid we aren't going to end up being friends after all," she said.

And she turned on her heel and left. She was crossing the threshold of the door when she heard the policeman's reply from behind her: "That's a pity."

That damn Lizard seemed to be one of those men who always insisted on having the last word.

CHAPTER ELEVEN

In fact, Bruna did have an appointment, although she'd almost forgotten. She had been going to a psych-guide every Saturday at 18:00 sharp for the past three months. Her problem had started a year ago. One afternoon Bruna was in her apartment watching a film when suddenly, reality disappeared. Or rather, she was the one who quit the scene. The screen, the room, the whole world seemed to move away to the other side of a long, black tube, as if Bruna were looking at things from the far end of a tunnel. At the same time, she broke out in a sweat and began to shiver, her teeth chattered, and her legs shook. She suddenly felt crushed by a horrific panic the likes of which she'd never experienced before. And the worst of it was that she had no idea what was terrifying her so much. It was a blind, indecipherable fear. Mad. Sanity suddenly switched off. The crisis barely lasted a few minutes, but it left her drained. And a permanent hostage to the fear of fear. To the fear that the attack would recur. And it did in fact recur a few times, always at the most unexpected moment: running through the park, eating in a restaurant, traveling on the sky-tram or the subway.

Initially, she resorted to a psych-machine, as she had done in the past during her years in the military. Combat troops used to use these "idiot booths" after a particularly tough fight or at times of heightened threats of war. You'd go into the psych-machine's little cubicle, sit in the easy chair, put on the electrode helmet, place your fingertips on the sensors and tell the booth what was happening to you. And it was assumed that the psych-machine would give you verbal advice, gently stimulate your brain with magnetic waves and, if that was not enough, dispense an appropriate pill. Androids went in search of them—the pills: tranquilizers, sedatives, stimulants, stabilizers, drugs that induced euphoria, anti-depressants. They knew what to say in the booth in order to get what they wanted, and the sessions only cost fifteen gaias, excluding the drugs.

But on that particular occasion, the detective didn't know what she needed, what she was searching for.

"You've had an anxiety attack," decreed the booth in a ringing baritone voice (Bruna had selected a male voice under the sound option).

"But why?"

"Panic attacks are the result of a fear of death," said the psych-machine.

As if that explained anything. The android's entire brief life had been spent weighed down by the awareness of death, and she'd obviously found herself in deadly peril many times without it provoking any crisis. On the contrary, that risk pumped her system full of a kind of lucid, cold calm. It was one of the contributions from genetic engineering; one of the hormonal improvements with which combat reps were endowed. But then, just like that, one afternoon while watching a silly film at home, she had gone to pieces. Why?

Given that the idiot booth hadn't soothed her anxiety, she considered the possibility of visiting a psych-guide. Ever since the Peruvian psychologist Rosalind Villodre had developed her post-Freudian master theory in the 2080s, her disciples had become very popular. Near Bruna's apartment there was a Health Arcade, one of those shopping malls specializing in therapies that were more or less alternative, and on the ground floor a psych-guide called Virginio Nissen had his consulting rooms. One afternoon the detective went in with the vague idea of getting some information, and left with the commitment to return every Saturday; in a somewhat inexplicable way, the man had managed to impose this obligation on her. It was now two months since the rep had had a panic attack, but she seriously doubted it was thanks to Nissen. It could perhaps be due to the eighty gaias that a half-hour consultation cost her: she had no alternative but to get healthy in order to save herself that amount of money.

And now Bruna found herself lying on a sensory-deprivation couch on top of a mattress of fine air bubbles and wearing virtual glasses that made her feel as if she were in the middle of the cosmos. She was floating pleasurably in the stellar blackness, weightless and incorporeal. The somewhat sickly sweet voice of Virginio Nissen reached her in that distant comfort zone.

"Give me three words that hurt you."

You had to answer quickly without thinking.

"Wound. Family. Harm."

"Let's discard the first one—too semantically contaminated. Think about *family* and give me three more words that hurt you."

"Nothing. No one. Alone."

"What does *nothing* mean?"

"That it's a lie."

"*What* is a lie?"

"We've talked a lot about this already."

"One more time, Husky."

"Everything is a lie...Affection...The memory of that affection. The love of my parents. My parents themselves. My childhood. *Nothing* swallowed them all. They don't exist; they never existed."

"The love you feel for your mother, for your father, exists."

"That's a lie."

"No, that love is real. Your despair is real because your affection is real."

"My despair is real because my affection is an illusion."

"My parents died thirty years ago, Husky."

"My condolences, Nissen."

"What I mean is that my parents don't exist either. All I have is a memory of them. Same as you."

"It isn't the same."

"Why?"

"Because my memory is a lie."

"Mine, too. All memories are lies. We all invent the past. Do you think my parents were really the way I remember them today?"

"I don't care, because it's not the same."

"Fine, let's leave it there. And the second word, *no one*? What does it mean?"

"Loneliness."

'Why?"

Look, you can't understand. A human can't understand it. Maybe I should look for a techno psych-guide. Are there technohumans doing this? Even rats...even the most miserable mammal, has its nest, its herd, its flock, its litter. We reps lack that essential group. We've never been truly unique, truly necessary for anyone. I'm talking about the way in which children are necessary for their parents, or that parents are necessary for their children. And then we can't have children, and we live for only ten years, which means that becoming a stable couple is very difficult, or agonizing."

Her throat suddenly became constricted and the detective stopped talking for fear that her voice would break. Each time she brushed up against the memory of Merlín's death, the grief overwhelmed her with an undiminished fury, as if almost two years hadn't elapsed. She breathed deeply and swallowed the knot of pain until she managed to recover an acceptable level of control.

"What I mean is that you're not important to anyone. You can have friends—good friends even—but even with the best of your friends, you wouldn't occupy that basic position of belonging to any one of them. Who's going to worry about what happens to me?"

It's marvelous, Bruna said to herself sarcastically. *It's truly marvelous to be paying eighty gaias to a psych-guide for the privilege of spoiling my afternoon and having a miserable time.* The astral space in which she was floating, previously so relaxing, was beginning to feel like a place of anguish.

"It's not, in fact, exactly as you say, Husky. Even the comparison you've used isn't correct. Not all mammals live in groups. Wild bears, for example, are totally solitary animals all their lives. They only get together briefly to mate. So..."

Wild bears be damned, thought Bruna. They were another lot of beings that didn't exist: there were only a few left in zoos. The rep flung off her virtual glasses and sat up on the couch. She blinked a few times, a little dizzy, while she returned to the real world. In front of her, lounging in an armchair, sat

Virginio Nissen, with his long, braided moustaches, his gold earring, and his shaved and waxed head.

"I've had enough. Let's leave it for today."

"Fine, Husky. It's time for our session to end anyway."

Of course. Nissen always had to have the last word. *Another control freak like Lizard,* the android said to herself mockingly as she transferred the eighty gaias from one mobile to the other. The man's computer beeped receipt of funds, the psych-guide widened his smile a tiny fraction, and Bruna walked out into the mall anxious to raise her spirits with a drink.

But no. She was drinking too much.

Instead of going into the bar opposite Nissen's consulting rooms, she set off through the main gallery of shops toward the Health Arcade exit. It was costing her little to leave; she fancied that untimely and solitary glass of wine too much, and the keenness of her thirst began to frighten her. She really must drink less. A lot of androids ended up as alcoholics or dependent on some other drug, no doubt spurred on by that same bitterness Bruna was unable to explain fully to Nissen. And that was also the reason why so many reps got into the dangerous illegal mems game. Though they were unable to live one real life lengthwise, at least they could try to live several lives widthwise. Simultaneous lives, one on top of another. Cata Caín was programmed to gouge out Bruna's eyes and then kill her. She felt another shiver and noticed that old scenes of blood and violence were flooding her memory, feverish snippets from her combat service days that she was normally able to block out. *Four years, three months, and twenty days.*

The shopping mall was packed with people; lately, there was nothing that obsessed people more than health. And not just the technos, but humans, too. Despite the optimistic scientific predictions of the twenty-first century, what was certain was that the life expectancy of the average human had not extended beyond ninety-six and, on top of that, it could not be said that conditions for nonagenarians were especially good. Transplants, bionic parts, and cellular engineering had improved the quality of life of younger people, but they hadn't managed to ease the implacable deterioration of old age. True, old people died wrinkle-free, converted into their own distorted death masks thanks to plastic surgery, but the passage of time was still eating away at them from inside. *At least the reps were saved from that,* thought Bruna—*from a slow and painful old age. Heroes die young, like Achilles,* Yiannis used to say to cheer her up whenever they came across those old people on the street, trapped in the prison of their deterioration: minds laminated by the years, drooling mouths, broken bodies transported hither and yon in wheelchairs, like dead meat. And yet, despite all this, the android reflected, she would have changed places with a human there and then.

The Health Arcade wasn't very big, but it had a bit of everything: hyperbaric chambers, antioxidant therapy centers, secondhand bionics stores, spiritual healers who claimed to be following the Labaric rite. And the usual host of anti-TTT quacks and visionaries. It seemed there was even a Gnés doctor on the upper level. The arcade was one of the few places where you could gaze at an alien close up—*apart from in my own bed, of course,* Bruna said to herself. She shook her head to rid herself of the thought of Maio's huge, translucent body, the annoying memory of which had just buzzed through her mind like a hornet.

Close to the exit there was a small tattoo bar that the rep had noticed previously. She wandered over to have a look;

the tattoo bar did essentialist tattoos. If she remembered correctly, the essentialist sect had sprung up in New Zealand toward the end of the twentieth—or the beginning of the twenty-first—century. Bruna didn't know a great deal about the sect's beliefs, though she had an idea they were based on ancient Maori rites. Whatever the case, its tattoos were famous. The essentialists considered them to be sacred, an external representation of the soul. People had to discover which was their tattoo, their primordial design, the visual interpretation of their intimate and secret being, and once the exact design had been found, they should have it engraved on their skin, as if they were writing the signs of their soul. According to the essentialists, tattooing the wrong image meant atrocious chaos, and brought with it no end of misfortune; applying the correct design, on the other hand, soothed and protected the individual and even cured multiple ailments. It wasn't surprising that these tattoos had become fashionable.

Bruna peered in through the narrow store window, adorned by a sketch on paper of a nude man whose skin was entirely covered with strange signs. The small store, a dark room with a wooden bench and some cushions on the floor, looked empty. The rep pushed against the door. It was unlocked, so she went in. She was immediately enveloped by a smell of oranges and an amber half-light. It was a pleasant spot. The bench, seen close up, looked old and was beautifully carved. Another piece of wooden furniture occupied the wall to the right. At the back, a curtain of clear beads stirred with a murmur like running water as the tattooist came through from the back room. Bruna made an effort to determine the sex of the diminutive, compact figure that seemed as wide as it was tall, and which had as hard a body as a ball of synthetic rubber. The person had very dark, shoulder-length hair and was wearing a long, tight, purplish unisex shirt over stretch pants, but seemed to have breasts…so the tattooist was probably a woman. The woman approached Bruna and, since she barely came up to the rep's navel, scrutinized her from below. She had the roundest face the android had ever seen, a fleshy, copper-colored face, strong, and in a certain sense handsome. For some strange reason, her intense curiosity wasn't offensive, and Bruna allowed herself to be examined without saying a word. When she had finished, the woman scowled and said: "It's splitting you."

Good grief, what a deep voice. So was it a male tattooist?

"*What's* splitting me?"

The man, if he was a man, pointed at Bruna's tattoo with a chubby finger.

"That line. How can you want to feel well if you're split in two? And the two pieces aren't even equal. And then it's done with a laser gun. Yuck!"

The gesture of revulsion was so spontaneous that Bruna started to laugh. Then she recalled that essentialists tattooed with a sharp reed and vegetable ink using methods that were a thousand years old. Apparently an extremely painful procedure.

"I don't know if I'll be able to help you. I don't know if I'll be able to discover your shape. That line you have makes a lot of noise." The tattooist spoke softly, and again, the feminine side predominated.

"It doesn't matter. I…I didn't come in search of my spiritual tattoo."

"Not spirit. It's not a question of spirits. It's your vital breath that has to be found."

"Fine, whatever it's called. My name is Bruna Husky and I'm a private detective."

The male or female tattooist nodded.

"My name is Natvel and I'm a Tohunga. I'm the one who searches out designs. The one who traps them. And who reproduces them."

The slightly emphatic statement sounded like a poem or a prayer, and the rep felt a little uncomfortable. She'd never much liked religions.

"Natvel, I'm investigating a murder, and the victim had a tattoo. It was a word and it was written in a very particular script. Lots of ink, very cramped, the letters almost overlapping. As if they formed a jigsaw puzzle and fit into one another perfectly."

"What was the word?"

Bruna hesitated for a moment.

"I can't tell you that. I'm sorry. But I thought you just might know what sort of writing I'm talking about."

Natvel scratched her thick lower lip thoughtfully.

"Was the calligraphy beautiful?"

"It was...suffocating."

The tattooist nodded and, with a matronly swing of the hips, walked toward the wooden piece of furniture, opened a deep drawer, and took out a handful of papers.

"Sit down," she ordered Bruna, pointing to the bench.

They sat down at either end of the piece of furniture and the essentialist deposited the papers on top of it, in the space between them. They were a pile of drawings done by hand in pencil or a red iron oxide crayon. Ancient tattoo designs, without a shadow of a doubt. Natvel leafed speedily through the sheets, as if looking for something, and eventually took one out and showed it to the rep. An eagle of sorts—a beautiful creature with open, geometrical wings—was holding a word between its claws as if it were a serpent that the bird was killing. The word was partially obscured by the eagle's talons, but the end of it was still clearly legible: *athan*. And it was written in the same script as the one used to write *revenge* on the bodies of the victims.

"That's it. Identical."

Natvel scrunched up her big, round moon-face with a look of concern.

"It's the Labaric writing of power. Filthy, wicked signs. This tattoo belongs to a boy called Jonathan. He was a slave on the Kingdom of Labari. Like all the other slaves, his name had been tattooed with the script of power to subjugate and humiliate him. But he had something within him. A special force. Thanks to that, he managed to escape from the Floating World and reach Earth. I could see that inner strength, and it was like an eagle. I tattooed it on him, devouring his slave name, and Jonathan recovered."

A Labaric script! That was a real surprise. Bruna had been on Labari once, following a lead in an old case; she had to disguise herself as a human in order to gain entry and she had very bad memories of that cruel world of fanatics.

"Well, well. Thanks a lot, Natvel, you've been a great help. How much do I owe you?"

"Nothing. Fighting against the shadows is good for you," said the little creature solemnly.

It really was impossible to figure out her gender. And it wasn't a case of Natvel being an androgynous, indefinite being, but rather that she seemed to offer successive, ever-changing images. One minute it was clear she was a woman and the next, there was no question that he was a man. Bruna wondered if Natvel might not really be a mutant; if that fluidity of sexual identity could have been caused by the atomic disorder of teleportation.

"Thank you very much, but you are..."

The rep hesitated, choosing her next words carefully so as not to betray her uncertainty as to the tattooist's gender.

"You are an authority on the subject, and the work of an expert deserves recompense. And on top of that, if you charge me, I'll be able to ask you for your help again if I need it."

Natvel raised a chubby finger in the air and said, "Stop."

And Bruna stopped talking.

Then the tattooist climbed up on the bench and put her hands on the rep's temples. Bruna started, but didn't move away. They were gentle, hot hands—padded, universal, maternal hands. Natvel dropped her head between her outstretched hands and remained in that position for a good while, concentrating, with her eyes closed. Rigid and uncomfortable, Bruna asked herself if she should be feeling something special—a certain energy flowing from those hands, an inner tremor, the hint of a trance; in short, one of those esoteric sensations that enthusiasts of this sort of ritual were always talking about. But she just felt ridiculous. After a while, Natvel released the android and straightened up.

"I know who you are; I know what you are like. I have seen you."

"Oh, yes," mumbled the rep.

"I've seen your essential form."

Bruna stood up.

"Well, I'd rather not know what it is. Thanks again for your help, Natvel. Tell me what I owe you."

"I've already told you—nothing. We're even. But come back when you want to know yourself better."

The detective nodded her head in agreement and left the store somewhat hurriedly. Once outside she heaved a sigh of relief: too many healers; too many therapists for one afternoon; too many people who seemed to know what she needed or what she was. At that moment, she decided to abandon going to the psych-guide, give up drink, abandon her messy life, give up her rage, abandon her anguish, give up being a rep. She let out a short, bitter burst of laughter that sounded like a sneeze. At least Natvel had been useful. Labaric script.

Screams drew Bruna out of her self-absorption. A short distance away, at the entrance to the Health Arcade, a small disturbance was unfolding. The detective walked toward it to see what was happening. Two big, strong, disagreeable young human males—one white and the other black, with heads shaved in stripes in the manner typical of supremacist thugs—were pushing and shoving a billboard-lady, toying with her and her humiliation.

"Shut up, once and for all, parrot! We're sick of your advertisements!"

"I can't switch it off," whimpered their victim.

"I can't switch it off, I can't switch it off…Can't you say anything else, you smelly old bag? You revolting old woman, you beggar, you…Shove yourself in a hole, then, so I can't hear you!"

The billboard-lady was the Texaco-Repsol woman who sometimes stopped off in Oli's bar, but even before Bruna recognized her, she'd been galvanized into action by a flood of hormones, was already tense and vibrating from her head to her toes, was already prepared for the confrontation and invested with that wonderful, clear, and preordained calmness, that burning coldness that possessed her in tense situations.

In two strong strides she had placed herself between the two louts so that the slumped body of the woman landed in her arms as one of the thugs was tossing her to the other.

"Game over," Bruna said quietly.

And delicately, she lifted up the trembling victim, moved her away a few yards and sat her on the ground next to the wall. "Clean energy for everyone, renewable power for a happy future," chirped the screen on the woman's chest. Bruna turned around to confront the aggressors, who hadn't managed to react to the speed of the detective's movements.

"Well, well. This is becoming more amusing by the minute. A rep! Which test tube are you missing from, lab monster?" hissed the black man, his features twisted in anger.

The two characters were rocking nervously on their feet, their arms rigid and out from their bodies. It was the typical animal dance, the primordial attack-and-defense ballet. Bruna, on the other hand, remained quiet and seemingly relaxed.

"Why are you interfering, monster? Hey! Who told you that a genetic monster has permission to speak to us?" the dark-skinned man, who seemed to be in charge, continued to spit out.

"Jardo, hold on...I have a feeling she's a combat rep," whispered the other one.

"As far as I'm concerned, she might as well be a whore on hormones," said the leader defiantly.

And, taking an electric stun gun out of his pocket, he threw himself at Bruna ready to fry her. He was quick, but not quick enough. Moreover, the android thought calmly as she jumped to one side and disarmed the lout by hitting his arm with the edge of her hand. He'd lost critical milliseconds amusing himself with taking out the Taser just when he should have been concentrating fully on his attack. It had been a really foolish decision, she determined as she was turning around, kicking her leg out behind her and hammering her heel into the thug's genitals. He collapsed in a heap, gasping for air. The other character, as Bruna had predicted, had already taken off.

The detective went up to the Texaco-Repsol woman, who was curled up against the wall, shivering.

"Calm down. It's all over."

"Thank you. Thank you so much…I…I know you," stammered the billboard-lady.

"Yes. We know each other. From Oli's bar."

Bruna helped her to her feet. They were surrounded by a small circle of bystanders, all humans. And some of them seemed to be looking at her with fear. At *her*. For crying out loud, they should have been grateful to her. The person they should have been scared of was that shit of a lout who was still cringing and sniveling on the ground, but no, the one who was intimidating them was the rep, the one who was different, the lab monster.

"The show's over," she grunted.

The crowd meekly dissolved.

"Are you okay?" Bruna asked the billboard-lady.

"Yes…just a little…shaken."

"Thank you, dear consumer! Between all of us, we've achieved happiness for families," said the advertising screen.

"My name is RoyRoy."

"And I'm Bruna Husky."

The billboard-lady must have been a bit over sixty, but she looked withered and a lot older. And she showed no signs of plastic surgery, so she was undoubtedly very poor. Her face was still pallid and her mouth was trembling. She was the picture of helplessness.

"RoyRoy, what would you say to us going to Oli's bar? To have a drink, calm down and recover. At least we know that we're both welcome there."

They caught a cab to the bar because the woman was still too dazed to walk. When they entered the bar, fat Oli Oliar immediately detected a problem; she possessed an uncanny sixth sense for when empathy was needed.

"What's happened, Husky? Come in, sit in that corner, where you'll be left in peace…Over there with your friend Yiannis."

The old archivist was indeed at the end of the counter and was delighted to see Bruna; he had heard nothing of her since the day before, when he had woken her up to tell her about Chi's death. The rep filled him in on what had happened. Oli—who had served them two beers and a bowl of french fries and then, her body spilling over the countertop, had stayed to listen to the story—screwed up her bright, coffee-colored face and passed judgment.

"That damned thug. He should keep in mind that a century and a half ago, our people were the ones being lynched and persecuted. But the renegades are always the worst."

"I'm starting to get worried about this supremacy business," said Yiannis. "Lately, I've been coming across some terrible sentences in the archive."

"Which I assume you're correcting."

"That's what they pay me for."

"Texaco-Repsol, always in the vanguard of social well-being!"

Bruna and Yiannis exchanged glances. It was difficult to maintain a normal conversation with the constant chatter of the advertisements interrupting all the time. RoyRoy noticed the look and got up from the stool, embarrassed.

"I'm sorry. I know it's torture. I don't want to go on being a nuisance. You've already done too much."

"What are you saying, woman? Sit down."

"No, no, really. I wouldn't feel comfortable if I stayed. Thanks, Bruna. Many, many thanks. I won't forget it. I think I'll go and have a sleep; I'll take my nine hours now. I need to rest. Please, let me pick up the tab."

"It's on the house today," growled Oli.

"Oh…well then, thanks again. It seems to me I have too much to thank all of you for today." She gave a faint smile.

Yiannis and Bruna followed her with their eyes as she was leaving. A little bird boxed in between the screens.

"She has one of the saddest looks I've ever seen," murmured the archivist.

It was true. She did. The rep yawned. She suddenly felt drained. She always did after she'd taken a candy. The neuropeptide and alcohol cocktail had to have a huge impact on the body. Moreover, she'd only had one beer all day, the one Oliar had just served her. And that was fine. She wanted to continue like that, and for that reason, the best thing would be to leave now.

"I think I'll head for home, too, Yiannis. I'm ready to drop."

She felt so tired that she took a cab again, although she worried she'd get used to this bad habit. She arrived in five minutes, paid and got out. The street was full of people; it was Saturday and the night had just begun. But Bruna could only think of her bed, of drinking a glass of chocolate-flavored milk, and of sleep. She activated the entry to the lobby with her fingertip and was pushing open the door to go in when a strange impulse made her glance to her right. And there he was, about five yards from her, leaning up against the wall, shoulders slumped. The alien, the Omaá, the greenish *bicho*. There he was, waiting for her like an abandoned and eager dog, an enormous dog wearing a T-shirt that was too small. Bruna closed her eyes and took a breath. *It's not my problem*, she said to herself. And went into the building without looking back at him.

CHAPTER TWELVE

Cata Caín's door was still sealed with a police security beam, although Bruna assumed the police had simply forgotten to remove it. Nine days had passed since the rep's death and the seals usually didn't stay that long. The only thing that the beam's continuing presence showed was Caín's extreme loneliness: no one had wanted to enter the apartment after her death; no one had shown the slightest interest in her belongings; and there was probably nobody who would remember her. Not even the police, who should have removed the seal. A short and wretched life.

Bruna easily switched off the electronic beam with a small pair of tweezers and opened the door with a key decoder. The detective possessed a good collection of small, illicit tools that served to disarm alarms, wipe traces, and decipher codes— effective as long as it wasn't a question of very sophisticated security systems. In this case the lock was the cheapest and most basic on the market, and it opened in a flash. She glanced up and down the corridor before going in. It was Sunday, 16:00, and the building was quiet. The detective, accompanied by one of the janitors, had already been in Caín's apartment the same day she had gouged out her eye. On that occasion Bruna had only checked out the place superficially, looking for basic information about the victim. Now she wanted to carry out a much more thorough examination. She needed to know why her own death was programmed into Cata's mem. She didn't have a clear idea of what she was looking for, but she did know how to look. The detective was good at searches; it was as if for some reason, the evidence leapt out in front of her eyes of its own accord.

Caín's apartment was identical in layout to hers, except that it was a mirror image and on the second floor rather than the seventh. Bruna remembered it as impersonal, empty and dusty, and her impression as she went in again now, nine days later, confirmed her recollection. It was still a very sad place. The blind on the large window was lowered almost completely, and the room was submerged in a quiet, dirty semidarkness that seemed almost funereal.

"House, raise the blinds," Bruna requested of the screen that was flickering weakly in the dark.

But the computer didn't respond; clearly it didn't recognize her as an authorized voice. So the rep crossed the lounge room to use the manual control and immediately noticed something unusual. She hurriedly raised the blind and turned around to inspect the room. It was a complete mess. There was no way the police would have left it like that. Ever since the state had been ordered to pay two million gaias in the scandalous John Gonzo case a few years back, the police followed very strict orders regarding tidiness. Which meant that someone else had been hunting around here. You could see shreds of clothing everywhere, probably taken out of Caín's closet and then ripped and left looking like rags. A corner of the carpet had been torn off and was nowhere to be seen, so perhaps the intruder had taken it with him. What would you need six inches of cheap carpet for? To stuff in someone's mouth and choke him to death? On the table, a cushion was sliced open and the stuffing removed. Could he have taken it with the carpet? Two drawers had been pulled off their runners, their contents scattered onto the floor and the drawers smashed, but three other drawers were still in place. Bruna went over to them and looked inside. The contents were neatly arranged, so the drawers probably hadn't been opened. Whoever had been here must have found what he was looking for.

The rep poked around a little inside the untouched drawers. Family photos, colored ribbons, cheap necklaces, teenage paper diaries. All the fake memento paraphernalia. Caín had it stored away out of sight, but she hadn't gotten rid of it.

The unmistakable sound of glass breaking could be heard close by. Bruna turned around with a jump and rested her back against the wall so as to be protected from behind. She stayed very still. It had come from the bedroom. Or maybe the bathroom. The seconds passed slowly while the silence stretched like elastic. The rep was on the verge of deciding it had been a false alarm when her enhanced hearing again picked up something: a furtive noise, a tiny tinkle of glass. Something was moving in the bedroom. Someone was in there. Then she realized that if there were still some unopened drawers, that was because she'd surprised the intruder hard at work.

Bruna stealthily made her way to the bedroom door, wishing she had her plasma gun. As she went through the kitchen area, she grabbed a knife from the countertop; it was just a small table knife, but she was capable of doing a lot with that. She scanned the bedroom from the doorway. The bed was unmade, the closets were half-open. The window was partially ajar. The intruder must have come in through there.

And it was likely he'd also end up going out that way. The detective held her breath for a moment to concentrate fully on any sounds, and she heard a tiny rubbing again on the other side of the bed, next to the closets. No, he hadn't gone. Bruna weighed all possible movements. She could move slowly, she could move quickly, she could go around the bed, or jump on top of the mattress, or roll along the floor. She could even turn around and try to leave Caín's apartment without offering any resistance. But the fact that the intruder hadn't attacked her so far suggested that he wasn't feeling very sure of himself. It was likely that he was neither armed nor very dangerous, and he might in fact be a good source of information. Moreover, he clearly had to be lying on the floor between the bed and the wall, without a weapon; this left him at a considerable disadvantage.

"I know you're over there. I have a gun," Bruna said, lying. "Stand up with your hands in the air. I'm going to count to three: one..."

And as soon as she said the first number, Bruna leapt onto the bed and threw herself toward the intruder's hiding place. She landed on her feet, not on a body as she had expected, but on the floor.

"By the great Morlay!"

In front of her, among the remains of a broken mirror, a hairy thing was looking at her with a frightened expression. It was a small animal, about eighteen inches tall, with a body like that of a small monkey but minus the tail, potbellied and covered all over with curly, red hair. Then came a neck that was too long and a head that was too small, triangular, with huge black eyes. It vaguely reminded her of an ostrich's head, except that it was furry and had a squashed nose instead of a beak. On the top of the flattened head was a crest of stiff hair. The creature looked both helpless and amusing. Bruna recognized it: it was a…What did they call it? A greedy-guts. It was an alien domestic animal—she couldn't remember from which planet right now—and it had become fashionable as a pet. The little *bicho* was looking at her and shaking.

"And where have you come from?" she asked herself out loud.

"Cata," gabbled the animal in a fuzzy but understandable voice. "Cata, Cata."

Bruna dropped the knife and lowered herself to the bed, stunned. A talking monkey. Or a talking ostrich. Either way, a hairy thing that talked.

"Do you understand me?" she asked the *bicho* pet haltingly.

"Cata!" the thing repeated in its nasal and somewhat shrill voice.

The rep wikied the word *greedy-guts* on her mobile and an image appeared on the screen of a being very similar to the one in front of her, together with an article:

BUBI (pl. bubes, colloq. Erth. greedy-guts)
A creature native to Omaá, the bubi is a small domestic mammal that has recently been introduced to Earth with considerable success, because its resistant and adaptable constitution allows it to be reared easily on our planet and because it makes an ideal pet. It is a heterosexual species and lacks dimorphism: male and female are identical save for their genital equipment, and even the latter is difficult to distinguish externally. The adult bubi weighs about twenty pounds and can live for up to twenty years. It's a clean animal, easy to train, calm, affectionate toward its

owner, and capable of articulating words thanks to a rudimentary speech system. The majority of scientists consider that the bubi's speech is nothing more than an imitative reflex similar to that of parrots on Earth. Some zoologists, nevertheless, maintain that these creatures possess a high degree of intelligence, almost comparable to that of chimpanzees, and that there is an expressive intentionality in their verbal utterances. The bubi is omnivorous and voracious. Its main food sources are insects, vegetables, and cereals rich in fiber, but if hungry, it can eat almost anything, especially cloth and cardboard. This constant eating has gained it the nickname "greedy-guts" on Earth. Various animal associations, both regional and planetary, have presented legal arguments seeking the same taxonomic consideration for bubes as for our great apes, and therefore, recognition as sentient beings.

This was followed by several other articles with anatomical and ethological details, but Bruna skipped them. She looked at the animal again. It was still trembling.

"Calm down. I'm not going to hurt you," the detective said gently.

The *bicho* had blood on its arm: maybe a cut from a piece of the broken glass. The blood was red and shiny, like human and rep blood. Bruna stretched out her hand very slowly and the bubi squashed itself up against the closet even more and emitted a little moan.

"Shhh...Be quiet...Calm down...I just want to see your wound."

The animal's hair was thick and strong, but not nearly as rough as Bruna was expecting. She slightly separated the curls, which were stuck together with blood, and inspected the wound carefully. It wasn't much. A small, superficial cut that was no longer bleeding. Under the reddish hair, the skin was gray.

"Okay…it's nothing. See? Calm down."

She stroked the nape of its neck and its back a little. She could see why greedy-guts were so popular; they were cute little *bichos* that inspired affection. The animal's shivering was lessening under her hand, although it continued to stare at her with a watchful gaze. Bruna stood up.

"And now what am I going to do with you?"

"Bartolo. Cata. Bartolo beautiful, Bartolo beautiful," said the bubi.

And having said that, the creature took the torn corner of the carpet out from behind its body and, holding it delicately with its two little gray-fingered hands, started gnawing at it.

Cata, thought Bruna. Meaning that Cata Caín had a pet bubi? And Bartolo must be the animal's name. She'd have to get in touch with some shelter that took care of animals.

"Bartolo? You're Bartolo?"

"Bartolo beautiful," repeated the greedy-guts, still chewing.

Judging by the surrounding destruction, Bartolo had been on his own and without food for the past nine days. Frightened, he had probably escaped to the patio during the police search, and that was why the police hadn't found him, although when she'd come in with the janitor, she hadn't seen him either. Could he have escaped earlier? *Let's assume that Caín was assaulted and they injected the mem using force,* thought Bruna. *Let's imagine the bubi witnessed the attack and took off through the window. Would he be capable of recognizing the aggressor? Didn't they say the bubi was a very intelligent animal?* She observed him with a critical eye as he applied himself to chewing the carpet, and she wasn't very impressed with what she saw.

She decided to extricate herself from the pet for the moment and got down to searching the apartment with rapid efficiency. The bedroom, the bathroom, and finally the living room. She didn't find anything worthwhile. The bubi had followed her timidly into all the rooms, but would sit in a corner and not bother her. When she'd finished searching the kitchen area, which was lacking in even the basics, Bruna turned toward the animal.

"But what the…"

In two strides she reached the bubi and yanked her wool jacket from his hands; or rather, the half-eaten remains of her genuine wool jacket. She'd left it in the lounge room when she came in and hadn't noticed that the greedy-guts was eating it. She looked at him indignantly.

"Bartolo hungry," said the bubi with a contrite expression.

I'm going to call an animal shelter right now to come and take him away, she thought, enraged. But then she decided it would be better to check first where the pet came from. She bent down and picked up the animal. The bubi clung confidently to her neck. It had a hot, sour smell, not unpleasant. A smell of moss and leather. The rep left Caín's apartment, closed the door, and removed the tweezers so that the police beam would reactivate. Then she went in search of one of the janitors who lived in the huge apartment complex. She managed to find one, the same one who'd accompanied her to Cata's the day of the attack. She'd clearly woken him up from his nap, and he was in quite a bad mood.

"It's Sunday, Husky. You tenants think that because we live here we're your slaves," he grunted through a waft of bad breath.

"I'm sorry. Just one question: do you know if this animal belonged to Cata Caín?"

The man looked at her with sleepy, spiteful eyes.

"I don't know if it was this one, but Caín had one like it, yes."

"Then why didn't you say so when we went to her apartment?"

"Was it important? Anyway, it would have been better if it had disappeared. If it were left to me, I'd ban all those wretched pets. No dogs, no cats, no birds, no nothing. All they do is make a mess. And then who cleans it up? The slave, of course."

"Okay, okay. Thanks, and sorry for bothering you," said the rep, giving him a ten-gaia bill.

So Bartolo was indeed Cata's animal companion, Bruna thought. The detective stood in the middle of the landing with the greedy-guts in her arms, not quite knowing what to do next. Then she heard breathing, light and regular. A gentle snore. The bubi had fallen asleep, his head resting on her shoulder. *What the hell*, she thought. *I'll take him home with me for now, and then we'll see.*

CHAPTER THIRTEEN

Bruna woke up with one foot frozen and the other boiling hot, and when she sleepily sat up in bed to see why, she discovered with amazement that one of her extremities was uncovered and the other was covered by a sort of fluffy, red cushion. It took her a few seconds to recognize that the cushion was in fact an animal, and to remember the bubi she had rescued from Caín's apartment the previous afternoon. The greedy-guts was curled up on her right foot and was calmly chewing the thermal blanket. He had already made a considerable hole in it, through which her left foot was now protruding. With additional annoyance, the rep now verified with revulsion that her foot was soaked by the creature's drool, which explained why it felt so cold. The android let out a roar and sent the bubi flying to the floor with a kick. The creature yelped.

"Bartolo beautiful, Bartolo beautiful," he babbled.

"I'll give you Bartolo beautiful! I'm going to call that animal shelter right now," the android scolded as she put on her Chinese bathrobe and bent over to inspect the hole.

At that moment, a call from Nopal came in. Unconsciously, Bruna stretched, cleared her throat, and tried to look vivacious. The writer was very brief. He said he had some interesting information for her and asked to meet her. The rep expressed her delight at the news and accepted, but she couldn't avoid a stab of unease, a worry she failed to decipher to her satisfaction. The memorist made her nervous. Very nervous. Was that merely because he was a memorist? Or because of the way he was? Opaque and ambiguous, arrogant and at the same time, too amiable. There was something about the man that hypnotized her while still sending shivers up her spine. The fascination of a snake.

They had arranged to meet at 13:00 in the Bear Pavilion, and Bruna, who had gone to bed early the night before, had woken up feeling really well despite the business with the greedy-guts. It was the second morning in a row that she had awoken without the shadow of a hangover, a feat she hadn't been able to achieve for quite some time. Now she was standing in the middle of the lounge room, reasonably pleased with life, which was something she rarely felt. She looked at the frightened bubi and again felt sorry for him; the creature had in fact scarcely eaten the night before, because the rep had very little food in the apartment. It was no wonder that he had started to nibble. Never mind the anxiety he must be feeling because of the violent loss of his owner, the abandonment that followed, and so many other changes. Anxiety was something that Bruna could understand. She, too, often felt like chewing and biting, except that she resisted the urge.

"All right. You can stay here for now. You may yet be able to help me, but you have to behave better."

"Bartolo good. Good Bartolo."

Bruna was impressed. The little animal really did seem to understand what she was saying to it. She called a Super Express and ordered cereals with fiber, apples, and prunes for the bubi, and a small shopping list with a bit of everything for herself. Express stores were very expensive, but she didn't feel like going out. While she was waiting for the robot courier, she gave Yiannis a brief holo-call and introduced him to Bartolo, and she even had time to add four pieces to the jigsaw puzzle. Then the food arrived and they both ate a big breakfast. The bubi sat sprawled on the floor, his back against the wall, the living picture of satisfaction. Bruna squatted down beside him.

"Bartolo, do you know what happened to Cata? Did you see anything? Did someone hurt her?"

"Yummy, yummy," said the greedy-guts, a satisfied glow in his eyes.

"Listen, Bartolo: Cata? Hurt? Ouch? Pain? Cata Caín? Attack? Bad people?"

Bruna didn't really know how to speak to him or how to reach his little brain. She acted out an attack with gestures: she grabbed her throat and shook herself, rolled her eyes. The bubi watched her, fascinated.

"Dammit, do you know what happened to Cata or don't you?"

"Cata good. Cata not here."

"Yeah, I already know she's not here. But do you know what happened? Did you see anyone? Did someone hurt her?"

"Bartolo alone."

Bruna sighed, scratched the tuft of stiff hair on top of the bubi's head and stood up.

"Hungry!" yelled Bartolo.

"Again? But you've only just finished eating a huge amount of food."

"Hungry, hungry, hungry!" repeated the greedy-guts.

Bruna grabbed a bowl, filled it with cereal and handed it over.

"Take it and shut up."

"No, Bartolo no! Hungry, hungry, hungry!" repeated the animal while he kept pushing away the bowl.

The rep looked at the creature, taken aback. She offered him the food again, and again he refused.

"Hungry!"

"I don't understand."

The bubi lowered his head, as if discouraged by the lack of communication. But immediately afterward, he happily started to scratch his tummy.

"Bartolo good."

He's a scatterbrain, Bruna thought to herself; it would be odd indeed to be able to get anything useful out of him. When she got back from her appointment, she'd call an animal shelter to take care of him.

The meeting with the memorist was at 13:00. There was still a couple of hours to go and the rep was bursting with energy, so she tidied up the apartment a bit and did a set of exercises with light weights. She didn't want her muscles to deaden her agility. After that, while the bubi was snoozing (apparently they spent their days sleeping and eating), the rep spent an unusually lengthy period of time getting dressed. She even tried on several outfits. Eventually she chose a form-fitting, rust-colored jumpsuit with wide pant legs. She was almost on the point of heading out when, on the spur of the moment, she put on one of the only two pieces of jewelry she owned: a large, geometric pectoral made from a sheet of gold as light and as fine as tissue paper. It was the famous gold from the mines of Potosí, where it was subjected to a secret chemical process that ensured that the fine metal sheets wouldn't break. The pectoral had been a gift from a human whose life Bruna had saved during some riots, when the rep was still doing her military service and found herself stationed on the remote mine planet. Bruna had made two teleportation transfers, from Earth to Potosí, and back to Earth. Fortunately, she appeared not to have suffered any of the consequences typical of TP disorder. Although you could never be absolutely certain.

"Be sure you don't do anything naughty, Bartolo. And in particular, don't even *think* about touching the jigsaw puzzle! If you eat anything, I'll throw you out on the street. Do you hear me?"

"Bartolo beautiful, Bartolo good."

So Bruna left the apartment, dressed as if for a party and somewhat perplexed at the excessive care she'd taken with her appearance. But she was in high spirits, almost happy, feeling healthy and full of life, her TTT still a long way off. In complete control of the perfect machine that was her body. The feeling of well-being became somewhat tarnished when, having barely left the entrance to her building, she saw the wretched bluish-green extraterrestrial on the corner, in the same spot as the night before. The Omaá of canine patience. *Dammit!* Bruna had forgotten about him—that is, she had managed to forget him. But there was Maio, surrounded by a small circle of curious onlookers, and prepared to stand forever in front of her door. Was that the way things were done where he came from? A cultural misunderstanding? Should she have fulfilled some specific farewell ritual, like giving him a flower or scratching him on the head or who knew what? The rep bit her lip with concern, regretting that she hadn't paid more attention to the documentaries aimed at spreading information about alien cultures. All the Omaá fauna suddenly seemed to have decided to become part of her life. It was like a curse. Without stopping to think about it, she resolutely walked up to Maio.

"Hi. Look, I don't know how it is in your land, on your planet, but here, when we say good-bye to each other, we go. I don't want to be rude, but…"

"Calm down. I know. You haven't done anything wrong. You don't have to say anything else to me. I know the meaning of the word *good-bye*."

His sentence sounded like the hiss of a wave breaking onto the shore.

"So why are you still here, then?"

"It's a good spot. I can't think of a better one. No one is waiting for me anywhere else. It's hard to find friendly Earthlings."

The importance of what the *bicho* had said registered with the rep. *So, then, does that mean he thinks I'm friendly?* she wondered. *Me, the person who rudely threw him out and who's just thrown him out again.* The scene that Maio's words were conjuring up was too much for Bruna, something she didn't feel capable of handling. So with that, she turned on her heel and marched off without another word.

She was walking quickly and had gone about 200 yards when someone grabbed her arm from behind. Irritated, she turned around, thinking it was the *bicho*, but she came face-to-face with a pale, ghostly person whom it took her a few seconds to recognize.

"Nabokov!"

It was Chi's lover, the head of security at the RRM. The thick knot of her bun had come loose and her hair, tangled and dirty, was now hanging down around her shoulders. She seemed to have lost an incredible amount of weight in the three days since Bruna had last seen her, or at least her face had become sharper and her skin, grayish and withered, was stretched over a frame of prominent bones. Her feverish eyes were sunk deep within the rings around them, and her body was shaking violently. It was Total Techno Tumor in full flight. Bruna had seen it too many times not to recognize it.

"Nabokov..."

Valo continued to hang on to Bruna's forearm, and Bruna didn't move away for fear the rep would collapse if she lost her support. Valo was leaning to the right and didn't seem capable of maintaining her balance. Her huge fake breasts now looked like a grotesque addition to her broken body.

"Habib has told me...Habib has told me..." she stammered.

"What? What has he told you?"

"You know it too. Tell me!"

What do I know?"

"They're like scorpions, worse than scorpions; a scorpion gives a warning."

She had a wild look about her and her hand was burning into Bruna's arm.

"Nabokov, I don't understand you. Calm down. Let's go to my apartment. It's close by."

"Noooo...I need you to confirm it for me."

"Let's go to my place and we'll talk."

"The supremacists. They're like scorpions."

"Yes, they're absolute swine, but—"

"All humans are supremacists."

"You need to rest, Valo, listen—"

"Habib told me."

"Well, let's go and talk to him."

Bruna tried to move the arm to which Nabokov was still convulsively clinging in order to free her mobile computer and call the RRM to ask for help.

"Revenge!" moaned the woman.

The detective became alarmed.

"Did Habib tell you that? Did he mention the word *revenge*?"

Valo gazed briefly at Bruna with wild eyes. Then her mouth distorted in a grimace that was perhaps an attempt at a smile. Her gums were bleeding.

"Noooo," she whispered.

She let go of Husky and, in an extraordinary effort, straightened her battered body and managed to gather enough energy to start walking with a relatively firm and quick step. The detective went after her and placed a hand on her shoulder.

"Wait...Valo, let me—"

"Let go!"

The woman freed herself with a jerk and continued on her way. Bruna watched her walking away with concern, but she was already going to be late for her meeting with Nopal, and she didn't think she was the most suitable person to look after the sick woman anyway. She rang Habib's personal number, and he answered instantly.

"I've just bumped into Nabokov and she seemed very ill."

"By the great Morlay, thank goodness!" he exclaimed, relieved. "Where is she? We've been looking for her for hours."

"I'm sending you my GPS location right now...Have you got it? Nabokov has just taken off southward on foot. I can still see her."

"We're heading there right now, thanks!" said Habib hurriedly.

And he cut out.

Bruna had more things to discuss with the acting leader of the RRM, but she decided they could wait. Pressed for time, she caught a cab again, something that was turning into a disastrous and wasteful habit. Despite the expense, she was fifteen minutes late when she walked into the Bear Pavilion. Nopal was waiting for her seated on one of the benches in the garden inside the entrance, elbows resting on his knees, his lank hair falling over his eyes. He looked annoyed.

"Late again, Bruna. Allow me say it's a very bad habit. Did your memorist do a bad job with your upbringing memories? Didn't your parents ever tell you that it's bad manners to be late?"

The rep noticed that he'd called her by her first name, and that disturbed her more than his sarcasm.

"My apologies, Nopal. I'm normally very punctual. There was a last-minute complication."

"Fine. Apology accepted. Have you been here before?"

Pablo Nopal seemed to have a strange predilection for meeting in peculiar places. The Bear Pavilion had been built five years earlier, at the time of the Madrid World Expo. The city's symbol had always been a bear eating fruit from a tree, and Inmaculada Cruz, the many times reelected and almost permanent regional president, had decided to celebrate the exposition by updating the ancient emblem. A half century had passed since polar bears had become extinct through drowning as the arctic ice cap melted. A slow and agonizing death for animals capable of swimming desperately for more than three hundred miles before succumbing to exhaustion. The last polar bear to drown—or at least the last one anyone knew about—was followed by a helicopter from the organization

Bears at Risk, which had tried to rescue it, but the polar bear's final swim coincided with the outbreak of the Rep War. The result was that animal lovers were unable to gain the support or necessary funds to carry out their rescue plans. All they could do was film the tragedy. They also froze and stored in a genetic bank the blood of that last bear—a female. Thanks to that blood, President Cruz was able to get her new symbol for Madrid. Employing a similar system to the one used for the production of technohumans, bioengineers created a bear that was a genetic clone of that last animal. Her name was Melba.

"Yes, I know this place," Bruna replied.

She had always been aware of the existence of the rep bear, as they more or less shared the same birthday. She found the Bear Pavilion a poignant place and had visited it a few times; in particular, during those months of torment after the death of Merlín, when she felt she was degenerating from the pain of her grief in the same way that the original Melba had degenerated on her solitary and ever-smaller iceberg before finally drowning.

"I haven't been here for ages. Shall we take a look?" asked Nopal, standing up.

Bruna shrugged her shoulders. She didn't understand the urge to sightsee, but she didn't want to argue with him about something so insignificant. They crossed the small garden and entered the pavilion building itself, a gigantic, transparent dome. They immediately felt a blast of cold air. Around them, everything seemed to be made of ice or crystal, although it was in fact made of thermoglass, a synthetic, unbreakable material used to create thermal environments. They walked through a re-creation of the Arctic as it once had been, with huge glacial rocks and sparkling icebergs floating on seas of glass, until they reached a large, irregular, moat-like crevasse that separated the visitors from an intensely blue lake with some ice shelves that formed Melba's home. You could look at the animal from the edge of the moat if she was out of the water and hadn't hidden among the rocks, but it was better to go down inside the crevasse. That was what Nopal and Bruna did now. They walked onto the moving sidewalk like conscientious tourists and descended between slippery, crystal-clear walls. The walkway moved very slowly, and a film of the last moments of the original Melba was projected onto five successive and overlapping screens on the walls of the crevasse. You really felt as if you were there, watching the last small piece of ice that the bear was trying to hang on to breaking up; the animal swimming more and more slowly, snorting as it sank beneath the surface, then thrusting its dark snout out of the water with one last, agonizing effort and letting out a chilling wail, a furiously terrified growl. And then finally disappearing under a black, gelatinous sea. The life-size images left the spectators speechless. And surrounded by this imposing silence, you reached the bottom of the crevasse and in the darkness the walkway deposited you in front of a shimmering wall of water. It was Melba's artificial lake, viewed from the bottom of the tank through a thermoglass wall. And there, with any luck, you would be able to see the bear diving and playing with a ball and happily frolicking while releasing a trail of bubbles from its snout. And once in a while Melba would swim close to the glass, because she could sense the visitors, too, and was no doubt curious.

Today, however, the animal was nowhere to be seen. Bruna and the memorist waited a while, noses frozen, the intensely blue shimmer of the water dancing across their faces.

But Melba didn't appear. So they went back up on the exit walkway, which was considerably shorter and quicker, and emerged from the crevasse into the polar landscape. Thanks to her excellent eyesight, Bruna managed to spot Melba on solid ground. Or more accurately, Melba's hindquarters—her round, shaggy behind—lying well camouflaged in the shelter of some equally white rocks.

"Look. She's over there."

"Where?"

Of all the times that Husky had been in the pavilion, this was the only one when the bear hadn't been clearly visible. *Too bad, Nopal*, she thought with a certain malicious pleasure.

"Fine. Let's head out," said the man. "I'm absolutely frozen."

They went into the cafeteria, deliciously warm and bright under the transparent dome. It was half-empty, and they sat down at a table next to the curved thermoglass wall. Above the memorist's straight, bony shoulders, Bruna could see a procession of clouds scudding across the sky. *It must be windy out there.*

They were in an automated establishment, so they ordered two coffees for their table, and after a short while, a small robot arrived with the order and the bill, which came to the exorbitant sum of twenty-four gaias. Entry to the Bear Pavilion might be free, but the cafeteria was highway robbery. No wonder nobody was there.

"How can they charge this for two coffees?! And in a place with robots!" muttered the detective.

"You're right. But thanks to that, it's more peaceful. No, it's my treat."

Nopal paid, and for a while they focused on drinking their coffees in silence. You could certainly keep yourself amused with a coffee. You had to pour the sugar in the cup and stir it. Then you could blow on the liquid to cool it down, creating gentle waves. And play with the spoon, separating the foam. Bruna unwrapped the small biscuit that came on the saucer and nibbled at it. It was almost lunchtime but she wasn't hungry; she'd had too much for breakfast. The cafeteria was a nice place. You could do worse than this, calmly having a coffee without saying a word. Almost like a human family. Or one of those couples who'd been together for decades. The twisted, ghostly face of the dying Valo suddenly flooded her mind. Bruna shivered. Melba, the replicant bear—would she also suffer from TTT when she completed her ten-year existence?

"Do you think the bear will die, too?" she asked.

"We're all going to die."

"You know what I'm talking about."

Nopal rubbed his eyes in a weary gesture.

"If you're asking about TTT, it would seem so. As far as they can tell, the average life span of replicant animals is a little shorter than yours—only eight years. But when this Melba dies, they'll produce another one. An infinite chain of Melbas down through the ages. I read all that while I was waiting for you. Here."

Nopal took a pavilion brochure out of his pocket and threw it on the table. Bruna glanced at the brochure without touching it; it had a 3-D photo of the bear. A poor image, a cheap brochure. *Four years, three months, and eighteen days. That was all she had left to live.* She wanted to stop, she wanted to give up counting, but she couldn't.

"You're very beautiful, Bruna. Very elegant," said the memorist.

The rep gave a start. For some reason, the man's words hit her like a reprimand. Suddenly she felt overdressed. Ridiculous in her shiny jumpsuit and her gold necklace. She blushed.

"I have...I have a date later, that's why I'm dressed like this."

"A romantic date?"

They looked at each other, Nopal unperturbed, Husky disconcerted. But this rapidly gave way to boiling rage.

"I don't think who I'm meeting is of interest to you, Nopal. And we've come here for something more than to talk nonsense. You said you had news for me."

The man smiled. A cold, smug little grimace. Bruna hated him.

"Well, yes. Don't ask me how, but I came across one of those mem pirates who write the illegal mem implants. And it turns out the guy owes me a favor. Don't ask me about that, though. The thing is, he's prepared to talk to you when he gets back to the city. He's traveling. But he'll see you in four days—Friday at 13:00 sharp. I'm transmitting the address to you right now. I hope you're a good interrogator, because he's quite a tricky customer."

Bruna checked that the information had made it to her mobile.

"Thanks."

The large screen above the counter was showing a tumultuous scene—blood, flames, people running about, police. The sound system was turned off, so Bruna had no way of knowing where it was happening. It didn't matter much, either, to be honest. It was just another violent scene on the news.

"And there's something else, something I remembered after our meeting at the museum."

Nopal paused hesitantly and Bruna waited expectantly for him to continue.

"I don't know if it's relevant, and I'm not even sure it's true, but there's no question that when I was in the business there was a rumor running among the memorists that about twenty-five years ago, just before Human Peace and the beginning of the process of the Unification of Earth, the European Union was developing an illegal secret weapon that had to do with artificial memories...for humans."

"For *humans*!"

"And for technos as well, but primarily for humans. That's why it was a clandestine operation. The thing is, the implants supposedly took over the subject's will and made them do things."

"An induced-behavior program."

"Exactly. And after a few hours, the memory killed the carrier. It was that detail that made me think it might be related to the current cases. But that old story could also be an urban myth. You'll have noticed that it has all the ingredients: a memory implant that, rather than being for technos, is for humans, and kidnaps your will and then finishes you off. It corresponds really well to our unconscious fears, don't you think?"

The cafeteria's screen continued to show disturbing images. Now some people appeared in ash-colored tunics, their faces painted gray, holding a sign that read: "3/2/2109. The end of the world is coming. Are you ready?" They were some of those crazy Apocalyptics. Recently, they had become very active because their prophet, a blind physiotherapist called the New Cassandra, had predicted on her deathbed fifty years ago that the end of the world would take place on February 3, 2109—in other words, in less than two weeks. Bruna frowned. Judging by the images, the Apocalyptics were giving their fiery speeches right in front of the RRM headquarters.

"Excuse me for a minute," she said to Nopal.

She swiped her mobile across the electronic eye on the table, paid twenty cents, took one of the tiny earpieces out of the dispenser and put it in her ear. She could hear the chanting of the Apocalyptics and, over the top of it, the voice of a reporter who was saying: "impression of this tragedy which has shaken the Radical Replicant Movement again. This is Carlos Dupont from Madrid." And then a block of advertisements started playing. Bruna took out the earpiece, discouraged and somewhat concerned. Were they still talking about Chi's death, or was it something else? She'd check the news on her mobile as soon as she left the writer.

"Why is he following you?" asked the memorist.

"Who?"

"That guy."

Bruna turned in the direction Nopal's finger was pointing. Her stomach churned. Paul Lizard was sitting at one of the tables at the back. Their eyes met and the inspector gave a small nod of his head in greeting. The rep sat upright in her chair. Her cheeks were burning. She thought she could still feel the guy's eyes on the nape of her neck.

"What makes you think he's following me?" she asked, trying in vain to keep her voice sounding normal.

"I know him. Lizard. A wretched, persistent bloodhound. He was giving me grief when...when I had my problems."

"Well then, *you* could be his target."

"He came into the pavilion behind you."

Bruna blushed slightly. How could she not have realized that she was being shadowed? She was losing her faculties. Or maybe the encounter with the dying Valo had upset her too much. A black rock weighed on her chest. A profound premonition of misfortune. The rep stood up.

"Thanks for everything, Nopal. I'll keep you informed."

She walked decisively toward the exit and as she went past the inspector's table, she bent down and whispered in his ear, "I'm going to the RRM headquarters. In case you lose me."

"Many thanks, Bruna," the big man replied.

And he smiled, granite-faced.

CHAPTER FOURTEEN

Nopal watched Bruna as she walked off. He saw her stop briefly next to Lizard, whisper something in his ear and then continue toward the exit with a light, confident step. She was a beautiful creature, a rapid, perfect machine. Thirty seconds later, the inspector got up and walked out after her, tall and sturdy, with the swaying gait of a sailor on land. His body was the exact opposite of Bruna's razor-sharp one, thought Nopal.

A gentle drumming above his head made him realize that it had started to rain. The drops were falling on the transparent dome and then tracing swift-running trickles of water across the cover. A pale ray of sunlight filtered through a gap in the clouds, and the sky was a tangle of mist in every conceivable shade of gray. It was a perfect sky to accompany sad feelings.

Sadness is a genuine luxury, the memorist thought to himself. He hadn't allowed himself that calm and unhurried emotion for many years. When you experience pain so acute that you're afraid you won't be able to bear it, there is no sadness but rather despair, madness, rage. He sensed something akin to that despair in Bruna, something of that pure sorrow that burned like acid. Of course, he had a clear advantage when it came to sensing her feelings. He knew her. Or rather, he recognized her.

In his time as a memorist Nopal had always behaved in the manner he'd described to the rep at the Museum of Modern Art. He'd always tried to construct solid, balanced lives with a certain sense of purpose. Lives that were comforting in some way. Only once had he transgressed that unwritten personal rule—and that was with the last job he did, when he already knew they were going to expel him from the profession. And Bruna was carrying that memory. The Law of Artificial Memory of 2101 strictly prohibited writers from knowing which specific technohumans would end up with their implants, and vice versa; it was assumed that such knowledge might generate various abuses and problems. But his work on Bruna's memory had been exceptional in every meaning of the word; it was a much more comprehensive, deeper, freer, more passionate, and more creative memory. It was the masterpiece of Nopal's life, because *it was precisely his own life*. In a literally re-created version, naturally. But the basic emotions, the essential events, they were all there. And since you are what you remember, Bruna was in a way his other self.

From the very moment he handed over the implant, Pablo Nopal tried to discover which technohuman was carrying it. All he knew was that it was a female combat model, and her age to within six months. He would have preferred the techno to have been a male, and a computation or exploration model, as these allowed for greater creativity and refinement, but the specifications were set by the gestation plant, and Nopal concurred. Anyway, he had been extremely free in creating her; he had ignored all the rules of his profession. Poor Husky:

by being his final opus, she had received the poisoned gift of his grief.

During the six years Nopal had been searching for her, he had investigated scores of technohumans. The only way to discover the recipient of his memory was to talk to them and try to winkle it out from their background, with the result that he had become a combat rep stalker. He discovered that some reps had a morbid fascination for memorists, and he ended up taking a liking to those quick and athletic women with their perfect bodies. He slept with several androids, but he only became truly intimate with one—Myriam Chi, who was not, in fact, a combat rep but an exploration model whom he met while he was hanging out with an RRM militant. So his relationship with Chi was free of any utilitarian considerations. She was a very special woman. Her memorist, whoever he might be, had created a real work of art. They ended up being friends and he spoke to her of his search. She made him promise that he would say nothing to the android when he found her, but she agreed to help him. Thanks to Chi, he had managed to draw up a list of the reps he still had to probe. There were twenty-seven, and Husky was among them. When the detective had spoken to him about Chi in the museum, Nopal had been unable to discern if Chi had sent Bruna to him in order to help him out or in order for him to help Bruna with her investigation. He had intended to give the RRM leader a call to ask her, but they had killed her before he could do so.

They killed *her*, the man repeated to himself, feeling that the hurtful, sharp edge of the word was slicing his tongue.

Nopal's father, too, had been killed by a criminal one night when the memorist was nine years old. That was one of the centers of pain he had implanted into the detective. But things had become even more difficult for the writer because, a few months later, his mother committed suicide. Then there was the year he spent in the orphanage and, just when he thought he'd reached the absolute depths of hell, his uncle appeared and adopted him—and that was when he learned there can always be something worse.

Nopal stirred in his seat, feeling too close to the abyss. Each time he thought about his childhood he remembered that child, Pablo, as if it weren't him, but some poor child they'd spoken to him about sometime in the past. He knew that they had hit that boy and had kept him in the dark in a cellar for days at a time, and that the child was terrorized. But he had no memory of those experiences from within, of the interminable darkness of the dirty cellar, of the dampness when he wet himself, of the pain of the burns. Inside Nopal's head that child who wasn't entirely him continued to be shut away and ill-treated. Just touching on that thought filled his eyes with tears at the pain and anguish that clutched at his throat like a hunting dog, preventing him from breathing normally. That was why Nopal tried not to think, not to remember.

The writer didn't really know why he had toned down his experiences when he translated them into Bruna's memory. Perhaps out of compassion for the rep who was going to become a life-size version of that young Pablo he carried inside him. Or maybe a professional obsession made him fear that if he included everything, the story would seem exaggerated and barely plausible. Or it could be have been that he had kept quiet about some of those things because authentic pain is indescribable. Even so, investing the rep with his own memories had helped Nopal to lighten the load of his own pain. Not only because he had, in a way, passed on some of his misfortunes to another, but also, more than anything, because that other existed, because there was someone who was like him. Because he was no longer alone.

The loneliness was worse than being locked up, worse than the sadism of the other children in the orphanage, worse than the beatings and injuries—worse, even, than the fear. Nopal had been left completely alone when he was nine years old, and the absolute loneliness was a terrifying and inhuman experience. After the murder of his father, the memorist had not been needed by, or important to, anyone. Nobody missed him. Nobody remembered him. Not even his mother had thought about him when she killed herself. It was the closest thing to not existing. But this replicant was, to a great extent, like him: she had a share of his memories, and she even possessed actual objects that came from Nopal's childhood. Bruna was, in short, more than a daughter, more than a sister, more than a lover. There would never be anyone as close to him as that android.

The afternoon at the museum, when Bruna's identity and the end of his search had finally been confirmed, he had come out in goose bumps. It had been a deeply touching moment, but fortunately he had been able to hide his feelings; he had spent his entire life learning to hide his emotions. Nopal had felt instantly attracted to the rep. She was beautiful, wild, and tough, and suffering and burning inside in the same way that he was. He found her fascinating from the first moment perhaps because he sensed the similarity, and when he finally confirmed that she was the one, he liked her even more. But he couldn't give in to that narcissistic impulse, the memorist told himself. He couldn't make love to the replicant. That would be an act against nature, something incestuous and sick. And the memorist, contrary to what many might think, considered himself to be a highly moral man, almost a puritan. It was just that his morals tended to be different from those of everyone else.

No, it was better to continue like this. He'd look after her from afar, as a benevolent god might look after his child. And for the few years of life she had left, he'd try to delight in her, in the relief from pain that Bruna's existence provided him. The memorist sighed, enfolded in a delicate sorrow. The cafeteria was empty and all you could hear was the soft drumming of the rain. It was a perfect day to experience the melancholy of the impossible. He would never be able to tell Bruna who he was. He would never be able to hold her in his arms and love her as only he knew how. Oh, what a refined luxury sadness was!

CHAPTER FIFTEEN

Bruna had just left the Bear Pavilion when she answered a call from Habib.

"I'm on my way over to you now. Can we catch up?"

Habib's well-proportioned face was distorted with distress.

"Don't even think about coming here. It's dangerous."

"Dangerous?"

"Because of the demonstrators. The police have already arrived, but I'm still wary. It looks like reps are being attacked all over the city."

"Attacked?"

Habib looked at her, astounded.

"Haven't you heard anything?"

"Anything?" repeated Bruna, unable to prevent herself. She felt like a total idiot parroting everything the man was saying.

"Husky, something terrible has happened. It's…it's…"

He was so upset that he seemed to be choking on his words.

"Valo has…has exploded a bomb on a travelator. There are many dead. Dead humans. And children."

Bruna could feel a chill running down her spine. And she suddenly realized that around her all the public screens were broadcasting the same images of blood and slaughter.

"But how? And what about her? Was she wearing the explosive device?"

"Yes, of course. She's blown herself up. Do you remember what we talked about, Husky? This is horrible. We need to find out what's happening. Check out Hericio! We've heard he's asking for a funding permit, and he's trying to raise funds for his party. He's getting ready for something. By the great Morlay, Husky, we have to do something or they'll finish all of us off. Listen, I have to go. It looks like the supremacists are trying to assault our headquarters. Be careful. The humans are enraged."

Habib's face disappeared. Bruna connected to the news on her mobile. Again, the flames, the confusion, the cries, the broken bodies being transported by medical services. But this time, the detective knew what she was looking at: the destruction caused by Valo Nabokov. *Revenge*, she'd said.

The news services were talking about the antirep wave of violence that had been unleashed throughout the entire region. Supremacists armed with clubs and knives had encircled the RRM building in a menacing way. It seemed to Bruna that the angry reactions of the humans were too well organized to be spontaneous. By all the damned species! The supremacists were even carrying 3-D banners! Once again, she was disturbed by the loathsome suspicion of a conspiracy in the making.

She felt the weight of someone's gaze on her and raised her head. A small child was looking at her with a frightened expression on his face. When their eyes met, the child clung to his mother's legs and started to cry. The woman tried to calm him down, but it was clear that she was as scared as her son. Bruna glanced around. The humans were avoiding her; they were switching sidewalks.

Dismay. It wasn't as if Bruna were an idealistic supporter of happy coexistence between the species; she did not in fact believe in happiness, and even less in coexistence. But she detested violence. In her years of military service, she'd had enough to last her lifetime. Now all she wanted was tranquility. She wanted them to let her be. And a society on the brink of civil disturbance wasn't exactly the most suitable environment for that.

Four years, three months, and eighteen days.

She couldn't rid her mind of the image of the wasted, spaced-out face of Valo Nabokov. Dying and lethal. The worst part was that children had died. Humans went berserk if you touched their children. Those children that replicants could never have.

Four years, three months, and eighteen days.

The detective felt she was on top of an avalanche. She felt she was caught up in a slippery mass that was hurtling into an abyss and growing exponentially by the minute, swallowing everything in its path. Scarcely a week and a half had passed since Caín had tried to strangle her, and things were moving with a terrifying speed.

Four years, three months, and eighteen days.

Enough, Bruna! she thought, cursing herself mentally. Enough of this mechanical litany, this nervousness and this anxiety. The detective was still standing in the middle of the sidewalk, and the passers-by were making their way round her like the sea around a rock. They were all humans; the technos must be hiding under their beds. The humans were looking at her and shivering. They were looking at her and whispering. A monster was reflected in the eyes of those men and women, and she was that monster. She missed Merlín with an acute longing. If he were still alive, she'd have a place to go to.

Four years, three…Oh shut up, you stupid rep, she said to herself, shaking her head. She suddenly realized she was hungry. The monster's stomach was empty.

She caught the sky-tram to Oli's bar, and as soon as she reached the rear section, the rest of the passengers began to migrate toward the front half of the vehicle, some brazenly and as quickly as possible, others with ridiculous stealth, moving one tiny step at a time, as if they were playing that ancient human game What's the Time, Mr. Wolf? Two stops farther on, the android was totally alone in her half of the tram and the remaining passengers were crammed into the other half. *I could put in some contact lenses*, thought Bruna. Of course she could disguise herself, wear a wig and cover her vertical pupils in order to avoid the humans' fear and anger. That wasn't hard to do, and there were bound to be some disguised technos out there already. Maybe one of those characters who had rushed to move to the other end of the tram was a camouflaged rep obliged to behave like the others so as not to give himself away. How humiliating. No, she would never disguise herself out of fear, she decided. She wouldn't pretend to be someone she really wasn't.

Just then, the sky-tram stopped abruptly next to one of the emergency staircases. The doors opened and a robotic voice ordered an immediate evacuation. It was a Risk Level 1 recording. Against a soothing background of harp music that had presumably been designed to calm things down, the soft voice repeated "Vacate the tram quickly and calmly, imminent danger" in the same banal tone used to read the results of the Planetary Lottery. Bruna always found the risk recordings counterproductive and ridiculous; each time people heard the harp riff, they panicked. The mob of passengers jumped chaotically onto the emergency platform and began to go down the stairs, pushing one another out of the way in their desire to distance themselves from the android. Suddenly, an explosion was heard somewhat farther down, shrieks, thuds. Then came smoke, a stinking smell, and information loudly exchanged by the passengers: "It's not reps; calm down, it's just an Ins who's blown himself up." *They prefer those damned terrorist morons to us*, thought Bruna. *Damned shit of a world!*

When the obese mulatto welcomed her with her usual smile, Bruna realized that it wasn't just physical hunger that had driven her to Oli's bar, but also a need to find an unaffected spot, a small refuge of normality.

"Hi, Husky. You were the only one missing."

Oli pointed with her chin toward the end of the counter, and Bruna spotted Yiannis and RoyRoy, the billboard-lady. And for some reason, she wasn't surprised to see them together. She went over to where they were. A sort of muffled whispering, a surreptitious murmur, was emerging from the woman's body: "Texaco-Repsol, always at your service."

"Did you notice? It was my idea. She bothers people a lot less like this," said Yiannis.

The advertising screens were taped over with various adhesive sheets of insulation.

"It was absolute torture," stressed the old man.

"I'm sorry," said the woman.

But she said it with a smile.

Without asking, Oli served everyone a beer and placed a platter of snacks on top of the counter.

"I've just taken them out of the oven. Don't let them get cold. And tell me, Husky, how's it going out there?"

"Looks bad."

A shadow passed over RoyRoy's face.

"They attacked a billboard-man, a fellow techno. They set him on fire and we don't know if he'll survive. The company has sent all the billboard-technos home. They say it's for their own safety, but in reality it's a mass layoff."

"Did you know Nabokov?" asked Yiannis.

"Yes. And I saw her just before the attack. TTT had taken hold and she was dying and totally insane. She must have had a brain tumor."

"It's a tragedy," reflected Yiannis sadly.

The screen in the bar showed the police charging the demonstrators surrounding the RRM. On the right of the screen stood Hericio, the leader of the Human Supremacist Party, who was being interviewed again.

"And what's unacceptable is that our police are protecting those monsters and attacking our boys, instead of protecting humans from those murderers who, at this stage—because there's no question some of the wounded will die—have killed seven people, including three children."

Seven victims! Including three children! Bruna shuddered at the thought of the enormity of the act. Oh, Valo, Valo. What a terrible deed. And meanwhile, here was José Hericio again, appearing opportunely on the scene and taking advantage of the drama. She thought about Habib's words and about Myriam's intuition regarding the involvement of the leader of the HSP. Her suspicion didn't seem so absurd now.

"Those supremacists should be investigated. I have to find a way of getting close to them," she said with her mouth full of a delicious little ersatz-partridge pie.

"There's…there's a bar in Colón Square where I know they hang out," said RoyRoy hesitantly. "As you know, I spend the whole day on the street thanks to these billboards. I once ran into problems at that bar and then I found out it was a supremacist hangout. In my line of work you really have to know where you can go, so I make myself a list of the good spots and the places to avoid. And that's one of the ones to avoid. Here, I'll give you the address. It's called Saturn. But be careful. If you're thinking of putting in an appearance over there now, who knows what could happen. They really scared me."

"And it's precisely because people feel this lack of protection that the populace is arming itself and taking on its own defense. A legitimate and absolutely necessary attitude, given the total absence of the authorities," railed Hericio emphatically from the screen.

"Oli, please, I beg you, switch him off," Bruna pleaded.

The woman muttered something at the screen and the picture immediately changed to a soothing panoramic view of dolphins swimming in the ocean.

"What's the matter? Don't you like listening to home truths?" screeched a nervous, high-pitched voice.

Silence spread through the bar like a bucket of spilled oil. Bruna kept chewing. Without moving, looking at him sideways from under her eyelashes, she studied the character who had just spoken. He was a small and fairly scrawny human. Possibly somewhat drunk. He was close to her, about three feet away.

"Does it bother you to know that we're sick of putting up with you? That we're not going to let you go on taking advantage of us? And on top of that, what are you doing here? Haven't you realized that you're the only monster here?"

It was true: she was the only rep in the bar. She bit into another canapé. The man was badly dressed and had the look of an unskilled laborer. When he spoke, he tensed his whole body and stood on his toes, as if he wanted to appear taller, more menacing. She almost felt sorry for him; she could knock him to the ground with one smack. But graveyards were full of people overly confident in their own strength, so the rep analyzed her options with all the caution of a professional. First, the exit. The guy was blocking her path to the door, but if push came to shove, she'd be able to jump over to the other side of the counter, which also offered her a perfect refuge. The most worrying thing, because of its very recklessness, was that a little man like this one would dare to confront a combat rep. Could he be armed? Maybe with a plasma gun? He didn't look the type to be carrying something like that, and she couldn't see a weapon anywhere on him. Or maybe he wasn't alone. Could there be other henchmen in the bar? She did a quick sweep of the place and rejected that possibility too. She knew just about everyone by sight. No, he was just a poor, slightly drunk idiot.

"Get lost, you revolting monster. Clear off, and don't come back. We're going to exterminate the lot of you, just like rats."

Yes, indeed, the most disturbing thing was that someone like him would feel confident and supported enough to insult someone like her. Bruna didn't want to confront him, didn't want to hurt him, didn't want to humiliate him, because all of that would merely strengthen his paranoid delusions, his antitechno fury. She preferred to wait until he got bored and stopped talking. But the little man was getting redder and angrier by the minute. His own rage was inflaming him. Suddenly, he moved one step toward her and threw an awkward punch that the rep had no difficulty in avoiding. *Damn,* she thought, annoyed, *I'm going to have no other option but to whack him*.

It wasn't necessary. Suddenly a wall of flesh materialized next to them. It was Oli, who had come out from behind the bar and was now grabbing the guy from behind and lifting him off his feet as if he were a doll.

"The only rat around here is you."

Fat Oli carried the little man—legs kicking—to the door and threw him out onto the street.

"If you show your ugly snout around here again, I'll split it in two," she barked, raising a menacing, chubby forefinger.

And then she turned around and looked defiantly at her clientele, like someone expecting a protest. But no one said a word, and people even seemed to agree with her on the whole. Oli relaxed, and a smile lit up her moon-face as she wobbled her way back to the counter. Bruna had never seen her away from the counter. She really was immense, colossal, considerably bigger in her lower extremities than in the majestic opulence on display above. A primitive goddess, a human whale. So gigantic, in fact, that Bruna wondered for the first time if she might not be a mutant, if that mountain of flesh was the product of atomic disorder.

Scarcely had the prickly waves of concern that any incident gives rise to died down within the bar when they heard a racket of sorts outside. Initially, the rep thought it was some kind of maneuver on the part of the recently expelled little man, so she headed to the door of the bar to see what was happening. A few feet away, a redheaded woman was shrieking and wriggling in an attempt to free herself from the grip of a pair of tax police, the feared "blues." A little girl, less than six years old, was observing the whole thing, wide-eyed with terror and clutching a grubby toy rabbit. A third blue, a woman, came up and grabbed her by the hand. It was an imperious gesture: she literally yanked the little girl by the wrist. The child began to cry and the redheaded woman softly followed suit, instantly abandoning her impulse to fight, as if the tears of the little girl—clearly her daughter—had been the signal to surrender. The police headed up the street with the two of them while the pedestrians kept watch out of the corners of their eyes, as if they were dealing with a slightly shameful scene, something it would be embarrassing to watch directly.

"*Moths*. Poor things," said Yiannis, beside her.

Bruna nodded in agreement. Almost all the moths had young children; if they were running the risk of living clandestinely in Clean Air Zones they couldn't afford, it was for fear of the undeniable harm pollution caused to children. They illegally abandoned their contaminated cities with permanently gray skies and appeared, just like moths, attracted by the sunlight and the oxygen, only for the vast majority of them to go up in flames, because the tax police were incredibly efficient. The woman and the child wore the same shabby clothes as the little man who had insulted Bruna in the bar. Fanaticism and racism fed on the same social stratum of the dispossessed and the desperate.

"First arrest, deportation and a fine; if they offend again, up to six years in jail," said Yiannis.

"It's revolting. It makes you ashamed to belong to Earth," muttered Bruna.

"*Cuncta fessa*," murmured the archivist.

"What?"

"Octavius Augustus became the first Roman emperor because the republic granted him enormous powers. And why did the Republic do that? Why did it commit suicide to make way for an empire? Tacitus explains it thus: *Cuncta fessa.* Which means 'the whole world is tired.' Weariness in the face of political and social insecurity is what led to Rome losing its rights and freedoms. Fear induces a hunger for authoritarianism in people. Fear is a really bad adviser. And now look around you, Bruna: everyone's afraid. We're living in critical times. Our democratic system is also on the verge of suicide. Sometimes nations opt to throw themselves into the abyss."

"A magnificent democratic system that poisons children who have no money."

"A disgusting democratic system, true, but the only one that exists in the universe. At least in the known universe. The Omaás, Gnés, and Balabís have aristocratic or dictatorial governments. As for Cosmos and Labari, they are both terrible totalitarian states. Our democracy, with all its flaws, is an incredible achievement for humanity, Bruna. The result of many centuries of struggle and suffering. Listen, the world moves on, society moves on, and the more democratic it is, the more progress there is and the greater society's capacity for change. On Earth we've had a dreadful century. Unification happened only fourteen years ago; our state is young and complex. It's the first planetary state; we're inventing ourselves as we go…We can improve. But in order to do that, we have to believe in the possibilities of democracy and defend it and work to perfect it. Have faith."

Four years, three months, and eighteen days.

"I don't think that girl will see any changes before the air makes her irreversibly ill," said Bruna, a knot of anguish tightening in her chest.

And after a few seconds of heavy silence, she angrily repeated: "No, she won't see them. And neither will I."

CHAPTER SIXTEEN

An hour later the detective left the bar and paused briefly to check out the scene. It had stopped raining and the sun was trying to show its face between the clouds. It was six o'clock on a Monday evening but the streets were unusually empty and the few people to be seen, all humans, were walking too quickly. It wasn't a day to be going for a walk. A vague foreboding of danger seemed to hang over the city.

Bruna called Habib. The man's troubled face appeared instantly.

"How are things around the RRM?"

"Better, I suppose. The police charged, so there are no supremacists outside the entrance anymore. But everything's a mess."

"One question, Habib. Do your spies know a bar called Saturn?"

"They certainly do. It's a nest of vipers. The HSP headquarters are nearby and all the extremists gather there. Why?"

"No reason. I was thinking about how I could get close to Hericio, as you were suggesting."

Yes, Saturn would be a good option. But be very careful. I'm not convinced it's the best day to go over there."

"I know. Oh, yes, just one more thing: what did you say to Nabokov?"

"Pardon?"

"When I bumped into her, Nabokov kept repeating that you had told her something: 'Habib told me that, Habib told me that.' Clearly something that really upset her."

The man raised his eyebrows, bewildered.

"I have no idea what you're talking about. I didn't tell her anything. I don't think I'd even spoken to her since Myriam's death. Everything's been so chaotic lately! She must have been delirious. In the end, she was totally beside herself."

"Do we know anything from the autopsy?"

"It's still too soon. But the weird thing is that they haven't taken Valo to the Forensic Anatomy Institute. We have no idea what the police have done with her body. Our lawyers are going to lodge a formal complaint."

"How strange."

"Yes, everything about this whole business is too strange," said Habib, his voice choking.

Bruna, uneasy, cut the link. Had they inserted an adulterated memory into the dying Valo as well? An induced-behavior program that included hallucinations, a supposed conversation with Habib, and the murderous idea of planting a bomb. Was that why she had mentioned the word *revenge*? And why the police were hiding her body?

"Get out of Madrid, you rep shit!"

The insult had come from a private car as it drove past her. She watched it speeding away and jumping the traffic lights at an intersection to avoid having to stop. The driver was yelling loudly, but he was undoubtedly frightened. Or maybe she should put it another way: he was undoubtedly yelling because he was frightened.

Bruna sighed. She looked around one more time, looking for signs of Lizard. He was nowhere to be seen, but the detective was not convinced. Her failure to register that the inspector was following her still irritated her. Naturally, tailing her was easy for him; if truth be told, all he had to do was track the rep's mobile computer. Totally prohibited for everyone else, of course, but apparently not for judicial inspectors. Legal trivialities happily ignored. Just in case, the detective switched off her mobile and removed the power source, which was the only way to prevent its being detected. Removing the locator chip was a crime, and that aside, the chip was installed in such a way as to make it very difficult to remove without destroying the computer. Next she walked around the block to see if anyone was following her and, in fact, she spotted a solidly built young woman who had police written all over her and who had to be one of Lizard's bloodhounds.

The android had various techniques for trying to lose a tail, and she opted for the subway one. Since she had to pay cash because her mobile was disconnected, her really dumb tail went through the entry control long before she did, so she had to wait on the other side, doing a bad job of hanging around until Bruna got her ticket out of the machine. Acting as if she were unaware of her tail's presence, the rep headed for one of the platforms. They were in the Tres de Mayo Station, one of the most complex hubs in the Madrid underground network, with five intersecting subway lines. The android waited patiently for the train to arrive while the solidly built young woman faked one ostentatious yawn after another a few feet away from her. Yawning was one of the first things they taught you to do in the introductory How to Follow a Suspect course: *yawning produces an instant feeling of lack of danger in the person being tailed*, the instructor used to say. When the train arrived in the station with a screech of metal, the rep got in and parked herself at the end of the last car, leaning carelessly against the small connecting door that allowed passage between the cars and which, in this case, was locked because it was last car. The yawning woman was four cars away. As the train started to move, Bruna took out her pin decoder and, in a flash, had released the lock's simple mechanism. The end of the train was just leaving the station when the rep opened the small door and leaped onto the tracks. She tried to push the door shut behind her, but in any case, even if she hadn't managed to, by the time the policewoman reached the door she wouldn't dare jump from the rapidly accelerating train. It would take incredible ability and training to land safely and avoid being incinerated by the high-voltage line. The android doubted that the human would have the necessary skills to do that—unless she was a circus performer.

While the train moved off into the darkness with a blast of hot air, Bruna headed back toward the Tres de Mayo Station and climbed up a ladder to the platform. A middle-aged human couple gave a start when they saw her emerging from the tunnel and launched into a pathetic little trot toward the exit. The android grunted in chagrin and considered the possibility of saying something to them: *Don't worry, there's no reason why you should leave, I don't pose any danger.* But they were already too far away, and if she started to call out loudly to them and follow them, she might well cause them to have a fit of hysteria. So much fear in the air couldn't lead to anything good.

She switched lines, got into another car and emerged from the subway two stations farther along. The multicolored plastic domes of a circus were in front of her. She didn't want to switch on her mobile, so she again had to pay cash to get in, mentally thanking again the customary corruption of those governing Earth, which ensured that the paper money of yesteryear would continue to be legal tender and still used by everyone, precisely because its use lent itself brilliantly to anonymity and impunity. It was invisible money that left no trace in its wake, unlike electronic transactions.

The show was halfway through and the tent was barely a quarter full. Bruna tiptoed in and sat down on one side, as close to the orchestra as she could. It was a dreadful spot with poor visibility, and all the seats around her were empty, so her arrival attracted attention. The violinist, who was the only woman in the group of six musicians, lowered her bow during a pause in the piece she was playing, looked attentively at the rep and then greeted her with a barely perceptible nod of her head. Bruna responded with a similar movement and settled patiently into her seat. She'd have to wait until the show was over. The acts followed one another with the boring repetition of their fake happiness. It was a mediocre circus, neither very good nor very bad—conventional and utterly forgettable. There was a human tamer of Gnés perrifants, those wretched alien animals the size of a horse that looked like greyhounds minus the ears, and had brains the size of a mosquito; but thanks to the different gravity on Earth they were able to turn the most astonishing somersaults. There was a troupe of reps with various biological implants: their stomachs were plasma screens and they could create holograms in the air with their hands—that is to say, with the microcameras surgically implanted into their fingertips. And there was the typical bloody act performed by the Kalinians, a sect of crazy sadomasochists who imitated the magicians of the classical circuses but without the tricks, because they were enamored of pain and exhibitionism. So for that reason, they really did cut their bodies with knives and pierce their cheeks with long needles. Bruna found the Kalinians revolting, but they were currently in fashion.

The Kalinians were the final act. As the orchestra was launching itself into its last happy chorus, it seemed to Bruna that Mirari was having difficulties playing the piece. The violinist had a bionic left arm, but she didn't have it covered with synthetic skin. It was a metal, articulated arm like those of the robots in the futuristic fantasies of the twentieth century, and something must have been happening with the implant because whenever Mirari could stop playing for a moment, she would try to adjust the prosthesis. The show finally ended, the feeble applause died down, and the musicians disappeared quickly backstage, Mirari among them—which surprised the detective somewhat as she'd imagined that the violinist would come to talk to her when the show was over.

Bruna leaped into the ring, trying not to step on the bloodstains left by the Kalinians, went through the gold curtains and entered the area where the dressing rooms were located. She found Mirari in the third cubicle she looked into. She was furiously banging her bionic arm with a small rubber hammer.

"Mirari—"

"This-damn-pros-thee-sis!" exclaimed the woman, enunciating each syllable, beside herself, not pausing in her delivery of the hammer blows.

But having said that, exhausted and red in the face, she threw the hammer on the floor and dropped into a chair.

"It serves me right for buying it secondhand. But a good bionic arm is incredibly expensive. Especially if it's for a high-level profession, as in my case. What are you looking for around here, Husky?"

"I see you remember me."

"I'm afraid you're quite unforgettable."

Bruna sighed. "Yes, I guess so."

Mirari was too, in her own way. Not just because of her retro-futuristic prosthesis, but also because of her pale skin, jet-black eyes, and round head framed by a halo of short hair, dazzlingly white and as stiff as wire. The violinist was a specialist, a supplier, an expert who operated in the underground world. She could forge any document, get hold of secret plans, or supply the most sophisticated and illegal equipment. Bruna had heard that there were only two things she refused to sell: weapons and drugs. Everything else was negotiable. People might think that her work in the circus was just a cover, but there was no question that she seemed to have a passion for music, and she played the violin well as long as her bionic arm didn't jam.

"And you were here for—?" Mirari asked again, for she was one of those people who get right to the point, who hate to waste time.

"I need a new identity. Papers and a past that will stand up to investigation."

"A thorough investigation or a routine one?"

"Let's say fairly thorough."

"We're talking about it being valid short-term, of course."

"Of course. A week will suffice."

"Class A, then."

"It has to be a human identity. And living a few hundred miles from Madrid. My age. Of high social standing. With money in the bank. And if you can add a touch of supremacism to the biography, fantastic. Nothing too serious, just an ideological sympathy rather than militancy. But so it's clear that racist ideas are a passion, though up till now, she's somehow managed to keep them private."

"Done. When do you want all this?"

"As soon as possible."

"I think I can have it ready by tomorrow. Two thousand gaias."

"I also want an untraceable mobile."

"That will be another thousand Gs."

"Fine. I don't have that much in cash."

"Transfer it to me electronically. I use a program that erases all signs of the transaction. Although there'll still be a record of the withdrawal of the funds on your mobile."

"That doesn't worry me. But my computer is switched off because I think the police are tracking me. I don't want to switch it on here. I'll do the transfer shortly, from the street, if that's okay with you. And if you trust me."

"I don't need to trust you. I'll just delay placing the order until I get the money."

Bruna smiled sourly. Of course. It had been an astonishingly stupid comment.

"But in case it makes any difference to you, let me tell you that yes, I do trust you," Mirari added.

Bruna's smile widened. The human's small kindness felt especially pleasing on a day marked by such bitterness among the species. Mirari had bent over to pick up the hammer from the floor. She had been opening and closing her bionic hand for a while. The fingers weren't moving in sync, and the ring and middle fingers weren't closing completely. The violinist gave them a few tentative taps with the rubber tool.

"How much does a new prosthesis like the one you need cost?" asked Bruna.

Mirari looked up.

"Half a million Gs. More than my violin. And that's a Stainer."

"A what?"

"One of the best violins in the world. By Stainer, the seventeenth-century Austrian instrument maker. I have a marvelous violin, but I don't have the arm to play it," she said with unexpected and genuine anguish.

"But the money can be raised?"

"Yes. Or stolen," Mirari replied dryly, with yet another closed and impenetrable expression on her face. "I'll call you when I have everything."

Bruna left the circus and decided to walk home. She hadn't exercised for days and her body felt stiff and her muscles were keen for activity. It was already dark and drizzling. The wet sidewalks shone under the streetlights, and the sky-trams thundered by, lit up as if for a party, and empty. When she reached Tres de Mayo Square, where she'd disconnected her mobile, she reinserted the energy cell and switched on the machine. She sent Mirari the money and then, after ruling out the option of going to Oli's bar for dinner, continued on her way in the direction of her apartment. She was so absorbed in going over the details of the case that she didn't see the attack coming until the last minute, when she heard the whirring and sensed a movement behind her. She jumped sideways, turning in the air, but she couldn't avoid the impact altogether. The chain hit her right forearm, which she'd instinctively raised to protect herself. The blow hurt, but the pain didn't prevent her from grabbing the chain and pulling. The guy on the other end of it fell to the ground. But he wasn't alone. Bruna glanced around and assessed her situation. Seven assailants counting the one she'd just knocked down and who was now getting up. Five men and two women. Big, strong, in good shape. Armed with chains and metal bars. And worst of all, deployed in a star formation around her—three closer to her, four one step farther back—carefully placed so as to leave no gaps. A professional attack formation. They weren't going to be easy opponents. She decided she'd try to break the circle by charging the blond male with the hoop earrings; he was sweating and seemed to be the most nervous. And wearing earrings while fighting was a sign of inexperience: the first thing the detective would do would be to rip them out of his ears. Bruna had the chain at her disposal as a weapon and thought she had a chance of escaping, but even so, she'd undoubtedly take a few hits. It was a most unpleasant encounter.

The entire analysis only took the rep a few seconds. The whole group still hadn't moved, motionless in that perfect, tense stillness that precedes an outburst of violence. And then a voice cut through the tense atmosphere like a hot knife through butter.

"Police. Throw down your weapons."

It was Paul Lizard, and his thick, calm voice emerged from behind a large plasma gun.

"I won't say it again. Drop those iron bars right now."

The surprised assailants let go of their bars and chains, producing a formidable din.

"You too, Husky."

Bruna snorted and opened her hand.

"So now what are you going to do, tough guy? Shoot us in the back?" asked one of the women, perhaps the leader of the group.

And as if that were a signal, they all took off, each in a different direction.

Lizard watched them go and put away his gun. He looked at Bruna with his sleepy eyes.

"You had a narrow escape."

"I could have handled them."

"Really?"

Lizard's tone made the rep feel ridiculous and a braggart.

"Yes, I could. What I mean is, I could have gotten away... though I would have ended up with a few bruises."

"No question."

"Hmmm, okay, thanks," said Bruna, and the troublesome word erupted from her mouth like a belch.

"You're welcome. Did you recognize them?"

"No. But they were professionals."

"Yes, maybe mercenaries paid by someone to whip up the disturbances."

Bruna looked at him, intrigued.

"Why do you think that?"

The policeman shrugged his shoulders.

"I don't know. I'm seeing too many strange things in this sudden antitechno rage."

The detective looked at him attentively. Under their heavy eyelids, his sparkling green eyes were very sharp.

"Seven people have died today, thanks to Nabokov's bomb," Bruna said.

"Eight. One of the gravely wounded has died."

"Eight victims then. Don't you hate reps, Lizard? Be honest. Not even a little?"

"No."

"And you're not afraid of us?"

"No."

And Bruna believed him.

"Go home, Husky. It's not the best night to be out walking."

"I thought I'd shaken off your plump girl. You can't be a good tail with that much flesh."

"You certainly lost her. But her visibility was my camouflage. You've fallen for a beginner's trick, Husky."

The rep bit her lip, mortified.

"Why haven't you taken Nabokov's body to the Forensic Anatomy Institute?"

"It was deemed a terrorist attack, and anti-terrorist investigations are classified as top secret. And the Forensic Institute, as you know better than anyone, leaks like a sieve."

Bruna smiled.

"You mean that you've hidden the body so that I can't find out anything?"

The inspector also smiled.

"How conceited you are, Husky. You're not the only person capable of stealing information. Moreover, how suspicious you are! I don't deserve it. I offered to collaborate with you, and you didn't believe me."

"Give me the results from Nabokov's autopsy and I'll believe you."

Lizard stood watching her. Those sleepy, sardonic eyes.

"Very well. I'll have the results tomorrow. If you like, we'll talk then. And now, once and for all, go!"

"Are you going to follow me again?"

"Lucky for you that I did."

"Seriously, are you going to do it again?"

"No."

Bruna didn't believe him.

**Central Archive, the United States of the Earth.
Modifiable version**

ACCESS STRICTLY LIMITED
AUTHORIZED EDITORS ONLY

Madrid, January 25, 2109, 11:05
Good morning, Yiannis

IF YOU ARE NOT YIANNIS
LIBEROPOULOS,
CENTRAL ARCHIVIST FT711, QUIT
THESE PAGES IMMEDIATELY

ACCESS STRICTLY LIMITED
AUTHORIZED EDITORS ONLY
UNAUTHORIZED ACCESS IS A CRIMINAL
OFFENSE
PUNISHABLE BY IMPRISONMENT UP TO
A MAXIMUM OF TWENTY YEARS

Submerged Lands
Keywords: global warming, Robot Wars, Plagues, Ultra-Darwinism, Demographic Laws, wet tourism.
#002-327
Entry being edited

Although **global warming** had already begun to melt the polar icecaps in the twentieth century and the sea level had been rising progressively for several centuries, it is clear that its devastating impact on society seemed to explode suddenly around 2040. "Just as a frog placed in water that is gradually being heated is unaware of the problem until it boils to death, so humanity was unaware of the catastrophe until the massive number of deaths became evident," said Gorka Marlaska, Nobel Laureate in Medicine, in 2046.

In reality, serious disturbances had already occurred much earlier, but they were seen as isolated incidents and passed by more or less inadvertently because, typically, they took place in overpopulated, economically depressed, and traditionally unstable regions, such as the no-longer-existent Bangladesh, a country whose territory was completely covered by water, except for a narrow strip of mountains in the east, and which was absorbed by India after the period of the **Plagues**. Toward the end of 2039, however, when between 13 and 14 percent of the Earth's surface was already submerged, a stampede of sorts began in the Irrawaddy Delta region (formerly Burma). In contrast to what had happened in other cases, the unrest did not remain confined to one region. Rather, it took off and multiplied rapidly in other geographical zones throughout 2040, turning into a planetary phenomenon. One must keep in mind that huge urban centers were located in the coastal strips, and that these were usually densely populated. As the sea advanced, cities like Venice, Amsterdam, and Manhattan disappeared completely, while others—Lisbon, Barcelona, Mumbai—were partially flooded. Even more damaging was the inundation of the most fertile deltas and the densely populated coastal farming strips. Hundreds of millions of desperate, hungry people who had lost everything climbed to ever higher places as they were pursued by the waters. But those high lands were already inhabited, and often the inhabitants were also suffering from hunger, given the terrible loss of the best arable land. Confrontations among these groups swept the globe. A blind violence overtook the whole world, and one massacre followed another for several years. It could be said that this was the first planetary civil war although it ~~must have been so traumatic that, oddly, it~~ lacks a formal name as such. Historians refer to this period as that of the Plagues, comparing the ferocious, massive, displaced hordes to the calamitous biblical plague of locusts.

It was a time of chaos, and reliable data are not available, but it is estimated that by 2050, after a decade of conflicts, two billion people had died through famine, disease, and direct violence. There were, moreover, other lethal factors to consider, such as the appearance of the Ultra-Darwinists. **Ultra-Darwinism** was a racist terrorist movement supposedly based on the theories of Charles Darwin~~, although a huge majority of the scientific community has always rejected the notion that the Ultras had anything to do with evolutionism~~. The Ultras believed that Earth could not sustain a human population of such magnitude—a fact that in one sense was self-evident—and maintained that the Submerged Worlds and subsequent Plagues were a process of natural selection of benefit to Earth, given that the highest mortality rates were occurring in the overpopulated, economically disadvantaged zones that, on the whole, were inhabited by individuals whose racial origins were non-Caucasian, and whom the Ultras viewed as defective and dispensable human material. In order to speed up this supposed process of "ethnic cleansing," the Ultra-Darwinists carried out countless attacks with conventional explosives, missiles, and even short-range nuclear warheads, until the organization was finally dismantled successfully in 2052. ~~That said, it has been demonstrated that the replicants took advantage of the Plagues to murder humans with impunity.~~

★★★★*Scandalously inaccurate! Technohumans had not even been invented during the period of the Plagues. I wish to record here my concern and revulsion in regard to certain seriously erroneous inserts that I am finding of late in the archive. I recommend an internal investigation. Yiannis Liberopoulos, central archivist FT711*★★★★

Although the worst period of Plagues was already over by the middle of the twenty-first century, the political and geographical landscape was so affected that the planet was plunged into explosive instability for decades. The **Rep War** (2060–2063) worsened the situation, ~~showing yet again the pernicious effect of the technos~~ and the illegitimacy of the new territorial borders became one of the elements that triggered the **Robot Wars** (2079–2090). This long period of general instability and violence caused the world's population to fall below four billion people. In the last quarter of the twenty-first century, some countries had already begun to limit the number of children their citizens could have, but it was post-**Unification** (2096) that the United States of the Earth decreed the **Demographic Laws** (2101) that regulate pregnancies so as to avoid renewed overpopulation. The objective is to maintain the number of inhabitants of the planet at four billion, to which should be added a further billion or so distributed between the two Floating Worlds, Labari and Cosmos. ~~Given that 15 percent of Earth's residents are reps~~

(six hundred million individuals), a further advantage to their extermination would be the ability to increase in a sensible manner the quota of human children.

★★★★*I recommend that the internal investigation be carried out as a matter of urgency. Yiannis Liberopoulos, central archivist FT711*★★★★

It was also post-Unification that the Planetary Government decided to exploit the Submerged Worlds to the maximum. Various sites were established, containing the most iconic of the flooded zones, and their management was auctioned among several leisure and tourism mega-enterprises. To date, about a dozen theme parks have been opened, and another twenty are under construction. The consortiums shored up the ruins of the Submerged Worlds and created artificial islands to accommodate hotels, restaurants, and other services. The flooded zones can be visited in a bathyscaphe, in one-person underwater bubbles, or using diving equipment. There are urban theme parks like the well-known Manhattan, or historical ones like the Nile Delta. These popular holiday destinations make up the so-called **wet tourism**.

CHAPTER SEVENTEEN

Merlín was a really good chess player. He was a calculation rep and had a formidable mind: mathematical, musical, a precise labyrinth of sparkling thoughts.

"I sometimes think about the wild little animal you'd be without me and I shudder in horror," he'd say to her occasionally, grabbing her by the scruff of the neck like someone handling an overly nervous young filly.

Merlín was joking, but he was in fact quite close to the mark. Bruna believed that the two years she'd lived with him, together with subsequent learning from her friend Yiannis, had made her into what she was—a combat rep unlike any other. Life was an unfathomable and mysterious thing, even the brief and preset life of reps. In fact, those genetic engineers who thought they were gods had no idea what they were doing. Yes, they could boost certain abilities in technohumans depending on the function for which were produced, but after that each rep was different, and developed capabilities and defects that no engineer had known how to anticipate in the lab as he cut up and mixed helixes of cloned DNA. Merlín was special, too: creative, imaginative, with a playful temperament that predisposed him toward happiness.

They met when she'd just been granted her license from the military and the settlement allowance was warming her pocket. So Bruna was still young, while Merlín was already 8/33. But he lived with no fear of death, as if he were eternal. Or as if he were human, because humans had the capacity to forget they were mortal. That was something Bruna failed to learn from her lover.

"Husky! Are you with me? You're not listening to me at all."

Habib's distorted face reflected weariness and impatience.

"Sorry. I was distracted for a few moments, thinking about—"

"Well, do your thinking on your own time. Given the expenses you're running up, you could try not to make me waste my time."

Habib had been like this all morning—extremely nervous, combustible, with an aggression Bruna had never seen in him before.

"You gave me carte blanche with expenses."

"And if you were offering some results, I'd consider it money well spent. But so far..." he grumbled.

And the worst of it was that he was right.

They were in the apartment Myriam Chi and Nabokov had shared. A spacious, comfortable but coldly functional apartment, as if radical ideology did not encourage too many decorative refinements. Or as if they didn't want to become too attached to things. There was only one personal touch: a photo of Myriam and Valo embracing each other, affectionate and smiling. It was laser-cut in 3-D, inside a block of glass. The photo was the typical souvenir done on the spot in many holiday destinations. Bruna and Merlín had had a similar portrait done in Venice Park during a wet tourism weekend they had given themselves as a present not long after their relationship began. After her lover died, Bruna threw out the glass block; she couldn't bear that picture of happiness. But then, coming across the picture of Nabokov and Chi, it had triggered something in her mind and she had started thinking about Merlín. Something she generally preferred to avoid.

Apart from that conventional glass souvenir, the room could have been the bland lounge room of any apartment. Compared with these surroundings, Bruna's apartment seemed even cozy. The rep reflected with a certain pride on her copies of two works of art: Leonardo da Vinci's *Vitrubian Man* and Jan Vermeer's *Lady Writing a Letter with Her Maid*. They were very good reproductions, not holographs but superrealistic, and they had been quite expensive.

"There's nothing here. I told you so," growled Habib, closing the drawers in the kitchen.

The police had just unsealed the apartment after searching it thoroughly. Bruna pictured the huge Lizard sniffing around and found the idea unpleasant, even offensive, and a bit obscene. Myriam and Valo wouldn't have liked having a human rummaging through their things, though they probably wouldn't have liked her and Habib being there either. When Habib had found out that Bruna wanted to inspect the apartment, he insisted on accompanying her, and now he was displaying a frenzy of totally useless activity, as he could have no idea what the rep was looking for. In point of fact, neither did she, but experience had taught her that her unconscious being was much wiser than her conscious equivalent. And simply by looking, she often saw things that others missed. Evidence that jumped out before her eyes as if it were calling to her. So Bruna walked along behind Habib, reopening and checking all the drawers and cupboards that he had dismissively just closed. Although it was true that so far they had found nothing revealing.

Then they went into the bedroom, and Bruna felt embarrassed but moved. This was a private room, a nest, a den, a sacred sanctum in which mortals took refuge believing they would be able to protect themselves from the desolation of the world. The enormous bed was covered with exquisite, brilliantly colored silk cushions, and along the wall facing the bed there were at least fifteen white orchids planted in gold baroque flowerpots and arranged in two groups. Lilac-colored strips of chiffon hung from the ceiling like banners, and the floor was covered with a glorious, soft, deep red Omaá carpet.

"Wow! Oh, my! Impressive," said Habib.

Bruna wondered which of the two, Myriam or Valo, was responsible for such a feminine and opulent decor: Chi with her painted fingernails, or Nabokov with her huge breasts and impossible bun? Although it was probably the two of them: an intimate, excessively ornate and secret world they shared. That was love, in reality: having someone with whom to share your quirks.

"I've been in this apartment before, naturally, but not in this room," murmured Habib.

On top of the bedside table there were traces of a living hell: countless bottles, subcutaneous injectors, patches, pills, disinfectants, dressings, ointments. All the medical paraphernalia, that foul flood of useless remedies, that illness leaves in its wake. When Merlín died, the room was full of all that miserable rubbish, too: double-strength painkillers; medication to treat the psychotic delirium, agitation, and violence caused by TTT; sedatives for anxiety. After he'd gone, there were still remnants of his suffering attached to those drugs, in the same way that you could follow the trail of Nabokov's death throes in that jumble of pills. Bruna felt a pinch of dread. The usual, ancient, and well-known dread snaking its way around her insides. *Four years, three months, and seventeen days. Seventeen days. Seventeen days.*

Habib was down on the floor on all fours, running his finger along the thin strip between the carpet and the wall. *He's taking it very seriously*, the rep said to herself half-jokingly. *If truth be told, he's taking it* too *seriously*, she thought right after that, somewhat surprised. In fact, he didn't seem to be searching the apartment as such but looking for something specific. That meticulous inspection, that acute agitation…

"Revenge!" she exclaimed.

"What?" asked Habib, turning toward her.

The detective had spoken on impulse, a sudden intuition, as if testing the waters. She looked Habib in the eye.

"*Revenge.* Does the word mean anything to you?"

The man frowned.

"Hmmm…not a lot. What should it be telling me, Bruna?"

He looked absurd, still on all fours with his head turned over his shoulder so that he could look at her. It suddenly seemed to her that he was being too pleasant. He had used her first name, and on top of that, his tone was too friendly, whereas he'd behaved obnoxiously all morning. Bruna was suspicious. She often was; she'd suddenly feel the cold wind of suspicion pass through her. She decided not to tell him about the tattoos. That was a secret she shared with Lizard.

"No. Nothing. It was something Nabokov said that last time I saw her. *Revenge.* And then she marched off to kill and to die."

Habib stood up and shook his head.

"She was delirious. Listen, Bruna, I don't know what we're searching for here. I don't think they inserted a memory in Valo. She was just very ill and mad with grief over Myriam's death."

The detective nodded in agreement. The man was probably right.

"And another thing, Bruna. Forgive me if I'm a little... tense. In two days' time, we're holding the RRM assembly to elect the movement's new leader. I thought it would be a given for me, but two other androids have turned up who are vying for the position, and they're mounting the dirtiest of campaigns against me. They're accusing me of not being sufficiently diligent in my attempts to clear up Myriam's death; they're even accusing me of being glad she's gone, as it allows me to take her position. That's why I need results as soon as possible—do you understand? As soon as possible!"

"I get it now. Especially the electoral results," said the rep somewhat sarcastically.

Habib looked at her angrily.

"Well, yes, that too. Does it surprise you? We're at a critical moment in the history of replicants and I know that I can help to improve the situation, that I can lead the RRM with a firm hand during this critical step. I didn't welcome Myriam's death as those wretches suggest—of course not—but in a certain sense maybe it was fortunate. Because I know what needs to be done. And I think I even know better than she did. Is it a crime to aspire to leadership when you know it will enable you to have a positive influence on society?"

He'd ended up holding forth in a grandiose tone. So that's what he was doing down on all fours, poking his nose into the corners: looking for votes. Even if it was at the expense of Nabokov's madness, Chi's blood, the horror, the fire, and the violence. Disappointing. She looked at the angry Habib with indifference. As Yiannis often said, *People's misery shines as soon as things start to go wrong.*

CHAPTER EIGHTEEN

Bruna got off the travelator, turned cautiously into the avenue and scanned from afar the area surrounding her apartment building as she clung to a faint hope. But no, there was the Omaá, with his translucent body and his ridiculous T-shirt. The *bicho*'s patient siege was turning her exits and entrances into a martyrdom. The night before, as she was approaching her building with adrenaline still pumping after her encounter with the thugs, Bruna mistook his huge shadow for that of an assailant and nearly gave him a kick in the groin. Or in the place where Earthlings have their groin. But the Omaá dodged it easily, as if he had predicted her movement.

"It's Maio, it's Maio. Sorry if I startled you," he had said with his murmuring voice.

And the rep had almost regretted that he wasn't an anonymous assailant. The alien was driving her mad. He was making her feel absurdly guilty and becoming an obsession to the point where the discomfort was making her think twice about going home. Right now, after completing her search of Chi's apartment, she would have preferred not to go home. But not daring to confront him seemed shameful to her. And then there was Bartolo, whom she didn't want to leave on his own for too long. So she had no alternative now but to start running, and race through the main entrance so as to avoid that persistent wretch Maio. The alien was turning into a problem.

Having successfully dealt with the first Omaá, she now had to confront the second one. The android opened the door to her apartment fearful of what she might find. How the devil had she managed to complicate her life in this way? Once again, she decided to get hold of an animal shelter right away and free herself of the bubi. She cautiously stuck her head inside; the place seemed to be in order. No half-chewed clothes on the floor. Relieved, she stepped inside and closed the door, at which point she caught sight of the greedy-guts glued to the far wall, very nervous, and with his head hanging down—the absolute picture of guilt. The rep's spirits plummeted.

"What have you done? You've been naughty, haven't you?"

Bartolo was wringing his gray little hands, desperately contrite. Bruna had a sudden terrible intuition and ran toward the table with the jigsaw puzzle. She gave a sigh of relief; everything seemed to be fine. But hold on a minute…There was one piece missing that had been extracted from what she'd already done. The hole was like a gaping wound in the middle of the picture.

"I told you not to touch the puzzle!"

The bubi whimpered.

"What have you done with the piece? Have you eaten it, you stupid animal?"

"Bartolo good," blubbered the creature.

And he started to run toward the bedroom. Bruna followed him and, to her relief, found the small piece of cardboard on top of her pillow, meticulously placed right in the center of it. The rep seized the piece—it was intact and didn't even seem to have been chewed. *It's undoubtedly a message, a warning, perhaps even a threat*, thought Bruna. *It's saying: I don't like being abandoned and I could have taken my revenge by destroying the entire jigsaw puzzle, but I've been generous and haven't done so.* It was a very sophisticated gesture, not that different from the just-decapitated heads of dogs that the Chinese mafia used to leave behind. The android tried to hide the smile lurking on her lips and turned toward the bubi, forcing herself to look stern.

"Bartolo alone," muttered the greedy-guts, twisting his fingers.

"I know. I know you were left alone and you don't like it. Okay, fine. This time, you're forgiven. But don't do it again."

The animal leapt up into her arms; Bruna felt his warm breath on her neck. Embarrassed and annoyed, she removed the bubi and put him on the floor. All she needed was to become attached to a creature she was going to get rid of right away.

"And don't ever do that again either! No climbing up and giving hugs!"

And, seeing the contrite face of the greedy-guts, she immediately added, "Come on, I'll give you something to eat."

That information instantly raised the bubi's spirits.

Just at that moment, a call came in from Mirari. The unusual face of the violinist appeared on the screen, her spiky white hair looking like a crown of thorns.

"It's done. I'm sending you a robot. Twenty minutes," she said and cut off.

Always so curt.

The rep poured herself a glass of white wine and dropped onto the couch in front of the picture window, exhausted, while Bartolo ate his bowl of cereal with noisy enthusiasm. *Four years, three months, and seventeen days.* She took a sip of wine. The arm with which she was holding the glass bore the imprint of the blow from the hooligan's chain, and the detective thought it was a symbolic mark. Events were leaving her bruised, wounded. For some reason, this case had stirred her up more than any other. It had become very personal.

It started to rain. The sky was a changing swirl of gray clouds, and the raindrops, slanted by the wind, beat against the pane of glass. Yiannis had once shown Bruna the old, mythical film from the twentieth century in which replicants first made an appearance. It was called *Blade Runner*. It was a strange, well-meaning film as far as the reps were concerned, although Bruna found it somewhat irritating. The androids bore little resemblance to real ones and on the whole, tended to be stupid, oversimplified, childish, and violent. Never mind the blonde techno who turned somersaults like an articulated doll. Even so, there was something profoundly moving about the film. Bruna had learned by heart the final words spoken by the main rep character on the rain-swept rooftop before he died: "I've seen things you people wouldn't believe. Attack ships on fire off the shoulder of Orion. I watched c-beams glitter in the dark near the Tannhäuser Gate. All those moments will be lost in time like tears in rain. Time to die." And then he lowered his head and died so easily. So easily. Like an electric machine that someone unplugs. Without suffering the nightmare of TTT. But his powerful words reflected wonderfully the inconsistency of life, that subtle, beautiful insignificance that time was unraveling without leaving a trace. The rep in *Blade Runner* lowered his head and died, while the rain ran down his cheeks, perhaps hiding his final tears.

When he was close to the end of his 10/35 years, Merlín disappeared. He left. Bruna finally managed to locate him: he'd moved to a hotel. The detective, for whom eloquence had never been a strong point, nevertheless managed to make Merlín understand that watching him die from afar would be even more painful. So Merlín returned, and they were still able to enjoy a few months of serenity before his TTT manifested itself.

When the illness appeared, they went to the Scottish Highlands. Bare, wind-swept land, with brooks like threads of mercury flowing through black banks. They both liked cold, remote, inhospitable places—one of those shared oddities that formed the basis of their love. That was why, when Merlín decided to withdraw into the dark like a wounded dog, he chose that distant corner. They installed themselves in a small, very old rented cottage, which they immediately filled with their pathetic cargo of medical equipment and medication. The smell of illness and poisoned time. The slow, oppressive time of dying. Death stalked them like a predator, tarnishing everything with suffering, but Bruna still remembered one night when it was raining, with raindrops drumming on the window just as they were now, and Merlín was dozing by her side in bed, momentarily relieved from his suffering while she, lying on top of the bedspread, read a novel by the yellow light of a small lamp. From time to time, she would glance over at her lover—his back, so familiar but now so bony; his emaciated features; the beard he had acquired. Because the nails and hair of the dying keep growing: while everything else is collapsing, those small cells continue to weave their substance with a blind and desperately tenacious vitality. A useless organic effort that cast a shadow over Merlín's cheeks and made his beautiful face seem ever more gaunt. Bruna knew that, just before the end, the profile of sick people became sharper, as if to cleave the darkness, penetrate the shadows like the prow of a ship. Her lover's face had already begun to sharpen. But they were together and they were still alive; and outside, the wind whistled and the rain whispered its desolate song, turning the bedroom into a refuge. That night, time stopped and there was a strange peace within the pain.

At times Bruna felt such acute pain that she thought she wouldn't be able to bear it.

But afterward, she always could.

Tears in rain. Everything would pass and everything would be quickly forgotten. Even suffering.

She took another sip of wine and looked at her reproduction of *Lady Writing a Letter with Her Maid*. The maid was waiting, arms crossed, for her mistress to finish writing so that she could then undoubtedly take away the letter. She wasn't in a hurry. While she waited, she wasn't required to work; it was a small break in her day. She was a young girl with a chubby face. She was standing in the background and gazing with quiet pleasure out of the window through which a clean, early morning light was entering. It must have been a lovely day outside. The girl was enjoying the sunshine, her youth, and her health, the perfect serenity of the moment, as if it were the most natural thing in the world. The joy of life captured in an instant. That painting moved Bruna because it was like a slice of time outside time. It made her feel the way she had felt that rainy night next to Merlín. That night, while her lover was dying, she was immortal. Almost like a human.

Just then a robot courier beeped at her door and Bruna gave a start. Her nerves were on edge. It was a high-security delivery, so she had to allow the robot to do a DNA check before she could pick up the sealed, waterproof container. *How the devil has Mirari gotten hold of my DNA?* the rep wondered, somewhat annoyed. The violinist was a dangerous woman. Bruna broke the seals and took out a wrist computer-mobile, a data chip, and an ID tag that was so perfectly made it was even a bit battered, as if it had been used a lot. She inserted the tag in the computer and confirmed that she was a thirty-year-old woman called Annie Heart from Tavistock, Devon, in what used to be Great Britain, and a professor of applied robotics at the Asimov Technical University in New Barcelona. This was followed by the usual encrypted files, which contained the remaining details about Heart: medical history; genetic profile; student record; employment history; dental record; financial and banking details; security reports; incidents involving the police or criminal acts; a list of activities and interests and the like—almost a hundred different references that could only be opened if you had the various authorization codes. Naturally, as the owner of the ID she could without a doubt consult all of them. She would have to study them carefully so as to know this Annie Heart, the woman she would become for a few days. But before doing that, she inserted the data chip into the slot in the computer. Mirari's face appeared on the screen.

"I only guarantee full cover for ID checks for six days. Five is better, to stay within the safe zone. As far as the mobile is concerned, I've bought you a month's usage with a clandestine satellite, so it will only be untraceable for that period. Check file FF3. I think I've done a good job," she said.

And she smiled a small, cheeky smile, totally out of character for the normally stern violinist. The chip switched itself off. File FF3 was a police report. Annie Heart had been arrested three days ago during a supremacist demonstration in New Barcelona and accused of having taken part in a beating handed out to a technohuman. But she had been released a few hours later because, apart from the confused testimony of the victim, there were no witnesses against her and Heart was neither politically active nor had she ever been in any radical human group, and she maintained that she had simply been passing by. Bruna smiled; it was a perfect touch, just what she needed. Mirari's work was impeccable.

The rep verified on the computer that, just as Habib had told her, the HSP had applied for a funding permit. Political parties didn't receive any funding from the state. They kept themselves afloat with party memberships and donations, but the latter were strictly regulated, and to receive them, they had to have a funding permit. FPs were valid for two, four, or six months, and during that period, the party could ask for and receive donations from private individuals or companies, subject to the prior payment of a certain amount of money to the Tax Office. It was assumed that this money was to pay the inspectors who controlled the transactions, but in reality it was a type of indirect tax whose imposition caused considerable resentment. That a party such as the HSP, so reluctant to recognize the legality of the state, would compromise itself by asking for an FP suggested deep financial need, or imminent plans, or both. The Supremacists' FP was valid for two months, and there were only two weeks left. *They'll probably be keen to collect as much as possible before they run out of time*, thought Bruna. And that might suit her very well.

The rep spent the next hour and a half studying the details of her false identity and eating a huge portion of precooked rice with tofu. Bartolo was snoring. Then she tidied the house, made the bed, placed three pieces in her puzzle and listened to a Brahms concerto. The greedy-guts continued to sleep like a log. Then the rep was struck by a sudden intuition. She sat down in front of the main screen and did a search on the word *hungry*. The seventh entry in the list of options read

> HUNGRY
> The best multi-entertainment center in Madrid
> A multipurpose venue to satisfy every conceiv-
> able craving.
> 12 Iris Avenue. Open 24 hours, 365 days of
> the year.

So Hungry was the name of a club. In fact, she now had a vague recollection of having seen it in ads or on the news. It was a *multi-e*, as they were referred to colloquially: a mega-entertainment center that accommodated diverse tastes, with restaurants, bars, discos, virtual games, all of them with the latest technology, always emphasizing the spectacular, and with zones dedicated to the tastes of reps and aliens. The rep had been in a multi-e in Paris. And it was quite entertaining. Maybe that was what Bartolo had been referring to with his incessant "hungry"; maybe Cata Caín had hung out in the place. There would be no harm in taking a stroll out that way and checking it out.

Four hours later, Bruna left her apartment wearing a lilac dress, one of her favorites, with the ethereal and luminous gold pectoral hanging around her neck. She was very elegant, maybe overly so, she thought, when she got to Iris Avenue. It was an industrial zone on the outskirts of Madrid. Number 12 was a round, six-story tower. There were no windows except on the top floor, which was occupied by the main restaurant, and the outside walls had a luminous, opalescent overlay that slowly changed color. On the roof there was an enormous sign that said "Hungry" in fiery letters. It must have been some holograph trick. Night had already fallen and the huge lobby of the multi-e was quite full with a motley crowd of people, from young boys who seemed barely over the curfew age, to Kalinians with safety pins stuck into their cheeks, and middle-aged, well-heeled, conventional-looking couples. Bruna stopped in front of one of the interactive information boards and checked out the various options on offer. Above her head, on a public screen, Inmaculada Cruz, the regional president, was furiously talking in the chamber. It seemed that the opposition had moved a censure motion against her. The whole situation continued to unfold with an inexorable escalation in tension. The detective looked around and couldn't see any other technohuman. She was on her own with her elegant outfit and her gold necklace.

She approached a young man with shaved eyebrows at the information booth in the middle of the lobby and showed him a picture of Cata Caín.

"Does she ring a bell?"

"Oh, yes, poor Caín...We were all horrified," answered the man matter-of-factly.

"Oh, yes? She was that well known around here? Did she come often?"

"What do you mean, did she come often? Caín worked here...in the lunar disco."

Bruna frowned.

"Really? Since when? And why didn't anyone say so? As far as I was aware, Cata had an administrative job with a hotel business."

"Well, what she did here was just part-time work. She helped with the management of the disco—maintenance, logistics, accounts. She'd been coming here to do a few hours in the afternoon for about four months. Until one day she stopped coming. And two days later she was dead. But ask on the next floor; they had more to do with her."

Taking the young man's advice, Bruna went up one floor to the lunar disco. She held her mobile against the electronic eye and was charged thirty Gs. It was a very expensive place. The metallic doors opened with a pneumatic sigh and the rep found herself on a small balcony of sorts that overlooked a vast circular room. The dance floor was at one end, and next to it, slightly elevated, as if it were suspended in the air, was the gleaming, opal-like bar. And the rest of the space was filled with comfortable floating sofas on which people could sit or lie as they drank and chatted. A dark luminosity, a restrained brilliance, prevailed, and the décor mimicked outer space, with stars and planets spinning slowly in the distance. It was really well done: you felt as if you were floating in the blackness of the cosmos, and that effect was heightened by the gravity that was lower inside the disco than outside. Bruna started to go down one of the two staircases toward the disco and felt the drunkenness of a relative lack of gravity—that wonderful, deceptive lightness. Despite the club's name, there was no doubt its gravity was not as low as the moon's, a sixth of the Earth's. But it might be at two-thirds. Bruna had to make a real effort to stop herself from taking off and tumbling down the stairs.

She headed for the bar with springy, elastic strides and had to grab the counter to come to a halt. The low gravity was entertaining. It was very entertaining. It created a sense of bubbly light-headedness and irresponsibility. As if nothing bad could happen to you while your body weighed so little.

Bruna spilled her entire first glass of white wine all over her face because she lifted it up too quickly, and her fit of laughter lasted some minutes. The barman laughed along with her in a friendly way, although you could see that he was used to such disasters. Still with tears in her eyes, the rep asked him about Cata Caín. She seemed to be a nice person, the man answered. Timid, reserved, hard-working. She didn't have any friends. She didn't confide in anyone. She didn't go out with anyone. There was nothing special to say about her. Or maybe there was, the barman suddenly added, throwing a discreet glance at the other end of the bar; she had a drink a couple of times with that woman over there.

Bruna took a look. She was a gangly woman, maybe as tall as Bruna, but very thin, wrapped in a purple habit of sorts, with lank hair parted in the middle falling on either side of her bony face. She was leaning on a corner of the bar, staring vacantly into her drink, a tall glass with a phosphorescent pink liquid. There was something sad and slightly repulsive about the woman. The detective grabbed her drink and went over to her.

"Hi."

The woman gave her a hostile look and didn't answer.

"My name's Bruna."

The woman remained silent and managed to do it in such a way that the silence became menacing. Her hair was lank because it was very dirty: two curtains of heavy, greasy hair consuming her face. In the hollow of her neck, there was a small, dark green tattoo: the letter *S* in heavy ink curved over itself, oppressive and contorted. It was a Labaric script, for sure. And the purple color of the shapeless habit.

"That's a letter of power...and you're a Labarian. I'd never have expected Ones to hang out in Earthling discos. I thought you were forbidden such excesses."

The woman looked at her angrily and then downed her drink in one gulp. The drink seemed to calm her down a little.

"I'm not a Labarian. Not anymore. Hey, you, same again."

"Let me get it. And I'll have the same, too. What is it?"

"Iridescent redcurrant vodka with oxytocin. The strongest dose allowed by law," said the barman.

"You don't say. I could do with that."

Oxytocin in small doses encouraged empathy and affection. That was why it was called the love drug. It must have been having an effect on the greasy-haired collection of skin and bones as well, because she now seemed more approachable. The barman brought over two tall, luminous glasses, and the rep hastened to have a drink, hoping that the woman would do likewise, and the drug would soften her up a bit more. It worked. When the gangly woman put her half-empty glass down on the bar, she turned toward Bruna and pulled back one of the curtains of hair covering her face. She leaned forward slightly, showing the rep the right-hand side of her face: there was a third eye on her temple or rather, the beginnings of an eye—an eyeball only partially covered by a rudimentary and rigid eyelid, a grayish-white film covering the iris and the pupil. She let her hair fall back again and sat back.

"You're a *mutant*," said Bruna.

"That's why they expelled me from Labari. I was doing TP transfers for them. I was working in the mine the Kingdom has on Potosí, and when I was deformed by atomic disorder, the Ones threw me off the Floating World."

"How many transfers did you do?"

"Eight."

"How barbaric! That's illegal! The Agreements of Cassiopeia forbid more than six teleportations!"

"But the Kingdom of Labari didn't sign the agreements. People TP indefinitely there. They assume that the One Sacred Principle defends you from everything bad. If you're a pure enough person, the principle will protect you. The Ones who are good never suffer from atomic disorder."

"That's idiotic. It's not a matter of faith but of statistics and science."

"Well, that's what I thought…and I think that sometimes, I still believe it," observed the woman darkly. "On Labari they use TP disorder for their sacred trials. If two people from the upper castes—priests or masters—have a serious lawsuit to resolve, they put themselves under the protection of the One Principle and begin to TP themselves, and the one who suffers TP disorder is the guilty one. The sacred trials are open to the public, and I've attended a few and I can assure you that they work."

"What do you mean by *they work?*"

"That one of the contestants is unscathed and the other is punished with a deformity."

"By all the damn species, what nonsense! The contestants in those trials undoubtedly transfer, and continue to transfer, until one of them mutates, right?"

"Right."

"Well, that has nothing to do with the Sacred Principle. The likelihood of suffering TP disorder multiplies with each transfer. It's sheer luck who gets it first, bad luck pure and simple. And I assume that sometimes both contestants return deformed. Starting with the eleventh transfer, the incidence of disorder is one hundred percent in all living organisms."

The woman looked impressed. And relieved.

"Really? One hundred percent?"

"Where have you been hiding, not knowing that? Even five-year-olds know that."

It was a stupid question, Bruna realized as soon as she'd formulated it, because she knew the answer: the Kingdom of Labari kept its subjects totally uninformed.

"I've only been on Earth two months," said the woman with an air of embarrassment.

And the rep felt a sudden, warm, intense current of sympathy toward her. A result of the oxytocin, she reminded herself with an effort: *Don't make a mistake; don't lose your distance. She's not your friend.*

"Hey, by the way, what's your name?"

"Sun."

"Sun, I think you knew this woman, Cata Caín."

The mutant looked at the picture on Bruna's mobile.

"Yes, she was a rep. Like you."

"You were friends, weren't you?"

Sun looked down and concentrated on the pale glow of her drink.

"Well, we shared a few drinks. I found her interesting. I've never seen reps before I arrived down here. There aren't any on Labari."

"I know."

"And then I felt more comfortable with her. And you. We're all monsters, aren't we?"

A bitter aftertaste tarnished the drug's sweet gentleness. *She's not my friend*, Bruna repeated to herself.

"Do you know if Cata was scared of something? Did she talk to you about anything strange? Do you know if she was seeing anyone else, maybe someone new?"

The mutant shook her head, her stiff, glued-together hair swaying lightly on both sides of her face like two heavy sheets of metal. But then she looked up at the ceiling, like someone remembering something.

"Hang on though, yes. It was the last day I saw her, I think…I didn't talk to her. But she was at a table with two people."

"Humans?"

"I don't know. They were some distance away and it's quite dark here, but I'm almost certain at least one of them was an android."

The disturbing presence of reps again. Bruna finished her drink, thanked the woman, and paid for another drink for her before leaving. But as she was heading off, she turned back toward her.

"By the way, that tattooed letter you've got…"

"It's the *S* for *serf.* I belong to the serf caste."

"And what does that mean, exactly?"

"Higher than a slave, lower than an artisan."

"It's a script of power."

The woman lowered her head.

"That's why I'm still a serf. I can't liberate myself."

Bruna grunted, activated her mobile, and sent Sun the name and address of Natvel, the essentialist in the Health Arcade.

"Go and see this…this person I'm sending you to. Say that Bruna Husky sent you. Natvel will help you."

Sun looked at her skeptically.

"Thanks," she said.

But it was clear that she would do nothing. *That's her problem; she's not my friend*, the detective reminded herself again.

"Just one more thing: Do you know of anyone who could give me information about Labaric power writing?"

"It's a highly secret wisdom. Only the priests have a mastery of it. I don't know, maybe at the embassy? All Labaric embassies are dual run. They're managed by a master and a priest."

The rep thanked her again and left the bar, relieved to get away from the gloomy, tormented woman.

She walked—or rather, skipped lightly—to the edge of the dance floor, which was polished like a mirror and lit up by a shimmering half-light that gave it a certain underwater look. As you stepped onto the dance floor, you became immersed in the music. The disco used the latest Soundtarget system, technology that allowed you to direct the sound to perfection; just a foot or two from the dance zone you could barely hear anything. Now, with one foot on the dance floor, the android allowed herself to be enveloped by a sonorous vortex of sound. She closed her eyes and stood still, swaying internally to the rhythm, but someone tapping her on the shoulder brought her out of her brief rapture. She turned her head; it was Nopal. Bruna swallowed hard and stepped backward, returning to the silence.

"Hi, Husky, what a surprise to find you here," said the memorist, smiling.

And without further ado, Pablo Nopal grabbed the android and leapt onto the floor to dance with her. The music suddenly filled the rep's ears like pressurized water, an intoxicating swirl of dazzling notes. Bruna hated to dance and was incapable of allowing herself to be led, but now she was unable to resist. Nopal and the melody were sweeping her along, dissolving her in a swirl of rhythms. Their first steps were quite clumsy, hindered by the rep's stiffness and the chaos caused by the low gravity, but gradually they began to adapt and relax. Slowly, they assumed enough control over their bodies to be able to let themselves go. Now they were flying across the dance floor, soothed by the lack of gravity, feather-light, beautiful, impossibly precise in their movements. She and Nopal—the same height, the same weight, similarly slender—the rep and the memorist spinning round and around to a stunning waltz: *Waltz from "Masquerade"* by Aram Khachaturian, the rep read in luminous letters above their heads. And they danced clinging to each other without stepping on each other's feet, without missing a beat, as if they were part of a single organism, free of Earth's humiliating weight, everlasting, miraculous.

The rep moaned as the waltz exploded in her veins, her eyes blinded by light, her skin burning. She moaned with life and with desire, supported by the man's warm hands, weakened by the oxytocin, and she gazed at the memorist. But she was taken aback by Nopal's face, with its firm, transparent expression, and the android knew without a shadow of doubt that she and the writer would never have a deeper relationship. Then, embarrassed, she buried her face in the hollow of her partner's neck and, carried away by the disappointment, the fever, and the fire, she sank her teeth into Nopal's shoulder until she tasted his blood on her tongue, while the music rained down on them like a deluge. The memorist started and stifled a cry of pain. He stopped for a moment and contemplated the rep with understanding, without any surprise.

"Ah, Bruna, Bruna," he murmured.

And then he hugged her even more strongly, and they went on dancing.

CHAPTER NINETEEN

B runa went over the information on Annie Heart's false ID
tag again and verified that she was sufficiently well versed
in it. She was ready. It was time to get going. Bruna stood up,
grabbed Bartolo by the neck and removed from his mouth a
wad of paper napkins he was eating, and then called Yiannis.

"Hi, I'd like to see you. How are you doing for time?"

The old man's face looked strained and nervous.

"I'm glad you called, Bruna, I've got lots of things to tell
you."

"What things?"

"Not like this. In person."

"Oli's bar in two hours' time?"

"Perfect. See you then."

The rep cut the link, ordered the computer to play music
(playlist 037, hyperacoustic themes that were relaxing but at
the same time had a slightly euphoric effect), and then pulled
out the small oven that was built into the kitchen. She put her
hand inside the cavity and opened the little trapdoor right at
the back in which she hid her box of secrets—all those things
she didn't want anyone to see, like the little plasma gun for
which she didn't have a permit. And her supply of silicon
skin. It had been a while since Bruna had disguised herself,

but it was something she had always been good at. The first thing she did was strip naked, then she warmed up a little bit of dermosilicon until it liquefied and rapidly spread the delicate pink film over the line of ink that ran around her body. The bit at the back was probably not so well applied, but that would, after all, be hidden by her clothes. She stood under an ultraviolet light with her arms and legs outstretched like Da Vinci's *Vitrubian Man*, and two minutes later the thin film had already dried and fused perfectly with her skin, completely covering her tattoo. Now, she could only remove the silicon with dermosolvent. Next, she put in contact lenses. She had chosen dark green ones that looked very natural and camouflaged her distinctive feline pupils. Then came the wig, ash blonde and autoadhesive with body heat, and fake eyebrows of the same color, a little thicker than her own. She padded her cheeks with the help of two prostheses made of anatomical rubber, and then put on padded underwear that increased the size of her buttocks and added two sizes to her small Amazonian breasts. Then came the makeup: a trifle exaggerated, slightly retro, with bright red lips and eyes highlighted using gold eye shadow. She chose a dress with a culotte skirt, a boringly conventional outfit that she wore only on these occasions, and she carefully styled the wig's silky hair, which fell to her shoulders. She looked at herself in the mirror. The best thing about having such an eye-catching appearance was the speed with which she could alter it. It had only taken her twenty-five minutes to transform herself, and even her own mother wouldn't have recognized her. If her mother had existed, of course. She was so blonde, so seemingly feminine; would Nopal like her more if she were like this? The memory of the writer slipped across her mind, leaving behind a fiery trace.

She found that thinking about him was too troubling. She was sickened by memorists and she found Nopal intimidating and ambiguous. But the previous night in the disco, in the warmth of his embrace, with the exhilaration of the music and the oxytocin, Bruna would have given herself to him. The rep savored again the taste of Nopal's blood on her lips. Uneasy and confused, she shook her head. She would, in fact, prefer never to see him again.

She picked some discreet, comfortable shoes—because you never knew when you might have to run for it—and removed her own ID tag from the chain around her neck, replacing it with the one Mirari had given her. Then she put what she needed into a handbag and headed for the door. Just then, a call came in. She checked the caller identification; it was Lizard.

"Damn!"

She switched her screen to invisible mode and answered. The policeman's fleshy face appeared on her screen.

"Husky, are you there?"

"I'm here."

"Why have you turned off your image?"

"Are you calling to give me the results of Nabokov's autopsy?"

"Why have you turned off your image? According to the GPS signal from your mobile, you're at home. Is someone holding a plasma gun at your head?"

"Could you do me the damn favor of not tracking me?"

"It's a serious question, Husky."

He said it with a small sardonic smile and yet it seemed to Bruna that, deep down, there was a degree of genuine concern. As if the inspector had faked that smile in order to hide the fact that when he said he was talking seriously, he *really was* talking seriously. The rep shook her head; everything seemed so ridiculously stupid with Lizard.

"Believe me. Nothing's going on."

"So why can't I see you then?"

He was as stubborn as a mule. Nopal had already said so.

"Because I don't want you to see what I look like."

"Why not?"

"Hmmm…Let's just say it's because I'm not looking attractive enough for you."

The detective had spoken sarcastically, but it suddenly crossed her mind that maybe she was being sarcastic to cover up that when she spoke about being attractive to him she really did, in fact, want this to be the case. *Oh, by all the damn species,* muttered Bruna to herself.

"Listen, Lizard, I haven't got time for this nonsense. If you've got nothing to tell me, I'm off."

The policeman rubbed his heavy jaw.

"Actually, yes, I do have things to tell you. But hang on…"

He leaned forward and the picture disappeared.

"Lizard?"

"I'm still here. It's just that I like to be on an equal footing."

He had switched to invisible mode, too. *Damned, arrogant, pigheaded man*, thought Bruna.

"Fine by me. Though you could just send a robot messenger," she grumbled disdainfully.

But it was true that she found it somewhat irritating not to be able to see his face.

"Nabokov's body was too destroyed by the explosion. They can't even establish if she was carrying an artificial memory. She was in the terminal stages of TTT and had massive cerebral metastasis, so her behavior could well have been due to her illness."

"We already knew that. Is that all you've got to tell me?"

"Almost."

Then there was silence, during which the detective couldn't stop herself from staring at the empty screen, as if the nebulous blur of pixels was going to reveal an important secret.

"We found something in Nabokov and Chi's apartment."

Bruna's imagination again pictured Lizard's massive body hunting among the filmy, lilac banners in the bedroom. It was not a pleasant image.

"It was a data chip hidden in a ring underneath the stone. An ingenious hiding place. We might never have found it if the stone had been pressed shut properly. When the ring was moved the chip fell on the floor."

"And?"

"It's some sort of supremacist pamphlet. There's no reference to Hericio's party, but it claims to speak on behalf of some vague panhumanism. It maintains they have a plan to exterminate the reps, and what's most important is that there are pictures of all the victims, including Chi, showing the tattoo with the word *revenge*. Which suggests that the chip was made by the killers."

Bruna frowned, trying to slot in this new piece of information.

"And why do you think Nabokov had that, Lizard?"

"I don't know. But I think someone might have sent it to her to mess with her head."

It was a good hypothesis. If Nabokov, as ill as she was, saw that rubbish, her violent reaction was much more understandable.

"That was why she spoke to me of revenge when we bumped into each other."

"By the way, there was also no way the medical examiner could tell if Nabokov had any tattooed word. There's nothing on what's left of her."

"They're done in the Labaric script of power. The tattoos, I mean."

Bruna was somewhat surprised at herself. Amazed at the ease with which she'd given that piece of information to the inspector. Clearly, the fact that he had saved her from a beating fostered a certain trust. She barely hesitated before she told Lizard everything she knew. She told him about Natvel, and Caín's other job at Hungry, and what the mutant with the third eye had told her. In the end, she told him everything except that she had disguised herself as a human, and that she was getting ready to infiltrate the HSP. It didn't seem wise to reveal that she was breaking a whole slew of laws.

"Since you have an official role in the investigation, you could demand that the priest at the Embassy of Labari provides you with information about the tattoo on the victims."

"Not a bad idea, Husky."

"By the way, did you run the two dead reps through your anatomical-recognition program to see if there was a match with the eye in the knife?"

"Yes, I did. And no, no matches. It wasn't them. I ran you through the program too, to see if it was you."

Bruna stared at the blank screen with indignation. A few seconds later, she heard the man's thick, calm voice again.

"There was no match with you either."

Thanks for the show of confidence, thought the rep.

"Well, that's good news," she said icily. "Bye, Lizard. I've got work to do."

There was no response. The screen was humming faintly. Had he disconnected without even saying good-bye? But the green connection light was still on.

"Lizard?"

Then his voice was audible again. Slow, fuzzy, heavy.

"Be careful, Husky."

And the line went dead. The rep frowned; it was as if the policeman knew something. As if he sensed something. She breathed out, ridding herself of the awkward thoughts. The lengthy conversation had held her up; she was going to be late for her rendezvous with Yiannis. She took off her wrist mobile and removed the battery. Then she took out the untraceable mobile, and when she switched it on, saw the screen welcoming Annie Heart; Mirari thought of everything. She switched the computer off, put it in her bag and raced out of the apartment. As she was going down in the elevator, she thought to herself with a certain degree of delight that at least this time the *bicho* wouldn't know it was her. But when she passed by Maio, the alien looked at her with his sad eyes and said, "Be very careful, Bruna."

The sentence had a watery softness to it, but it resonated shrilly in the rep's ears. By all the damn species, was her disguise useless? And why had that weirdo told her to be careful? Did he suspect something too, like Lizard?

Furious, she stopped a cab and gave the address of Oli's bar. Here and there, on the street corners, you could see pairs of soldiers on the alert. Not a single combat rep, just humans. Which was pretty unusual.

"Since they brought out the army, things seem to be a bit quieter. Just as well," said the driver.

The detective made a scarcely encouraging grunt of agreement. She loathed idle conversations with cabdrivers. The man turned toward her.

"Although at least the disturbances have made those damn reps disappear. There isn't a single one on the streets! It's great, isn't it?" he said, giving her a complicit wink.

Bruna thought, *I'd love to smash his face.* Thought: *This means my disguise is working.* Thought: *Control that anger, conceal it.* But she must have shown something, because the driver backed down a little.

"Well, it's not that I wish them ill, you understand. I don't want them lynched or anything like that, but why don't they go, and leave us in peace? Let them build themselves a Floating World. Speaking of which, you have the people of Cosmos and Labari, who don't allow technos on their worlds. They sure are smart. And why do *we* let them in? Because we're wimps. Because we have a government of replickers and wimps."

The cabdriver had set the autopilot and he was still leaning over the back of his seat, spewing his xenophobic, racist views. Bruna thought, *I want to strangle him.* Thought: *Concentrate on remembering that your disguise works.* Thought: *Four years, three months, and sixteen days, sixteen days, sixteen days...*

She walked into the bar, frustrated and nervous. Fat Oli scrutinized her with half-closed eyes, as she always did any new customer. The detective saw that the mulatto was taking mental note of the striking bruises on her forearm, which the rep had chosen not to cover up. Big Oli missed nothing.

"Hi. What can I serve you?"

"Vodka and lemon with two ice cubes."

She said the first drink that came into her head, something well-defined and yet totally removed from her usual tastes to reinforce her disguise. Clearly Oli hadn't recognized her. She felt optimistic. She grabbed the glass and walked to the end of the counter, where the archivist was already waiting for her.

"Hi. I think I know you from somewhere," said Bruna, smiling.

Yiannis looked her up and down, barely showing any sign of interest.

"Well, I don't know. I don't think so. You don't look familiar."

"And I'm telling you that I do. You're Yiannis Liberopoulos."

The old man straightened up, surprised.

"Yes, I am, but…"

"Yiannis, Yiannis, do you really not know who I am?"

Up to that point, Bruna had been forcing herself to speak with a deeper voice, but she said the last sentence with her normal voice. The man's mouth and eyes opened wide in a perfect caricature of surprise.

"Bruna! It can't be. Are you Bruna?"

The rep smiled.

"Shhh, don't speak so loudly. I see my disguise is working. Yiannis, I want you to know where I'm going in case anything happens. I'm hoping to infiltrate the HSP. I'm going to go to Saturn, the bar RoyRoy told me about, and I'm going to try to get an appointment with Hericio."

Oli approached with a cloth in her hand and, while she pretended to clean the counter, asked, "Is everything okay down here, Yiannis?"

"Everything's fine."

The mulatto walked away and Bruna looked affectionately at her monumental back. The big mother hen always looking out for her chicks.

"That seems very dangerous to me, Bruna. Really dangerous. Are you sure of what you're doing?" whispered the old man anxiously.

"Absolutely sure. And don't say another word, Yiannis, or I'll never tell you anything again."

The archivist frowned but didn't say anything, because he knew her too well. The rep sighed. In fact, she herself wasn't all that clear about what she was going to do. Infiltrating the supremacists seemed reckless, and it could be a disproportionate and pointless risk. Of course, it could be that it was risk she was looking for; maybe by putting herself in danger she was placating her guilt for living and her despair at being condemned to die. To kill herself ahead of time—young, like Achilles—and thereby save herself the horror of TTT. The rep shook her head to allow that troubling thought to escape, to make it as light as a balloon and rid herself of it, and her biosynthetic blonde hair brushed her shoulders. It was an unexpected and unpleasant sensation, one that caused her to shiver.

"I wanted to tell you something, too, Bruna. I've been keeping an eye on it for some time, but it's getting worse. And this morning, it was something truly scandalous. I've asked for an official investigation."

"What are you talking about, Yiannis?"

"The archive. Someone's manipulating the documents, falsifying the facts in order to stir up the revolt against the technohumans."

The central archivists worked under a strict confidentiality clause that forbade them from talking about their work, and old Yiannis, who was a meticulous and somewhat obsessive man, had always kept strictly to this rule. But now he was so worried by the drift of events that, for once, he felt released from his obligations—or, rather, indebted to an even greater obligation. So he spelled out the blatant alterations that he was finding in the articles.

"And that's why I've asked for an urgent investigation."

"And how did they reply?"

"They haven't replied yet."

"You don't say."

That was alarming indeed. Mercenaries, spontaneous demonstrations that appeared to be carefully organized, the collusion of the news media...and now the archive as well. So many fronts at once. It was like a dance, a sinister, well-rehearsed dance. On her way to Oli's bar, Bruna had noticed the public screens: nine out of every ten messages were diatribes against reps, with varying levels of anger and intransigence. Some of the comments were so violent that even a month ago, they would have been censured by the Department of Harmonious Coexistence. She recalled a couple of poisonous statements, and the bile rose in her throat. She had to make a real effort to reflect calmly, and she looked at Yiannis and Oli to prevent herself from being swamped with hatred for humans. The rep was well aware, moreover, that the public screens, despite their name, were not at all public; citizens had to pay a monthly fee if they wanted to upload their pictures and messages. It was a private company, easily controlled and manipulated. A company that anyone could hire and use to launch a poisonous campaign. Bruna couldn't believe—didn't want to believe—that nine out of every ten humans wanted to destroy her.

"And another thing: they killed one of RoyRoy's sons," added Yiannis.

"The supremacists?" asked the detective, appalled.

"What have the supremacists got to do with this?" replied the archivist, mystified.

Yiannis and Bruna looked at each other in confused silence for a few seconds. *How can you have faith in communication between the species if friends can't even understand each other?* thought the android with misgiving.

"No, no, Bruna, forgive me, it has nothing to do with what we were talking about before. What I meant was that RoyRoy has also lost a son."

Also? She realized he was revealing a personal matter.

"A sixteen-year-old boy. He was shot by mistake during a police operation. He was walking past, quite by chance, and the shot shattered his skull. Poor RoyRoy. That's her heartache, you know. That sorrow you can always sense within her. It was a long time ago, but it's never over."

He likes her, the rep thought with surprise. She had a sudden intuition—not entirely pleasant—that old Yiannis liked the billboard-lady. Of course. Another grieving mother, another wasted son. In the months after Merlín's death, when Bruna was lost and devastated, Yiannis had taken her into his home; he'd taken care of her and managed to get her back on her feet again. The android was enormously grateful to him for all he had done, but she'd always had an unsettling suspicion that his friendship was based on the pain of bereavement, that Yiannis had turned his life into a temple to the memory of his son, and what attracted him to Bruna was her grief at the loss of Merlín. As if they could share the emptiness. But the android didn't want to dedicate her short life to memories. Let Yiannis befriend RoyRoy; let them exchange sorrows; let them build an enormous cathedral to honor the children they had lost. It was all the same to her.

"You see, Bruna, everyone drags along their own little bundle. Sometimes, it seems to me that we humans—and you technos, of course—we're like ants, all walking along with the overwhelming weight of our lives on our heads."

The rep hated the tone of self-pity in his voice.

"But you once told me that what distinguished us is what each person does about it," muttered the rep.

She couldn't bear seeing the archivist so mournful, so adolescent. *Falling in love makes you stupid*, she thought with a certain bitterness.

Yiannis sighed.

"Yes, I suppose it all depends on what you do."

A short time later, when Bruna left the bar, she was still feeling annoyed. She'd always believed that her friend was as sealed-off from emotional fickleness as she was. Yet again, she felt odd. Different from everyone else. She was rare, even among the reps. A genuine monster, as the supremacists maintained. *But hold on a minute, hold on! It's me who's falling into self-pity now.* By the great Morlay! It was a wretched vice, weak and contagious.

CHAPTER TWENTY

Tall, hips swaying, her dress clinging to her exaggerated curves as convention dictated, her blonde hair wafting just above her shoulders, the detective didn't go unnoticed when she walked into Saturn, which turned out to be a retro-style bar with marble pedestal tables and pseudomodernist wall lights. A sufficiently old-fashioned atmosphere for reactionary types. It was eight o'clock in the evening and the place was half-full: all humans, more men than women, the majority of them young. Bruna strolled slowly around the place as if she were trying to decide where she should sit, while covertly studying the clientele and allowing herself to be checked out. When she was sure that everyone present had taken note of her arrival, she sat at a table near the door and again ordered vodka and lemon with two cubes of ice. She liked to develop the fictitious personalities of her creations and be true to the tiniest details, to the point where she almost believed them. Right now, for example, she was beginning to feel that there was no better drink than a vodka and lemon. She took a sip from the glass the robot brought her and glanced around through the veil of her eyelashes. A couple of women and half a dozen men were gazing at her invitingly, trying to catch her eye and initiate some sort of interaction. After a brief analysis, she decided that none of them seemed very useful, although two of the young men formed part of a more promising group seated around a couple of the tables. Just then one of the two young men got up and came toward her, swaggering and swaying like a cocky little idiot. He stopped at her table.

"You're new around here," he declared.

"Yes."

The youth grabbed a chair and sat down, full of self-importance.

"I'll tell you what we're going to do. We're going to have another drink—I'm buying—and while we're drinking it, you'll tell me all about yourself," he pronounced.

"No! I'll tell you what you're going to do," Bruna replied. "You're going to go back to your table, and you're going to tell that man in the green vest that I'd like to have a word with him."

The man in the vest was a few years older and seemed to be the one in charge of the group. It was that air of strict hierarchy that had led Bruna to suspect that they might be militant supremacists.

"And why the hell do you think I'm going to obey you?" said the youth, infuriated.

"Because if you don't, it's possible the man in the green vest will get mad at you."

The young man gave an angry snort, but he got up like a lamb and went straight to his table to deliver the message. *There's a boy who knows how to do as he's told*, thought the rep.

The guy in green listened to the message and took his time. *Better*, thought Bruna to herself. *The longer he takes, the higher up he must be in the chain of command.* She saw him order something from the robot, and she ordered another vodka, too. Five minutes later, after he'd had a few sips of his fresh beer, green vest got up and came toward her.

"What can I do for you?"

He was very short and plain-looking, with muscles all over, probably silicon implants. Bruna smiled. She was blonde, she was shapely, she was retrograde. How did ultrafeminine, ultraconventional blondes smile? Not with eyes blazing like Bruna's, of course, but as if making an offering, with moist tenderness, demonstrating that her mouth was yet another cavity. With promising submissiveness. Bruna-Annie smiled coquettishly and said, "You see, they told me that people from the HSP meet in this bar, and clearly you're the most important person in the bar right now. That's why I think you can help me. I want a meeting with Hericio."

The man screwed up his face in a comical manner, caught between two opposing emotions: personal flattery and suspicion at the request. Uncertain, he dropped into the same chair the youth had occupied earlier.

"Let's assume for a moment that I am from the HSP. Why do you want to meet Hericio?"

"Because he's the only one who seems to know what to do in these times of danger and insanity. Because we're condemned to disaster at the hands of a government of useless replickers. Because like all good people, I can see the abyss into which we're headed if we don't remedy the situation. Because I want to collaborate in the defense of the human race, which is what's at stake, nothing more, nothing less," she railed emphatically.

And then, in a moment of absolute inspiration, she added, "Because I don't want to leave any future child of mine with the legacy of a corrupt, perverted, heinous world."

And she smiled her most maternal and helpless smile.

Bruna-Annie's fiery speech seemed to have some sort of an impact on the man, who scratched his chin hesitantly— or, rather, the implants in his chin, which made his jaw look more manly and powerful. Under the soft skin of his arms, his silicon biceps moved up and down like tennis balls. But all the same, he still wasn't entirely convinced.

"Sure. And you suddenly turn up here from nowhere, saying all these lovely words, and you want us to believe you. Where have you come from? Who the hell are you? I've never seen you around here, nor at any of our events."

"I was born in the Britannic region, but I live in New Barcelona. Here, I'm transmitting my ID number to you. Three days ago I took part in a supremacist demonstration and the police arrested me for assaulting a rep. They finally let me go for lack of evidence. But I'm a university professor and I can't afford this sort of thing or they'll fire me from the university. You know how strict they are about these things. That's why I've come to Madrid to offer my assistance. Better to be active here and live in New Barcelona. So the right hand doesn't know what the left hand is doing."

The man agreed.

"But you don't need to see Hericio to collaborate with the cause. I'm Serra, one of his deputies. Won't I do?"

Bruna tried to look like a pussycat, softening her usual tiger look as much as possible. Her cheek padding helped because it rounded her mouth and made her look insipid.

"I'm delighted I wasn't wrong; I knew you were some-one important. I could tell. However, I still have to speak to Hericio. Because I'm thinking of making a donation to the party. I know you're in a period covered by an FP. Well, I want to give some money to the cause. But I want to be certain that

Hericio is all he makes himself out to be. That we're inspired by the same ideas."

Serra nodded his head. The talk of money seemed to resolve all his doubts.

"Okay. I'll see what I can do. Where can I find you?"

"I'll be at the Majestic Hotel. But only for three days."

"I'll get back to you," he said.

And he walked away, his tennis balls wobbling like jelly with each step.

Bruna noticed they were following her as soon as she hit the street. She had assumed that they'd tail her and she tried to make it easy, because the tail, one of the boys who had been with the man in the vest, was not at all good. He was so clumsy that she was almost tempted to ring Lizard so he could give him a few pointers on how to tail someone without being seen.

She entered the Majestic and asked for a room as Annie Heart. The hotel was from the middle of the twenty-first century but had recently been replastered and converted into a lower-range establishment. Bruna had stayed there when she first arrived in Madrid and, as was always the case with her, had taken note of what the hotel had to offer. She went up to her room, which was on the top floor, and checked that everything was still as she remembered it. If you were a guest of the hotel and had a key, you could get down to the street via the external fire escape at the back of the building. It ended up at a lung park that hardly anybody ever used. She left her bag in the room and went downstairs to the hotel bar, which was half-full. It was eleven o'clock at night and she was hungry. She asked for a gigantic real-chicken sandwich and a vodka and lemon with two ice cubes, even though the two drinks she'd had earlier on an empty stomach had left her with an unpleasant throb in her head. But consistency was consistency. She saw her tail at the back of the place doing a disastrous job of hiding behind an interactive screen and decided to put on a good show for his sake. Just then, two Apocalyptics came into the bar, handing out brochures and promoting their cause.

"Brothers and sisters, listen to the word. Here you are losing your most precious asset—your lives—in alcohol and recklessness. The world is ending in one week. Don't close your minds to the truth!"

There were vague rumblings of annoyance, and the barman rushed from behind the bar to throw them out, which he did quite easily. They were fairly docile visionaries.

Bruna swallowed her mouthful of sandwich and spoke loudly enough to be heard throughout the bar, taking advantage of the momentary attention the business of the Apocalyptics had attracted.

"They might seem like a couple of crazies to you, and they certainly are, but it is true that the world is ending. That's to say, the world as we know it. Do you want those technological freaks to finish off the human race? The reps are our creatures! Our artifacts! We made them! So are we now going to let them exterminate us? They're our mistake! Let's put an end to this dangerous error!"

Some applause was heard from the other end of the counter. It was an endorsement that left Bruna with a bitter taste in her mouth. She had completely lost her appetite, so she paid and, pretending to be a little more inebriated than she was, went up to her room, supposedly to go to bed.

But she still had much to do. She pulled off the wig and the false eyebrows; she removed all the padding and undressed;

she opened her bag, took out the solvent and removed the dermosilicon covering her tattoo. Next, she took out the contact lenses and got rid of her makeup, and had a quick vapor shower. She sighed with relief on rediscovering Bruna in the steamed-up mirror. After she had dressed in her usual clothes—a dark purple latex jumpsuit—she put away the items of her disguise and went out into the corridor with considerable stealth. She crossed the deserted corridor and, using the key to her room, opened the service door that provided access to the fire escape. It was twelve thirty at night now, 00:30, she was on the fourteenth floor, and on the external metallic platform an unpleasantly cold wind was blowing that raised goose bumps on her skin, still damp from the shower. She again swiped the chip in her key across the electronic reader that controlled the emergency staircase and the steps quickly unfolded ahead of her descent, making a worrying metallic screech that could have betrayed her presence. Just as well that the tinkling of the nearby lung park served to cover it up. Bruna hadn't thought of any of that, neither the noise of the staircase nor the unexpected help from the artificial trees. She was irritated by her lack of foresight; she was too tired to think properly. Thank goodness she'd had luck on her side.

She reached the bottom, jumped onto the sidewalk, and the staircase folded itself back up above her. The keys only worked to go down, never to go up. That was why the android was forced to do what she was about to do now. She walked around the corner, entered the Majestic, walked up to the reception desk and asked for a room. The manager, a pale man with prominent cheekbones, looked at her in a strange way. In a flash of inspiration Bruna realized, *He's going to tell me there's no vacancy.* The android felt feared, felt hated—more hated and more feared than ever before. She felt segregated and a sudden, distressing premonition made her imagine a world like that, an Earth where reps couldn't go into hotels or travel on the same sky-trams as humans, or even mix with them. A drop of cold sweat slid down her skull, following a line parallel to her tattoo. And at that same moment, just when the immobility of the receptionist was starting to become unnatural, the man broke his absolute stillness, cleared his throat uncomfortably and asked Bruna for her details so that he could check her in. *He doesn't dare*, said the android to herself; the idea of refusing her had probably passed through his mind, but he hadn't dared. Discrimination between the species was still illegal.

He gave her a room on the twelfth floor, two down from Annie Heart, and the rep went up to her new room, for which she'd registered with her real name, dragging her feet and feeling vaguely disconsolate. She went into the room and, suddenly feeling all the exhaustion of her overlong day, allowed herself to fall flat on her back onto the bed. She could sense the tiredness building up in her muscles, in the lower parts of her legs and arms, as if the fatigue were water weighing down on her body and pressing her into the bedspread. She was tempted to close her eyes briefly and sleep right there, but she knew it would be better to go back home. With a force of will, she spun around on the bed and scrunched up the sheets and the blanket so that the robot cleaners would have something to do the next morning. Then she got up, grabbed her gear and left the building, again using the emergency staircase.

She walked a few blocks so that they couldn't connect her to the hotel and to check that she wasn't being followed, and then she caught a cab; she was too tired to economize. She got out in front of her door and, as usual now, came face to face with the alien in the middle of the night, so alone, so different. The rep felt the anguish rising up inside her again and blocking her throat. Poor Maio. Poor Nabokov. Poor victims of Nabokov. Poor everyone. She crossed in front of the *bicho*, not wanting to look at him, and rushed to put the imprint of her finger on the lock to open the door. Her fingers must have been stained with the cosmetic silicon, because she had to repeat the action several times. An unease was growing inside her and already turning into an ache in her chest. *Four years, three months, and sixteen days*, she thought, like someone whispering a refrain. A private mantra for moments of anguish. *Four years, three months, and sixteen days.*

"It's fifteen days, Bruna. It's almost two in the morning. It's Thursday already," babbled Maio's liquid voice.

The rep stood paralyzed. The sound of the lock opening resonated in the silence, but the detective didn't push open the door. She turned her head slowly toward the alien and they looked at each other for a few seconds without saying a word.

"Yes. I can read your thoughts, Bruna. I'm sorry. Perhaps I should have told you," whispered Maio.

And his words sounded like grains of sand tumbling gently inside a hollow tube.

I'll be damned, thought Bruna. *Well, I don't care. The* bicho *has won. Let him sleep at my place. We'll find him a place to live. But he'd better not think he's sharing my bed again.*

"Don't worry, Bruna, I can sleep on the couch. Thanks a lot," said the alien.

The android sighed, somewhat exasperated: *Heavens above*, she thought, *so—*"

"So I don't need to talk to you; you can guess everything without me saying a word?" she concluded out loud.

"Oh no, no, Bruna, it's much better to talk normally; it's more comfortable, because that way we're on an equal footing. And often, what you humans think isn't what you end up saying. And what you say is what you want the world to hear. I prefer to hear your words, and that way, I know who you want to be on the outside."

His reasoning seemed far too confusing for Bruna, given how late it was and how tired she was.

"Fine. Forget it. Let's just go in. Are you hungry?"

"No, thank you."

"Good. I have no idea what you aliens eat. And don't tell me now. I don't want to know. I just want to sleep."

She spoke sharply and grumpily, but it was true that, in some way, Bruna felt better for having told the Omaá to come in with her. Monsters united were somewhat less monstrous. *Four years, three months, and fifteen days. Fifteen days.*

CHAPTER TWENTY-ONE

Bruna had to admit that the Omaá was no trouble, despite the fact that the *bicho* was very big and the apartment was on the small side. Moreover, he and Bartolo got on really well: the bubi was beside himself with joy when he saw his compatriot, and from the moment the alien arrived, the pet didn't move from his side. The greedy-guts slept coiled up next to Maio's back, and was now perched on his shoulder. It was Maio who prepared breakfast for everyone, guessing exactly what the rep liked; reading her thoughts had its advantages. The alien ate some sort of powdered cereal for breakfast, which he moistened in a hot broth, making neat little balls from the resultant dough with his fingers. The rep watched him eat with fascination and then saw how he stored the rest of the food in his backpack.

"Omaá food. They sell it in the interplanetary section of some of the gourmet supermarkets, though it's pretty expensive. I can also eat your flours but they provide far less energy. I have to eat kilos of Earthling bread to get as much nourishment as these little balls give me. I also like cheese and fruit, and I've learned to eat eggs. They don't taste too bad, but if I think about what they are, they make me feel a bit ill. No corpses, please. Neither meat nor fish. Not even seafood protein paste.

They put shrimp and other creatures into it, as well as algae concentrate," he explained, as if he were answering a question.

And it was true that the rep was mentally asking herself just that.

"And the business of not eating dead bodies, is it a matter of principle or doesn't it agree with you? Physically, I mean."

"It really doesn't agree with us. It hardens the *kuammil*. It can even kill you over time. The *kuammil* is like your soul."

"We don't have souls."

"Neither do we. We have *kuammil*."

"I mean the soul doesn't exist."

"Well, it was to give you a simple comparison. The *kuammil* does exist. If you like, I can give you a summary of how our bodies work."

Bruna looked at the Omaá's translucent skin, pinkish and bluish, throbbing, as changeable as the sky at dusk, and she shivered. It had been a while since she had been conscious of the alien's difference—in fact, she was starting to get used to him—but she suddenly became uneasily aware again of how incredibly strange his body was. Just then, a call came through on the mobile Mirari had given her and Bruna welcomed the interruption, as she didn't have to answer Maio, and instantly thought, *How stupid, given that he's already sensed everything I've been thinking.*

She answered the call in invisible mode. The face of Serra, Hericio's deputy, appeared on the screen.

"Why can't I see you?" the man asked suspiciously by way of a greeting.

"I've rigged my mobile to prevent anyone from locating me; I don't want any evidence of this trip to Madrid. Remember what I said about the left hand not knowing what the right hand is doing. But I must have broken something in the process because I can't send images."

The guy nodded, reassured by the reply.

"Yes, we also couldn't understand why you were untraceable."

"It's illegal to track a mobile."

Serra smiled contemptuously.

"As Hericio says, there's nothing more legal than disobeying the laws of an illegitimate system. Okay, Annie Heart, I want to talk to you. In one hour's time, at Saturn."

And he cut off.

An hour! The rep grabbed her travel bag and raced off to the Majestic. She went upstairs as Bruna Husky, transformed herself quickly into Annie Heart, and headed back downstairs praying to the memory of the great Gabriel Morlay that she hadn't forgotten any detail of her disguise. When she got to the ground floor, she breathed deeply to reduce her agitation. She stepped calmly out of the elevator with a relaxed air, as if there were no need for haste, although it was almost the time the HSP deputy had set. And yes, she hadn't been wrong in her assumption. Her tail was back, the young man from yesterday, or maybe another one—all those supremacist pups looked the same. That was precisely what they valued: homogeneity, sameness. She allowed herself to be followed as she walked with studied calmness toward Saturn. Although it was quite close to the hotel, her lazy pace meant it was twenty minutes before she was within sight of the bar, but she didn't actually manage to enter. A car stopped beside her and raised its door with a pneumatic hiss. Serra was sitting inside.

"You're late," he grumbled.

Bruna settled into her seat and arranged her lips into a coquettish but contemptuous pout. —the sneer of a disdainful blonde, which she did well.

"I'm not accustomed to being treated with such rudeness. I'm not one of your little foot soldiers to be ordered urgently hither and yon."

Serra chuckled. Today, instead of a vest, he was wearing a sleeveless T-shirt made of a thin, shiny material that stuck to his artificially inflated muscles. *No doubt he wants to impress Annie*, thought Bruna. The car was on autopilot, without a driver. He didn't want any witnesses.

"Don't be offended, sweetheart, it's just work. And an element of basic caution."

"Why are we here?"

"Here?"

"In the car. Are we going somewhere?"

"We thought it would be best if we were seen together as little as possible. We're doing it for your sake. That's what you want, isn't it? All the trouble you've taken so your mobile isn't traceable."

Bruna cautiously agreed. She didn't like the slightly sarcastic tone she thought she detected in the man's words.

"Yes, indeed."

"Speaking of which, how did you do it? Can I have a look at your computer?"

Bruna could feel her shoulders tensing. Did they suspect something? Worse still, did they know something?

"Of course," she replied matter-of-factly.

And she immediately removed the thin, flexible, semitransparent device from her wrist and passed it to Serra.

The deputy took the machine, turned it over in his fingers a few times, and switched it off and turned it on again. The mobile restarted and the screen welcomed Annie Heart, and Bruna mentally thanked Mirari for her impeccable work. At that moment she realized with horror that she was carrying her own mobile in the pocket of her elegant trousers. In all the rush, she had forgotten to leave it in her hotel room when she was getting changed. And on top of that, she now couldn't remember whether or not she'd switched the mobile off. And if a call came in? A sudden wave of anxiety left her in a cold sweat. Luckily, Serra was too busy inspecting the computer, because the rep was convinced that her expression had changed. Vaguely, on the other side of her anxiety, she sensed that the man was saying something to her that she hadn't managed to pick up. She breathed deeply and felt the powerful cocktail of antistress hormones that strengthened her combat rep body kick in. An invisible line of lucid calmness descended through her body like a curtain of water extinguishing a fire. She put a smile on her face to distract him. Just in time. The deputy turned his face toward her and looked at her.

"Aren't you going to tell me?" he asked.

"What?"

"I was asking you how you did it. If you try to cancel the GPS and you don't have an authorization code issued by a judge, the machine self-destructs."

Bruna reflected coldly for a fraction of a second and decided what she was going to say.

"Well, you see, it's quite complicated. You can only do it in parallel sync with a central computer. You connect the mobile peripherally and then you type a virtual port link into your mobile's IDD; you manipulate the values until you access the residual profile of the HTC and the apex code. You can do this with a cryptorobot, but it's slow and difficult. Even though I used some special algorithms, I still needed to search through millions of numbers before I found the code…Are you with me?"

Serra nodded yes, even though his expression clearly showed that he'd become lost in the tangle of words. Bruna had no idea what she was saying, but she had assumed that the supremacist wouldn't be able to work that out.

"So, what you do is trick the mobile into thinking it's part of the mainframe."

"You seem to know a lot about all that."

"Well, I am a professor of applied robotics."

The man scowled and gave her back her mobile. The rep adjusted it on her wrist while she thought about the other mobile she was carrying in her pocket; she had to get out of the car as quickly as possible.

"I see we're going round the block. Are we waiting for someone? Why did you make me come?" she asked.

To sniff around in my hotel room in the meantime, she answered herself. Which wasn't a problem. Having anticipated that possibility, she had scattered the likely contents of a basic suitcase around the room. In reality, the fact that Serra had made the appointment in order to be able to search her belongings was a reassuring supposition; it meant her plan was working.

"It's just a security procedure. You have to understand our caution. The party finds itself in a very difficult position thanks to this puppet government," said Serra.

"That's precisely why I want to see Hericio. I'm beginning to think that you talk a lot but don't actually do anything. Like all the others," said the android.

The man stiffened.

"You don't know what you're saying. You know nothing."

"Oh no? What don't I know? What are you good for, apart from appearing on the news spouting big words?"

It was such crude bait that Bruna didn't expect the man to bite, but sometimes you get information in the most ridiculous way. Not this time. Serra frowned, annoyed, and touched the panel in front of him. The vehicle stopped next to the sidewalk and opened the door.

"We'll give you a call," the man grunted.

"It had better be soon. Tomorrow or the next day. I leave town on Sunday," Bruna answered imperiously; the cover Mirari had provided wouldn't last much longer.

Serra didn't answer. The car shut its door and sped off again. The detective watched it disappear and repressed the urge to take her mobile out of her pocket; it was possible that her tail was still nearby. Above her head, the public screen was showing dreadful images of combat androids slaughtering humans. They were old tapes from the Rep War. "Are you going to allow this to happen again?" the soundtrack kept repeating on a continuous loop over the massacre.

Back in the hotel, the detective took off Annie with a sigh of relief. This dual-personality work was eating at her nerves like acid. She checked and found that her own mobile had not only been switched off but deactivated. Then she put the power source back in its place and switched on, and instantly there was a call from Lizard. The policeman must have left his automatic reconnect activated.

"What are you up to, Husky? You've been switched off and untraceable for hours," he grumbled.

"Why are you so irritated? Because I get away from your bloodhound surveillance, or because you're concerned about my well-being?"

Bruna had fallen back on a very old trick: when you are asked a question you don't want to answer, reply with another question—an annoying one if possible. So she had behaved according to the manual, but she felt that she was gliding unstably over the words like someone slipping on ice. She felt she really wanted Lizard to answer. To reassure her that, yes, he was worried about what could happen to her in this world, which was ever more dangerous for her. But he didn't say anything like that.

"I was looking for you because I got an appointment with the chancellor-priest at the Embassy of Labari. In case you wanted to come. It was you who suggested I give him a call."

Yes, of course she wanted to. The legation was quite far from the Majestic, so she decided to catch a cab again despite her renewed intention to economize. But after wasting ten minutes standing at the edge of the sidewalk failing to get anyone to stop, she had to catch the subway. It was clear that the human cabdrivers didn't want to pick up a combat techno, and in Madrid the cabdrivers' union had prevented the adoption of automatic cabs like those that existed in other cities. As far as techno cabdrivers were concerned—they seemed to have disappeared. In reality, reps were hard to find anywhere.

She arrived at the appointment feeling exhausted; it had turned into a wretched day of nonstop rushing around. The headquarters of the representatives of Labari was an enormous, very old building located on Estados Unidos de la Tierra Avenue, next to the Prado Museum. It had been a Catholic church—San Jerónimo—for centuries, until it was burned down and half-demolished during the Robot Wars. The impoverished Catholic Church, driven to the wall by its internal crises, the progressive secularization of the world, and the fact that individuals eager for certainty preferred more radical doctrines, found itself obliged to sell the ruins to a consortium that was actually a front for their most vitriolic rivals, the Ones of the Kingdom of Labari, who constructed a heavy, cheerless version of the chapel. Now, gazing at that mass painted in ritualistic Labaric dark purple, the detective shivered. That archaic, overwhelming, and severe building represented a declaration of principles, a definition in stone of intransigence.

"Come on, Bruna, what are you doing? Don't lag behind. We're late," muttered Lizard.

And the rep forced herself to walk behind the policeman and into the embassy of a world on which her species was forbidden.

The interior must have been a soaring nave in its time, as the inside of Catholic churches used to be, but it was now compartmentalized like any other building, with various floors and normal living spaces. Or almost normal. As they passed from room to room, from the entrance to the security precinct and then to the waiting room, the detective felt a vague tightness growing in her chest. The height of the rooms was much greater than their width. They were, in fact, unpleasantly narrow and their never-ending walls were covered with thick, bruise-colored curtains that fell heavily from above.

"What a cheerful place," murmured Lizard.

Just then a man came to fetch them. His head was shaved and a chain had been driven through his earlobes and hung over his chest like a collar. *Maybe he's a slave*, the detective said to herself as they followed him. Up to that point, they hadn't seen a single woman. Before allowing them to enter the office, the possible slave turned to them.

"Call him *Your Eminence*. That's his title. And you must use the old polite form of address. You must address him formally. Don't forget."

The chancellor-priest received them in a room whose walls rose dizzily to a dark and distant vaulted ceiling. It must have been the height of the original San Jerónimo church, but the room was a relatively small space with a hexagonal floor, which made it feel like a stifling well. The purple hangings covered only the lower half of the walls, and farther up, the bare stones were lost in the shadows. The diplomat was a mature man with long, gray hair caught up in a ponytail on the top of his head in the style typical of Labaric leaders. He was seated behind a large, solid wooden table.

"The Sacred Principle is the principle," he said pompously, using the ritual greeting of the Ones.

"Thank you for receiving us, Your Eminence," Paul Lizard replied.

"It's my job," the man muttered with icy arrogance.

There was something odd about his face. At first glance, his high cheekbones, pointed chin, and elevated eyebrows—shaped like circumflexes similar to those in the old drawings of the devil—gave the impression of a long, severe, and bony face. But then you noticed the quivering chubby cheeks, the overall flabbiness of the flesh, and the roundness of his squashed face. It was as if a pudgy man with a big head were transforming himself into a thin, angular person, but the process had been halted by mistake halfway. The cheekbones, the chin, and those impossible eyebrows, which looked like two pointy little roofs, had to be the product of a surgeon's knife. Bruna had read somewhere that the Labaric religion didn't allow plastic surgery solely for aesthetic purposes, but it did if the operation had a moral purpose. Perhaps endowing this flabby, insipid person with a more imposing and spiritual appearance had been considered a sacred mandate.

Lizard took a holograph ball from his pocket and activated it. The word *revenge* floated above the One's table. The image was no doubt taken from the body of one of the victims, although you couldn't see what the word was written on in the holograph, and the tattoo had been enlarged four or five times.

"Is Your Eminence acquainted with this?"

The man glanced at the holograph indifferently.

"No."

"There's nothing about it that seems familiar?"

"No," the ambassador repeated without even bothering to look at it again.

The inspector manipulated the ball, and the image expanded until it was evident what it was: a tattoo on the back of a dead woman's naked body.

"And now?"

The legate considered the body for a second with a blank expression. Then he looked at Lizard.

"Now even less."

"But that script…Those letters are from the Kingdom of Labari," Bruna retorted.

The chancellor-priest didn't even look at her. He continued to address Lizard.

"At first glance, it might appear that that type of writing bears some resemblance to a certain script used on my world for ceremonial occasions."

"The Labaric script of power," stressed the rep.

The man ignored her interruption and continued.

"But I'm sure we're dealing with a copy."

"I've seen power writing and the script is identical," Bruna insisted.

"Why do you think...my apologies. Why does Your Eminence think we're dealing with a copy?" asked Paul.

"How do you know when a replicant is a replicant and not a real person, even though it's such a good imitation?" replied the One.

"By the eyes."

Bruna was furious with Lizard. She was outraged that he would answer a comment clearly formulated to humiliate her.

"Labaric writing has its own 'eyes' for those who know how to look. And this is a forgery, absolutely no question. Anything else?"

"Yes. Do you know whose dead body that is?"

The priest sighed in annoyance as if he were dealing with an idiotic question, although his expression of utter disdain was somewhat undermined by the wobbling of his chubby cheeks.

"I assume it's one of the replicants who was recently executed by other replicants."

"If the writing really is a forgery, who might be interested in implicating the Kingdom of Labari in a case as foul as this one?"

"The One Truth has more enemies than there are grains of sand at the bottom of the oceans. The Primordial Order is always being attacked by the henchmen of disorder, of whom there are many. But we are accustomed to it; they've been trying to distort our words for millennia. They have no effect."

"Millennia? The Labaric Cult began less than a century ago," interrupted the rep sharply.

The chancellor-priest continued to ignore her.

"The One Sacred Principle was the beginning of everything. Then, feeble man forgot who he was and what he
knew. We have merely gone back to uttering pure words,"
he declaimed.

He leaned forward and fixed his blazing eyes on Paul, and
his face became contorted with revulsion.

"Moreover, what do we care whether or not they kill those
things? They were not part of the Principle and they do not
count. They do not exist. They have no more significance than
the buckle on your shoe. You see, they seem so imperceptible
and irrelevant to us that we have even allowed you to bring
one of those things here—*here*, into the Embassy of Labari!
And what's more, a female."

The man stood up abruptly, although if truth be told,
you couldn't really tell; he was considerably shorter than was
suggested by his bulky head.

"May the Sacred Principle be your Law," he muttered
ritually.

And he left the room, dragging the shapeless, purple robe
that was too long for him along the ground.

Bruna left the building as quickly as she could, anger
adding to her speed. Lizard was following a few steps behind,
circumspect and phlegmatic, suspecting an outburst.

"Hold on, Bruna. Where's the fire?"

The rep whipped around and pointed a shaking finger at
the policeman.

"You...Thanks for your support in front of that miserable
racist," she roared.

"Professionalism, professionalism. A detective like you
should know that a major portion of our work consists of
interrogating nasty people, and nasty people are unpleasant.

You mustn't lose your composure, no matter what they say. They say all that to distract you. And it's worked in your case."

In reality, deep down the rep knew it. Lizard was right. But she was too enraged to stop.

"You humans are all the same. In the end you always support each other," she said venomously, still tasting the bitterness in her mouth.

The inspector's face darkened.

"That's not true," he muttered with a hint of annoyance.

Bruna had wanted to wound him and she had certainly done so. Now she was beginning to regret it, but she couldn't bring herself to apologize to him. Not yet. Not with all that adrenaline and humiliation still churning around inside. So they walked on together for a few minutes without saying a word, not knowing where they were going until Lizard stopped.

"It's time to eat. Let's grab something and that way we can talk a bit about the case."

Before Bruna could answer, a call came in from Nopal. She jumped, signaled to the policeman that he should wait for her and walked off a few feet to talk to the memorist.

"What are you doing with that bloodhound? Have you managed to be arrested by him?" asked the writer sarcastically.

And what's that to you? thought the detective, but for some reason she couldn't say it to him. She grabbed the wrist on which she wore her mobile with her other hand to stop it shaking. Nopal made her nervous.

"What do you want?"

"Your appointment tomorrow. The guy rang me. He wants you to get there an hour earlier."

Yes, of course. The get-together with the mem pirate who wrote illegal memories.

"So it'll be at…at 12:15, right? Same place?"

"Yes."

"Fine. Thanks."

Pablo frowned.

"Listen. That Lizard is dangerous. Don't trust him."

Bruna became irritated. Suddenly she felt she had to defend the inspector. She felt that Paul was her friend. *Paul*: it was the first time she had thought about him using his first name. In fact Paul seemed less of a risk to Bruna than Nopal.

"You're wrong. The other day he saved me from a beating," she said.

And she gave the writer a quick summary of her encounter with the thugs.

"Well, what a coincidence. They attack you and Lizard just happens to be there. And it's enough for him to take out his gun for everyone to run off. Because it turns out that—oh, what luck—none of the assailants is actually carrying a firearm. And no one is arrested, of course. I can write much more realistic scenarios."

"That's nonsense," said the rep.

But Nopal's words began to buzz around inside her head like menacing hornets.

"You won't believe me, Bruna, but I am your friend. I am now, and I always will be, on your side. And I worry about what might happen to you. It's clear that this escalation in antitechno violence is meticulously organized. I can see it, I know it. I've spent years re-creating life and I can tell when life is too perfect, more realistic than the real world! Everything that has happened has been prepared, is being controlled, is following a script. And you can't set up something like this without the involvement of the police as well."

The android didn't say anything. She didn't want to hear any more. But she listened.

"Isn't there anything about him that has surprised you? No strange behavior? He hasn't by any chance made an effort to become your friend? To gain your confidence?"

Bruna glanced over at Lizard and caught him watching her from afar with his arms folded. The android quickly looked away. She had indeed always found the policeman a little too friendly, too collaborative. Like today. Why had her taken her to see the priest?

"But how would it help him to become my friend?"

"As far as I'm aware, you're the only independent detective who's investigating the case on behalf of the technos. If he has you close at hand, he can find out what you're learning. And he might have something worse in mind. This script still contains many surprises, and it strikes me that it's a horror story. Be careful, Bruna, and don't trust him."

And he ended the conversation, leaving the rep full of despair and feeling like an orphan. The android walked slowly back to where Lizard was waiting for her, her spirits as heavy as her boots.

"What did he say to you?" asked the policeman sharply.

"Who?"

"Nopal. What did he say to you?"

"Why do you look over my shoulder to see who's calling me? Is total lack of respect an aspect of police brutality?"

"I saw you. I saw that sideways glance you threw me. It wasn't a nice look."

"Oh, by all the damn species! Stop bothering me with your paranoia!"

"Why did you become so nervous when he rang you? I've never seen you like that before. What's with you and that man? Don't trust Nopal, Husky."

Well, well! Earlier on he'd been calling her Bruna; now, he'd gone back to the more formal surname. The policeman's green eyes looked very dark, almost black. Two shiny, hard balls with a fearsome expression, trapped like insects under his thick eyelids.

"Pablo Nopal is an assassin. I know it. He killed his uncle and probably killed his secretary. Everything incriminates him beyond a shadow of a doubt, but he got away with it because we couldn't find the weapon. He used an old-fashioned gun, one that uses gunpowder with a 9mm metal bullet. Probably a P35."

"A Browning Hi-Power. That gun is more than a century old."

"Yes, it's an old piece of junk, but it can still kill."

Those sorts of guns had been withdrawn from circulation after Unification, with the famous Clean Hands Law, which also restricted the use of plasma weapons solely to security forces and the army. The old pistols and revolvers were traced with efficient scanners capable of detecting their metal alloys. And the fabrication of plasma guns required a sheet of celadium, a new mineral from the distant mines on Encelado, and each sheet was registered, numbered, and loaded with a locator chip. Despite all these precautions, there was no shortage of every conceivable sort of illegal weapon on Earth—from relics of the era of gunpowder to diverse types of plasma.

"What I'm trying to say is that he's a man with no scruples and no morals. A truly dangerous character. And he was a memorist. Perhaps he's the one who's writing the content for the adulterated mems. Why is he calling you? Maybe he's offered to help you? Doesn't that strike you as odd? I don't know what power he has over you, but I do know he's deceiving you."

"Oh, leave me in peace," spluttered Bruna.

What she wanted to say was, *Don't go on. Stop talking. I don't want to hear any more. I'm confused.* But her confusion caused insecurity, and the insecurity was making her angry.

"I've had enough. I'm off."

She turned her back on Lizard and, flustered, strode off down the street. She was about to jump onto a travelator when, out of the blue, she had a marvelous idea. An incredibly simple, brilliant idea. She turned her head; it took her a few seconds to locate the broad shoulders and sturdy neck of the inspector rising above the crowd. She caught up with him just as he was beginning the complicated maneuver of folding his large body into his car.

"Lizard...Paul...Please, wait."

She breathed in and gave a big smile. It wasn't difficult: she was so pleased with the idea she'd had that she felt like laughing.

"I'm sorry. I'm behaving like an idiot. I'm...on edge."

"You're unbearable," he said with a neutral, composed tone.

"Yes, yes, forgive me. That Labarian drove me crazy. The whole situation is driving me crazy. But let's leave it at that. You were talking about having something to eat. That seems like a good idea, but let's go to my place. I'll make us something to eat and at the same time, I want to show you something."

"What?"

"You'll see."

They got there quickly in the official car, but it seemed like an eternity to Bruna. She had difficulty containing her excitement. They went up in the elevator without saying a word, and when they got to Bruna's floor, the rep rushed to her door and opened it. A strange music filled the landing.

Standing upright in the middle of the lounge-cum-kitchen was the *bicho*, playing a sort of flute. He stopped and lowered the instrument.

"Hi, Bruna."

"Hi, Maio," she replied, really happy to see him for the first time ever.

The rep looked at Lizard. The man was stunned. She'd finally managed to breach his stupid air of a laid-back know-it-all. She looked back at the alien—huge, as tall as Lizard but even broader, with that incredible face of a big dog—and his bare torso, and the colors, shimmering viscera, and internal juices discernible through his translucent skin. Wow. Bruna was beginning to get used to the *bicho* and there was no question he was an impressive sight.

"Sorry," babbled Maio with his watery voice.

He picked up his old T-shirt and put it on.

"I took it off because it's annoying; I'm sorry."

It was not surprising that the T-shirt bothered him: it was stretched to breaking point across his large chest and seemed to be squeezing him like a corset.

"You must be a refugee, Omaá," murmured the policeman, still somewhat taken aback.

"That's right."

"Lizard, meet Maio. I met him one day in...the street. Anyway, yesterday I told him he could stay here on my sofa until he finds somewhere else. And Maio, this is Inspector Paul Lizard, who's helping me with my most recent case. Paul, please explain to him what you're doing."

"Explain *what*?"

"Well, you know, tell him that you're investigating the matter of the deaths of the reps. And that we've been collaborating."

While she was talking, Bruna was gazing intently into the Omaá's eyes, as if trying to send him a signal. Then she realized her stupidity, and began to speak mentally to the *bicho. Get inside his head. Get inside this guy's head and tell me what he's thinking. Tell me if he's hiding anything from me. Tell me if he wants to hurt me.*

"I can't," said the Omaá.

"You can't *what?*" asked Lizard.

"What do you mean you *can't?*" Bruna shouted.

"What is it that he can't do?" the policeman insisted.

The Omaá lowered his head and repeated, "I can't!"

It sounded like someone throwing a bucket of water against a wall.

"But why?" asked Bruna in despair.

The alien began to change color. He went dark all over, becoming reddish-brown.

"What's happening to you?" asked the rep, concerned.

"It's the *kuammil*. It's the result of an intense emotion. Like when you want to speak but you shouldn't."

"What's going on here?" growled Lizard in annoyance.

Something told Bruna she shouldn't pursue the matter further. Not right now.

"So you really can't?"

Maio shook his head. The rep turned toward the inspector.

"Look, I'm sorry, but it's better that we drop it and you leave. I haven't got anything to eat anyway. We'll talk another day."

Lizard looked at her, more wide-eyed than ever. Just then, he noticed that Bartolo was chewing on the cuff of his pants and with a shake of his leg, he sent the creature flying a few feet. The bubi shrieked.

"What are you doing, you brute?" yelled the rep angrily, squatting down to pick up the greedy-guts, forgetting that she had done the same thing two days earlier.

Indignation seemed to have swept away all of Lizard's lethargy.

"You're insane," he spluttered.

He said it with anger. With hatred.

"What's happening is that I don't trust you, Lizard."

"Nor I you. Because you're insane. Keep your interplanetary zoo and leave me in peace," he spat.

And he left, slamming the door behind him.

The android turned to Maio, who was slowly recovering his customary multihued color.

"And now, you, tell me why the devil you can't read his thoughts."

The Omaá turned slightly darker in color.

"I can only get inside the heads of those people with whom I've been close."

Bruna became worried.

"How close?"

"Very close. Totally close. *Intimately* close. As close as two beings can be. When two beings make *guraam*, their *kuammils* come into contact and from that moment, they can read each other's thoughts. *Guraam* means connection. It's what you call—"

Bruna raised her hand. "Don't go on."

"I won't go on."

He had turned reddish-brown again.

Four years, three months, and fifteen days, thought Bruna in order to concentrate on something other than the Omaá. She went to the bathroom to see if the nausea she was feeling might lead to her throwing up, but nothing happened. She wetted her face using her precious, meager supply of water. *Four years, three months, and fifteen days.* How Merlín would have laughed at all this.

She went back to the living room, where Maio was again blowing on his little piece of wood. Or something similar to wood. It was like a flute, except that on one side there were grooves that ran the length of the instrument. And it was played transversally, like a harmonica, by moving the lips across the grooves. It produced a captivating sound—a beautiful, delicate, liquid hiss. Bruna sat down on the armchair and allowed the alien music to relax her. The notes seemed to caress her skin, to enter through her epidermis, not her ears. After a while, Maio stopped, as opaline and multicolored as ever.

"Do all Omaás play this well?"

The *bicho* smiled.

"No. I am an *ambalo.* That means an *amb* virtuoso—that's this instrument. I'm a musician."

Then Bruna had another brilliant idea. The second big idea of the day. And she mentally prayed to Gabriel Morlay that this time it would work out well.

They reached the circus between the afternoon and evening sessions. On this occasion, Bruna didn't disconnect her mobile because she had a legitimate and understandable reason for visiting Mirari. The journey there was quite unpleasant. It wasn't the best moment in history for a shabby alien and a combat replicant to be crossing Madrid side by side. Never mind Bartolo, who had hitched a ride on the Omaá's powerful shoulders. They formed an eye-catching group, but the fear they provoked was much stronger than any rejection, and humans took off hastily at the sight of them. Streets, sky-trams, and travelators emptied at their passage, as if they were radioactive. If it hadn't been so depressing, it would have been amusing.

They found the violinist in her dressing room eating a pizza. She looked at them impassively, and Bruna envied her calmness, or maybe her experience. Mirari had probably dealt with aliens in the past.

"What's up?"

"Hi. This is Maio. He's a musician. I'd like you to listen to him play."

Mirari turned her head to look carefully at the alien. She resembled a bird, with her face crowned by her shining, thick, white hair, like a feathery crest.

"An Omaá flutist. They say they're good. Would you like some pizza?"

She fiddled with the small food dispenser she had in the room, and two steaming extralarge vegetable pizzas, and a small one for Bartolo, appeared instantly in the drawer. They all chewed in silence for few minutes until the last crumb had disappeared. Then they washed their hands in a jet of vapor.

"Let's hear what you can do," said Mirari, leaning back in her seat.

Maio raised the amb to his lips and began to blow. Liquid notes flowed from his mouth, threads of sound that seemed to glide around the room leaving a trail of light. Bruna held her breath—or, rather, she forgot to breathe for a few seconds, submerged in the music like a diver underwater.

A delicate, moving lament of a sound responded beside her. The rep turned her head and saw that Mirari was on her feet, playing her violin. The voices of the two instruments intertwined in the air, the flute sinuous and soothing beside the raw lament of the violin, creating such a profound, vast whole that Bruna felt she had sounds flowing through her veins instead of blood. Time dissolved, the past fused with the present, and Merlín was alive again because absolutely everything but death fitted into that primordial music. And then the horsehair bow slipped and the violin screeched, breaking the spell.

"Shit!" shouted Mirari, beside herself, throwing the bow to the ground.

She put the violin on the chair and began to hit her seized-up bionic arm with her other hand. She must have found it insufficient because she then walked over to the wall and, balancing her body, repeatedly smashed her arm against the doorjamb in a whipping motion. She was furious, and the sound of metal being pounded seemed to intensify her frenzy. Finally, she stopped, panting and exhausted, her extremely pale face flushed with fiery red blotches, her shattered artificial arm hanging limply from her shoulder. Mirari gasped, moved the violin aside with a trembling hand and fell into the chair. Maio and Bruna watched her in silence. The violinist gradually recovered her normal breathing rhythm. Then she looked at her orthopedic member with aversion and began to examine and move it. It squeaked.

"Now I'm in trouble," she murmured gloomily.

She bent over to pick up the bow.

"At least *this* isn't broken."

She raised her head and looked at the alien.

"You're very good, Omaá. You're fantastic. What a pity."

She grimaced, perhaps intending to look severe but actually looking desolate, and, opening a red box on the floor, took out an electronic screwdriver and began to poke around in the joints of the arm.

"Wait, Mirari. I know a bit about this. I think I can help," said Bruna.

And it was true. The standard package for combat technos included midlevel training as electronics technicians so that in an emergency they could repair weapons, peripherals, and vehicles in the field.

The violinist handed over the screwdriver and leaned against the back of the chair. She looked spent. Squatting down beside her, Bruna began to study the workings of the prosthetic arm.

"You told me the other day that your violin was a Stan...a whatever. Something very expensive. Couldn't you sell it and buy yourself a good arm?" she commented as she tightened some screws.

"A Stainer. Everyone used to say I was a good violinist. In fact, they used to say I was *very* good. I'm not telling you this out of vanity, but so that you'll understand what happened. The thing is, I was confident in my violin playing and wanted to improve...I'm sure you understand me, Omaá. I wanted to improve, and for that I needed a good violin. I fell in love with that Stainer and I couldn't think about anything else, so I borrowed the money and I bought it. But a few things went sour for me and all of a sudden I couldn't make the repayments, so I teleported myself a few times to the outer mines to earn the money. And what happened was that on the way back from my second trip, on my fourth transfer, cellular disorder destroyed the bones in this arm. The only thing remaining was the bone in the tip of my ring finger; the rest of the bone tissue had volatilized and the remaining extremity was a useless scrap of flesh that they had to amputate. So I lost an arm to get the violin, and now there's absolutely no way I'll sell the violin to get an arm. That's why I've become involved in underground deals: to accumulate Gs and get hold of a good piece of bionic engineering. Although, given my luck, I'm sure to end up in jail first."

Bruna had never heard such a long speech from Mirari. She carefully tightened a cable in the elbow and then looked at the violinist.

"You thought Maio was good, didn't you?"

"He's splendid. He could do it for a living. He'd earn good money. Omaá flutists are a much sought-after rarity."

"Exactly. That's what I thought. So I asked myself, wouldn't Mirari be interested in him for her orchestra?"

The violinist sat upright in the chair and focused. You could almost hear her thinking.

"Such a good musician, and an alien to boot," she said slowly. "Yes, that would be good. Our small orchestra would be greatly improved. We could renegotiate our contract. Even ask for a percentage of the takings. Are you interested?"

Maio nodded.

"All right then. We split everything equally. But I'm the one in charge, you understand? I still have to consult with the others, but they'll say yes. They always agree with whatever I say."

The alien nodded his head again energetically. His large body was lighting up in vibrant color. Maybe it was a demonstration of happiness.

"One more thing. Maio has nowhere to live. And then, I wouldn't like to separate him from the greedy-guts; they get on so well!" said the rep, hopefully. With a bit of luck, she'd be able to free herself of both of them in one hit.

Mirari shrugged.

"They can stay here in the dressing room. There's a bed behind that screen."

And without realizing it, she pointed toward the back of the room with her bionic arm, which unfolded itself obediently in the air.

"Oh! Hey, it's working now," she said, testing the metal joints with a finger.

"Yes, it's working. But try not to smash it against the wall again until you can afford a new arm."

CHAPTER TWENTY-TWO

*B*runa was standing in line in front of the ticket office. She had been there for a while and was beginning to get tired. It was hot, the room lacked ventilation; it was an oppressive and depressing place. Hundreds of people were squashed into a space that was too small, with low ceilings and faint lighting. There were old people sitting on bags, adults nervously walking back and forth, children crying. But apart from that crying, a strange silence prevailed, as if the people had used up all their words because of such a long wait. They looked like war refugees, stateless people in search of asylum, and the rep somehow knew this to be so. She looked around and told herself that all those people filling the room, technos and human, mutants and bichos, were desperate beings, although it was a cold, passive, resigned desperation. Suddenly Bruna found herself at the ticket window. Finally she'd made it. A woman took charge of her documents and a man led her toward a door.

"It's your turn," he said.

In front of her, a long way down, in a panoramic view beneath her feet, the marvelous spectacle of a multihued, ebullient city—a brilliant, multicolored pool—was spreading out under the dark vault of the sky. Excitement and vertigo. She took a step forward, but someone grabbed her by the arm and stopped her.

"He can't go through."

The android turned in surprise and discovered that Merlín was at her side. They were holding hands.

"Not him," repeated the voice, authoritatively.

Merlín looked at her and smiled. A small, melancholy smile. Bruna tried to speak to him, tried to turn around and go back into the room. But they were already in motion, nothing could be stopped now, and everything was happening very quickly. Bruna was flying downward toward the city and Merlín was being left behind; Merlín was a dead weight pulling on her. The rep gripped her lover's hand—gripped it so as not to lose him, so as not to become separated from him—but Merlín was floating like a helium balloon and he was being left behind, painfully stretching her arm.

"Nooo!" shouted the android, sensing that he was getting away from her.

In a desperate effort to hold onto him, she dug her nails into his back, but her sweaty hands were slipping, and suddenly they were no longer touching. Merlín, with all his extremities stretched out in the air like a star, was ascending toward the black, never-ending sky until he finally disappeared into the drift among the shadows of nothingness.

Bruna sat bolt upright in bed. She was drenched in sweat and gasping, because the nightmare's terror was still crushing her lungs. She looked at the time projected onto the ceiling: 03:35. Thursday. No, Friday. January 28, 2109. One week out from the end of the world, according to the Apocalyptics. *Four years, three months, and fourteen days.*

She moaned quietly because the pain was killing her. The pain of Merlin's absence, the pain of remembering his pain. If people saw other people dying as a matter of course, if people were conscious of what it cost to die, they would lose faith in life. Bruna tensed her jaw and ground her teeth. *Enough*, she thought. She leapt up, put on her old military training gear and left the apartment to let off steam. Madrid was deserted, even lonely now that Maio was no longer to be found at his post on the corner. His presence had been so constant that now his absence seemed to have left a hole in the scenery. But the *bicho* had remained behind at the circus, with Mirari.

Bruna started jogging along the empty street, but immediately broke into a run, racing along without even waiting to warm up. She ran and ran, pushing herself beyond her capacity, and her muscles began to hurt and the air set her lungs on fire. One stride after another, her feet pounding the hard asphalt, her heart pounding in her throat, the sky above her head as black and menacing as the one in her nightmare. *Oh, Merlín, Merlín.* The sound began to push out through her clenched teeth, first as a grunt, then as a wail. And now Bruna opened her mouth wide and was shouting, howling with all her might, with her flesh and bone, every cell in her body combining to exhale that scream; running and shouting as if she wanted to kill, running and shouting as if she wanted to turn herself inside out. The thick military boots hit the sidewalk again and again, and the heavy thuds were vaguely pleasing; she seemed to be trampling on the world and actually kicking it. Bruna was running viciously.

Now and again, shadows as fleeting as cockroaches disappeared at top speed in front of her. Windows were opened as she went past, lights were turned on. *Four years, three months, and fourteen days*, thought the android as she yelled at the top of her lungs. Or 711 days. Almost two years had passed already since Merlín's death. Between the two vectors—the ascending sum of her memory and the descending one of her own life— the huge hole of all terrors was opening up, the unbearable incoherence. It was impossible not to despair, not to scream.

Right at that moment she saw a gun emerging from the dark in front of her.

"Stop! Police! Identify yourself."

He was an FCP, a member of the Freelance Contract Police, a mercenary service hired by the regional government, which was always in a state of economic crisis and incapable of maintaining its own security forces. FCP companies varied a great deal in price and quality; this extremely young policeman with his hesitant voice and shaking weapon had to be part of a very cheap and very bad contract. Without stopping, Bruna took advantage of the impetus of her fury and her running speed to kick the gun out of the FCP's hand and throw herself on top of him. The young man fell backward onto the ground with the rep above him, grabbing him by the neck. The policeman didn't even try to defend himself; he was ashen, paralyzed with fear. In a moment of sanity, the android saw herself with another's eyes, her face twisted with rage, bellowing. Because the deafening noise she was hearing was her own howl—the threatening howl of an animal.

"Please, please, please," stammered the half-choked policeman.

He was a child.

"Why did you point the gun at me?"

"I'm sorry...I'm sorry...The neighbors alerted us, and I was the closest one."

That meant that others would arrive soon.

"How old are you?"

"Twenty."

Twenty! Bruna had never been twenty, although she had a memory of that age. She was startled by a sharp, unexpected twinge of hatred, an infinite hatred toward this privileged human who didn't even know how much he had. Her hands twitched momentarily with the desire to tighten her fingers, to close her hands, around the boy's neck. It was like a shock, like the instantaneous and galvanizing passage of an electric current. But then the impulse left without a trace. All that remained was a young man, almost a boy, about to burst into tears beneath her claws. And a very black sky over their heads.

So Bruna released the policeman and stood up.

"Forgive me. I'm really sorry. I hope I haven't hurt you."

The policeman sat up on the ground and shook his head.

"It was a reflex action when I saw you coming toward me with the plasma gun. My nerves are on edge, as I'm sure you can understand. You're pursuing us reps, you're marginalizing us, you're hating us, you're killing us. And yet you were the ones who created us."

Two tears, dense and round like drops of mercury, rolled unexpectedly down Bruna's cheeks. Where was the water coming from? How was it possible to have experienced so much pain without any tears and now cry for no reason? Then, as she tried to control and contain herself, the rep saw that the FCP was also crying. Sitting on the ground, he was crying like a little boy, his eyelashes damp with tears. So different, the two of them, yet suddenly united by tears on this dark and solitary night. It was a very strange moment. The strangest in Bruna's life.

CHAPTER TWENTY-THREE

What with the early morning run and the time it had taken Bruna to get to sleep, she hadn't slept much at all. She got up feeling more tired than she had when she went to bed, clumsy to the point of exasperation, slow and groggy. She hit the wrong button on the food dispenser and instead of coffee ordered soup, which she had to throw out. So then she decided to grab one of those disposable espresso coffees that reach the perfect temperature with just a shake of the container, but when she took the lid off the cup, the liquid spilled out all over her. She was in a bad enough mood already, but then on top of everything else, the vapor shower suddenly stopped working and the android had to rinse herself with water. An expensive outlay, especially given the calamitous state of her finances.

At that stage, the only thing that appealed to Bruna was getting back into bed or maybe even crawling under the bed for fear of what else such a clearly disastrous day might bring. But she plucked up courage and set to work unwillingly. She spoke to Habib to tell him about her progress with the investigation, which had not in fact advanced at all. But at least she could tell him about her upcoming meeting with the mem pirate. She spoke with Yiannis to tell him that everything was fine, because she assumed that he'd be worried about her infiltration of the HSP, and discovered to her amazement that the old man not only seemed unconcerned but also probably didn't even recall their conversation about it. He was in too much of a state about the manipulation of the archive and the lack of response to his complaints. More irritated by the minute, Bruna checked her bank account with Bancanet and confirmed that her situation was even worse than she had expected, because they had withdrawn the third repayment on the personal loan she had taken out months earlier when she found herself out of work and out of sorts. Next, she rang the person in charge of maintenance in her building to tell him about her broken vapor shower, and the man replied that, according to the autoanalysis records, there was nothing wrong with it. So the android took advantage of the moment to give him a piece of her mind, very loudly. Then, still trembling from the adrenaline hit, she went into the kitchen, pulled the built-in oven out from its cavity, and dropped it on her foot. Or rather she didn't drop the oven, as the appliance simply slipped from her hands; but it missed her foot only because her rapid reflexes allowed her to jump into the air and save her toes. And the oven crashed loudly onto the floor, and the door cracked and came off.

"A curse on all the wretched species," she muttered in desperation.

She'd have to buy a new oven, and buy it very quickly, despite the parlous state of her finances, because the appliance no longer fit into the hole and she couldn't risk having someone come in and find her secret hiding place—the hiding place from which she now removed the small plasma gun, putting it in her backpack. She had a vague but persistent feeling of danger, and she decided to take a weapon with her to the meeting with the mem pirate. Then she went to her main screen and checked manually one last time to make sure that she hadn't received any call or message from Lizard.

"That damn stubborn mule," she muttered.

Bruna was ready, and she had to leave now if she wanted to use public transportation to get to her appointment with the mem pirate. But instead of doing that, she flopped into the chair and told the computer to call the inspector. The man's face filled her screen, more impenetrable than ever.

"What do you want?"

Clearly, he wasn't in a good mood. The android had no idea what she wanted; maybe to apologize somehow for her behavior the day before. But Lizard's unpleasant curtness instinctively made her adopt a similarly harsh tone.

"A question: Do you think what the ambassador said about the tattoos being forgeries of Labaric writing is true?" she improvised.

Paul lowered his heavy eyelids a little farther.

"What do you think?" he replied in a somewhat irritated tone.

The rep thought for a moment.

"It infuriates me to say he's right, but I think that's the case. Lies tend to come with lots of unnecessary details, and he made no effort at all to embellish what he said."

"Could be. Anything else? I'm really busy."

"I'm going to meet a mem pirate this morning."

Bruna heard herself saying it and was amazed. Why was she telling the inspector such an important detail? *Because I don't want him to hang up*, she answered herself. *Because I want us to go back to being friends.* But in reality, it had been a stupid thing to confide. Lizard would undoubtedly start talking about Nopal again and advise her against going to any meeting arranged by him.

"Fine. I hope it goes well."

And he cut the link. The rep was left staring at the screen, flabbergasted. What? He wasn't even going to bother to argue with her? *Four years, three months, and fourteen days. Four years, three months, and fourteen days*, she repeated mechanically. But she didn't feel any less devastated.

Just then a call came through on Annie Heart's mobile from the supremacist Serra. *Of course*, Bruna thought gloomily. *No doubt my meetings with the supremacist and the pirate will coincide.* When things were going badly, they usually got worse. She answered with the screen switched off.

"What can I do for you?"

"You're lucky. Hericio will see you. In half an hour's time, in front of Saturn."

The detective caught her breath.

"No."

"No?"

"No, not today. Tomorrow."

She could sense the man's stunned silence.

"What do you mean, not today?" he said, finally.

"Look, you're the lucky ones, not me, because I could be a good contributor to your cause. If Hericio wants to see me, it means you've already checked out my good intentions. Fine, so now I want to check out yours. Since I'm going to give you a tidy sum of money, I want you to treat me well, politely, even with a little respect. What's this business of expecting me to come running like a dog when you whistle? It will be tomorrow or not at all, because I'm leaving the day after tomorrow. And since I'm generous, I'll let you choose the time. I have all the time in the world for Hericio tomorrow."

She stopped talking and held her breath, amazed at her own audacity.

"All right. I'll see what I can do," grunted Serra before disconnecting.

Bruna slowly released the air from her lungs. She hoped she hadn't ruined everything. She pushed the chair back to stand up and the wheels jammed: they were caught up in some frayed rags. Intrigued, the detective pulled on the fabric, and tight little balls of half-chewed cloth began to emerge. She had just discovered one of Bartolo's secret stashes of food; the chair's hollow leg was filled to bursting with a haul of various rags. Bruna emptied the tube—initially with irritation, then with a certain tenderness, and finally with something akin to longing. But her mood turned foul when she realized that she almost missed the silly animal and that she was even contemplating storing the rags somewhere. *This is definitely not my day,* she said to herself as she threw the rags into the incinerator.

At least she left her apartment on time, and after catching the subway and two sky-trams, she reached the designated location on the outskirts of Madrid. It was a former industrial zone that had fallen into disrepair. Almost all the premises were closed and a good number were in ruins. Weeds were growing in the cracks in the walls, and small mountains of ancient refuse had fossilized in the roadways, creating a soggy mess that time and rain had leeched of color. There was hardly any traffic moving on the streets, which were full of potholes and laid out in a grid. In the ten minutes she spent wandering around until she found the warehouse, she didn't meet a single pedestrian. A charming place.

Warehouse 17-B in Sector 4 looked like just another ruin, which was why it took Bruna some time to find it. The whole zone lacked GPS tags, which showed its age and degree of deterioration. The detective had to find the warehouse by sight, as almost all the signs were either ripped off or covered, making them illegible. In fact, the brass plate for 17-B was on the ground next to the warehouse door. It looked as if it had fallen off, but when Bruna tried to pick the brass plate up, she discovered that it was bolted to the pavement. The sliding front door of the warehouse—the only visible entrance—was misshapen, rust-ridden, and twisted, and looked as if it hadn't been opened for years and would never be opened again.

"Hello? Is anyone here?"

She banged on the rusted metal panel a few times without much enthusiasm, asking herself if she'd gotten the address wrong. She was about to ring Nopal to confirm the location of the appointment when suddenly the door lifted upward, silently and easily. Bruna stepped inside and the door noiselessly lowered itself again behind her. Clearly, it was a new system and in good shape; the broken, rusted exterior was merely a facade. The detective looked around. She was in a small, white, empty vestibule.

"Enter the lift and push button B," ordered a computer-synthesized voice.

It was a gray freight elevator, an industrial relic from the twenty-first century. There were only three buttons: A, B, and C. She pressed the one she'd been told to press, and the box shook and started to rise very slowly. When it stopped and opened its doors, she found herself in a large living room, richly decorated in neocosmic style. Floating divans and form-hugging sofas in the latest style shared space with select antique pieces—an art deco desk, a small Chinese chest of drawers. The walls displayed animated images of panoramic vistas: a beautiful deserted beach and, in the background, a white village at the foot of a mountain. The design of the landscape artwork was ingenious and it seemed as if the walls of the room were actually huge, outward-looking windows. The pictures even maintained continuity, so that if a dog was running across one wall it moved on to the next wall without losing appropriate perspective. A really expensive piece of work.

"Come in. Over here."

The space was so big and so full of furniture that initially Bruna had trouble working out where the voice was coming from. Eventually she located its owner in a group of red divans. They studied each other as Bruna walked toward him. He was a young man and very slender. But when she reached him, the rep realized that the smooth, childlike little face was the product of surgery. He was undoubtedly much older than he seemed to be at first sight. Close up, he had a plastic, inexpressive appearance. Unpleasant.

"Looks like being a mem pirate is pretty lucrative," said Bruna by way of a greeting.

The man's mouth formed what was presumably a smile. But it was so tightly stretched that the corners couldn't bend.

"Yes, business isn't bad. I'll take your remark as a compliment, since I'm doing you the favor of seeing you...to give you certain information that is of interest to you. So I won't assume that you are so stupid as to insult me as soon as you arrive. No, I'll presume you have been surprised by this beautiful apartment, and your sentence is an implicit recognition of how lovely it is."

Bruna swallowed. The man was right. She cursed herself for being a big mouth and, in particular, she cursed the aggression that memorists aroused in her. The memory of Nopal, and Nopal's arms as they were dancing, flashed through her mind like a searing wind. It was even worse if memorists didn't bring out her aggression.

"You're right, it was a compliment. It's just that we replicants aren't very good at social niceties. Of course I'm impressed with your home. May I sit down?"

The man nodded his assent and Bruna dropped into the divan facing him. The piece of furniture swayed slightly in the air as she lowered herself into it.

"I'm even more impressed by the fact that you have agreed to see me. Why did you?"

"For that, you have to thank Nopal," the memorist answered, waving a skeletal hand in front of him.

"Are you friends?"

The man snorted sarcastically.

"Friends. I wouldn't say that. Hmmm...not exactly friends, no. But I'm seeing you because he asked me to."

"Then Nopal must be very persuasive, because on top of everything you've received me in your own home. Extraordinary. Very...intimate."

The man made the same attempt at a smile as before. His excessive, crude plastic surgery didn't match the exquisiteness of the apartment. His clothing seemed vulgar as well: ostentatious and loud black velvet, never mind the gold necklaces strangling his skinny neck. Clearly the guy was out of place in this refined environment.

"I don't have much time. Are you going to waste it talking about Pablo Nopal?" he growled.

"I'd rather we talked about the mems."

"Which ones?"

"The doctored ones. The ones that make the replicants go mad and then kill them."

"I know nothing about those. I never killed anyone. Pirate, yes; murderer, no. I only work with traffickers I trust. Reliable people. They have the customers, they get a hold of the hardware; I restrict myself to writing the content."

"Right. And I assume you know nothing about who might be behind the deadly implants either."

"Well, you do hear things out there. I know it's someone from outside."

Labari was Bruna's immediate thought.

"Outside Earth, you mean?"

"Outside the profession."

"Yours is a profession?" she asked, disappointed.

"As much as yours, with the difference that I am more professional than you."

Bruna sighed.

"I don't doubt it. Forgive me. But if you really are so good, you would have been asked to write the killer mems."

"I've already told you I didn't."

"How many are you? I mean, how many illegal memorists like you are there out there?"

"Like me, there's no one. I'm the best. But apart from me, maybe a half dozen."

"And which of them might have done it?"

"Of those, none."

"Why not?"

"The majority of the mem pirates are very bad. They use random plots bought on the black market and images synthesized by a computer. Their mems are garbage. But those killer memories are incredible. Unusual, very unusual. I've never seen anything like them. Very violent and full of hate, but also full of truth. There's definitely a writer behind them. Someone who's desperate to express himself. They're short—barely forty scenes—but they're good. The pirates I know would never have been capable of making them."

"You astonish me. How do you know about the content on the killer mems?"

"Well, we all have our contacts...and it's my profession. What's more, you could say that my life depends on it."

"You say they're unusual. Is that why you think there are new traffickers in town?"

"No, no. I didn't say that. That's what's so strange about the whole business. There aren't any new traffickers. There aren't any new memorists. There's no adulterated consignment. No one's putting killer mems on the market. No one's selling them. It's not a commercial operation. It's not drug related. Do you understand what I'm saying?"

Bruna thought for a moment, processing the man's words.

"You're saying that the victims didn't buy the implants voluntarily, that the memories were inserted by force, and that they probably weren't random victims but they've been chosen for a reason."

"That's it."

Which meant that not just Chi but also all the other replicants were likely to have been carefully selected according to some plan.

"Then why are they killing the regular traffickers as well?"

The memorist scratched the tip of his ear nervously.

"Hmmm...That's a good question. I'd love to know the answer."

He was scared. The man was frightened, the rep suddenly realized. That explained a few things.

"You're frightened that they'll kill you too. That's why you wanted to talk to me."

"I've already told you that seeing you had to do with Nopal. But it's logical that the deaths alarm me. As the saying goes, there's no smoke without fire."

"And you don't have a theory?"

"What about you? You're the detective, after all."

Bruna furrowed her brow in thought.

"At first I thought it was a battle for the market, to get rid of the competition."

"No. It doesn't look like they want to finish everyone off. They've only killed one of my regular colleagues. I was in his company, together with another trafficker, when they killed him, but they didn't touch the other one. It would seem that they also pick and choose."

"Perhaps because of something they know?"

The memorist went pale. *That's why he's had such savage surgery*, said Bruna to herself. Everything was starting to make sense. It wasn't plastic surgery but a complete change to his looks and his identity. Here was a man who intended to hide, a fugitive.

"Because of something they know," the mem pirate repeated gloomily.

"That secret project to implant induced behavior, those artificial memories for humans."

The idea had suddenly occurred to her out of the blue. The android tended to run with those sudden flashes of intuition. She was convinced that sometimes those thoughts worked their way into her mind because somehow she had picked them up from her surroundings. The batch of combat replicants to which Bruna belonged had been provided with an experimental enzyme, nexin, which supposedly boosted their ability to empathize, to make links. The experiments hadn't been conclusive and the enzyme was officially considered a failure, but whatever the bioengineers might say, it seemed to the detective that nexin worked—at least from time to time. The memorist cringed.

"How do you know about that?" he asked, lowering his voice.

"As you put it, we all have our contacts."

The man seemed uncomfortable.

"It's a very...ahem...I took part, yes. I don't mind telling you that. I took part in those experiments. They were secret, true, but official. A matter of state. And then, when they hurriedly and unpleasantly shut down the program, they made my life impossible. They accused me of things I hadn't done. They expelled me from the profession. They didn't allow me to return to my work as a memorist. And I was the best. I *am* the best. That's why they hired me."

"That doesn't seem fair."

"It was an outrage!"

"And who were the people who did that to you?"

The man grimaced.

"I don't intend to say any more. I've already said too much. It's dangerous."

"But those wretches who hired you and then destroyed your life, they deserve to have people know what they've done."

Furious, the man retorted, "If it were known, I'd already be dead! Do you think I'm an imbecile? Don't try to make me feel indignant. You won't get any more information out of me by using such a crude tactic."

Bruna raised her hands in a gesture of appeasement.

"Okay, fine, my apologies. It's true that I was trying to ingratiate myself...somewhat. But it's also true that I find it a terrible story. And it could be the reason for the murders. Who was running the project? Who did this to you?"

The memorist screwed up his eyes and bit his lower lip. But he was too angry to be able to contain himself.

"It wasn't the fault of the person leading the scientific section. In fact, the scientists were also..."

The man suddenly stopped speaking and stared at Bruna wide-eyed, with his deformed mouth wide open. It all happened in a fraction of a second—the immobility, the shocked expression—and then a stream of blood gushed from his mouth. By that stage, the rep had already flung herself headlong onto the floor and rolled under the floating divan. The air smelled of burnt caramel—the smell of plasma—and of the sickly sweet smell of blood. Plasma shots don't make a sound, so you only know someone is shooting at you when the cold light opens up a hole in you. Bruna crawled under the sofas and sought protection behind the Ming chest of drawers. She took out her own gun, which seemed so small in her large hand, and tried to weigh her options. From behind her precarious barricade, she couldn't see anyone. The memorist had fallen facedown on the floor; the shot had entered through his neck and seemed to have split his windpipe. They must have used a black plasma gun, an illegal weapon of the sort that turned its luminous impulse into a broad beam when it hit the target. That was the reason so much blood had come out of the memorist's mouth, the reason for the instant destruction. Anyway, the shot must have come from the door. It was the only entrance to the place, right next to the elevator, and it clearly led to the stairs. She held her breath and listened carefully. She couldn't hear anything other than the liquid bubbling of the dead man's blood. And she couldn't see anything either.

But the assailant, or assailants, must still be there.

Or maybe they'd only wanted to kill the memorist?

She waited.

And waited. *Surely they're gone already*, she thought. Against a black plasma gun, the Chinese chest of drawers she was trying to shelter behind was of no more use than a sheet of paper. If the assassin had wanted to kill her too, he would have done so already. Cautiously, and following the route she'd previously worked out, Bruna moved from the chest of drawers to the big armchair, from the big armchair to the table, and from the table to the desk. There she stopped, because the worst part came next, an unobstructed and relatively long stretch to the door. The warehouse didn't have any windows but instead was illuminated by solar panels, so she'd have to leave the same way she had come in, but taking the staircase rather than the elevator, which could turn into a cramped trap. By the same route that the assailant had no doubt taken.

She filled her lungs with air and sprinted for the door. She kicked it open. Nobody. Exhilarated, she thought, *I've nearly made it*. And at that moment, she smelled sweat and adrenaline and sensed a slight vibration in the air behind her. She thought about turning around but there was no time; something hard hit her head and shoulder. Her vision blurred and she opened her legs wide to prevent herself from falling. Hazy assailants, emerging from who knew where, threw themselves on top of her. *It's not possible*, she thought for an exasperated moment. *Where are they?* Where the hell had they been hiding? She fired her plasma gun at a shape, but a searing pain in her wrist forced her to drop the weapon. Half-stunned, she defended herself against her attackers with the fury of a wild animal. She hit, she kicked, she bit. The blows she was receiving didn't hurt, but she was conscious of them landing on her. *Too many blows*, she calculated. *I won't be able to take many more.* Then her knees went out from under her and she found herself on the floor. *It's the end*, she told herself coldly. Without any fear. Without surprise. And she thought about Merlín.

CHAPTER TWENTY-FOUR

"Bruna…how are you feeling?"

The rep didn't recall having fainted. She thought she had been conscious the whole time—perhaps a bit stunned, but conscious—and yet she must have missed something, because there was no one around now. At least, none of her assailants. Only Lizard was there, leaning over her. He made a large, pleasant shadow, like a protective cave.

"How are you feeling?"

"Perfect," answered the rep.

Or that's what she tried to say. In reality, it sounded something like "purrffcc."

"Bruna, do you know who I am? What's my name?"

Irritation got her going.

"Oh, by-aw-the-speeshies, you're Paw. Paul. Wha-you-dooo-here?"

She was recovering by the minute. And with lucidity came pain. Her neck hurt. Her hand hurt. Her kidneys hurt. Her head hurt. Even the air going slowly in and out of her lungs hurt.

"I tracked you. Just as well. You were taking a long time to come out so I decided to have a quick look around. The door was open and I found you lying here. They've given you a real beating. Unfortunately, I didn't see anyone. There's a hidden door in the entrance hall that leads to a back staircase. They must have escaped that way."

Bruna tried to sit up and groaned.

"Hold on."

Lizard raised her up as easily as if he were lifting a doll and left her sitting with her back against the wall. That hurt, too. Her back, or maybe the wall.

"How do you feel?"

"Dizzy."

She carefully felt her mouth with her hand.

"I think they've broken a tooth," Paul announced.

"You're joking."

Bruna spit a clot of blood onto the floor. Which reminded her of the mem pirate.

"There's a man here who's—"

"Dead. Yes. They shattered his neck with a shot," replied Lizard.

A pair of scared young FCPs appeared at the door.

"It's about time you turned up. There's a present for you over there," said the inspector, signaling with his head toward the body.

"I've already alerted the examining magistrate. Nobody touches anything until he gets here."

"Yes, sir."

Meanwhile, Paul was examining the rep's body with experienced hands, moving her legs, her arms, feeling her ribs.

"You're covered with blood, but I think most of it is his."

"I'm fine," said Bruna.

"Sure. Come on, I'll take you to the hospital."

"No, not the hospital. To my place."

"Okay. To your place, but via the hospital."

Lizard picked up one of the android's shoes from the floor—it had come off in the midst of the maelstrom—and raising her leg, he put the shoe on her foot with exquisite gentleness. And then Bruna felt that something was breaking inside her, that something was beginning to hurt her more than all the other aches in her bruised body.

"I'm fine," she repeated, barely resisting the ridiculous temptation to cry.

Oh, what was going to become of her? To make love with someone was easy. To sleep with the inspector, for example, would have been a very simple and banal thing to do. A gymnastic triviality quickly forgotten. But that someone would place a missing shoe on her foot, that someone would put the shoe on her foot with such gruff care, with such awkward tenderness—that was impossible to surpass. Lizard's small gesture had left her defenseless. She was lost.

CHAPTER TWENTY-FIVE

At the hospital they gave Bruna a full body CT fluoroscan and, surprisingly, there was no major damage. Her organs were fine, there was no internal hemorrhaging, and the knock on the head hadn't produced any lasting trauma. She had a couple of cracked ribs and a superficial wound on her wrist from the plasma shot; luckily it wasn't black plasma so it hadn't affected the bones. In summary, there was nothing that couldn't be cured with a round of subcutaneous paramorphine injections. As far as the broken tooth was concerned, they dealt with that in the same emergency cubicle by extracting the stump, inserting an implant and screwing on a new tooth that was totally indistinguishable from Bruna's own. She was undoubtedly benefiting from being there with Paul Lizard. Bruna was paying with her own mediocre health insurance, but the inspector knew half the hospital personnel and he had managed to arrange for her to receive first-class treatment.

"It's the medical center the Homicide Squad uses; that's why I brought you here."

I brought you, Bruna repeated softly to herself as Lizard was helping her into his car. The rep had the feeling that he was making too many decisions for her. Under other circumstances, she would have found that situation infuriating.

But she was exhausted and the paramorphine was deadening her nerves, so she sank back comfortably into her seat and allowed herself to be taken away without saying a word. As they left the hospital parking station, a blast of gale-force wind rocked the car.

"Siberian wind. I don't know if you're aware of it, but we're in a state of emergency. There's a polar crisis on its way."

Not even the peacefulness of the drug could prevent the android from feeling a deep irritation at the news. Although climate change had caused the annual average temperature to rise several degrees and had turned previously temperate, wooded zones into desert, an inversion of the so-called Arctic Oscillation—a phenomenon Bruna had never managed to understand—periodically caused brief and unusual waves of extreme cold, with one or two days of heavy snowfalls, howling gales, and plummeting temperatures that in Madrid could easily reach minus four degrees Fahrenheit. Although the crisis had only just started, the temperature was going to drop still farther. The pedestrians, their faces cold, were struggling to walk against the wind, and were standing in line to buy provisions or, even worse, heaters and thermal clothing. The rep was always amazed at people's lack of foresight; there were at least two polar crises each year, but people lived as if they were a one-off occurrence, something abnormal that would never happen again. And so, every time a cold snap arrived, supplies of thermal articles sold out.

"Look, it's snowing already," said Lizard.

And he was right. Half-dissolved snowflakes were crashing against the windshield. Deadly snow, thought the detective; the icy cold always left a trail of victims: the very old, the very sick, the very poor. The android breathed deeply, feeling incredibly good in the warm, soft interior of the vehicle, in the fuzzy calm of the drug, in the protective company of Lizard.

"You're going the wrong way. It's straight ahead."

"We're not going to your place, Bruna. I think it would be better, at least for today, if you rested in a safe place, and I'm not convinced that your apartment is it. You could say that in recent times too many people have been bent on assaulting you."

True, thought the android. Before the memorist killers, there had been the thugs who had intercepted her on the way to her apartment, and before that, the attack by her neighbor Cata Caín, who had the scene of Bruna's murder written on her deadly mem. The image of the rep gouging out her own eye lit up briefly in Bruna's mind like a lightning flash of blood. She shivered.

"So where are we going, then?" she asked, though she already knew the answer.

"To my place."

The android gave a slight frown. That wasn't a good idea; it wasn't at all good to give in to the inspector's wishes, to assume the passivity of a wounded animal, the comfortable weakness of a victim. It wasn't at all good to allow Paul to make decisions on her behalf without even pretending to consult her, to allow him to control her, no matter how gently he did so. On any other occasion, the rep would have refused, would have argued and protested, but now she allowed herself to be led, feeling a rare pleasure in her compliance. A perverse pleasure. *What difference did it make?* she thought.

"What difference does it make?" she growled softly.

Suddenly she remembered that, a few days back, she had left her panties on the hood of this very car, and she gave a little smile. What had the inspector thought when he found her gift? Had he guessed that it was from her? It was the night she met Lizard for the first time. A mad night; her body had been burning from the candy. Just the thought of the oxytocin cocktail made Bruna feel as if her body was slightly on fire. Indistinct but searing memories of her carnal rapture began to ignite in her head. But then she also remembered that she'd ended up in bed with the Omaá, and the mild, erotic excitement she was feeling suddenly vanished. All that had happened eight—no, seven—days ago. Friday, January 21. How many things had happened in that short time! If she were capable of living every day of her life with such intensity, her short technohuman existence would seem very long indeed.

She tipped back her seat and closed her eyes. *Four years, three months, and fourteen days.* Today was Friday, January 28, 2109. Merlín had died on March 3; it would be the second anniversary of his death in just over a month. Bruna wondered what the exact date of her own death would be. Her obsessive countdown only provided the time left before she reached the fateful ten-year border, but as of that point TTT could take two to three months to finish her off. She figured it would be in April or May, or perhaps even June.

She must have fallen asleep, because she suddenly opened her eyes with a start and saw that the car had stopped and Paul was saying something to her.

"Come on! We're here."

The snow was beginning to settle in, and as she got out of the vehicle, the intense cold pierced through her thin clothes like a thousand pinpricks. Lizard flung an arm across her shoulders and leaned his large body in close to hers. He did it so naturally that Bruna didn't find it at all odd; on the contrary, her own body automatically adapted itself to the inspector's as if it had made that move a thousand times in the past. And just like that, holding tightly on to each other, leaning into the cutting edge of the wind and protecting each other, they covered the distance to the building.

As she was going through the entrance, however, the detective, somewhat embarrassed, immediately disentangled herself. The movement produced a sharp stab in her injured ribs.

"So this is where you live," she remarked foolishly, just for something to say, as she tentatively felt her rib cage with her fingers.

It was one of those old houses in what used to be the heart of Madrid, renovated on the inside a few decades earlier but not very well maintained. The narrow space next to the worn stairs housed a single, vintage elevator. Lizard opened his mailbox and a few holograph flyers emerged, shrieking. He crushed them with his hand and put them into the sealed bin. Then he opened the elevator door for Bruna.

"You take it. Fourth floor. I'll take the stairs."

It was no surprise that he should walk up, as the cage was so small that the two of them would have fitted in only if they were tightly embraced. *A pity*, thought Bruna with a small smile as the elevator rose, shaking suspiciously. When it stopped on the fourth floor, Lizard was already there, only slightly out of breath. He wasn't in bad shape, especially considering his bulk.

"Come in. Make yourself comfortable."

How the hell was she going to do that? Her entire body ached. She entered hesitantly. The apartment consisted of only one room, but it was very large. Large and distressingly austere. An enormous bed, a work table, a couch, bookshelves. Everything as bare and impersonal as a technohuman's apartment. *Or the majority of technos' apartments*, Bruna mentally corrected, remembering Chi's exquisite but excessively ornate bedroom, and even her own apartment, with its pictures and its jigsaw puzzle. Here there were so few decorative objects that the three ancient balconies with their iron railings constituted the biggest adornment in the place. But the street was very narrow and the building opposite—a cheap and ugly apartment building in the Unification style—seemed to be forcing its way in through the windows.

"You can sleep over there," said Paul, pointing toward the spacious couch. "It's even comfortable for someone my size—I've tried it out a few times. You'll see."

Bruna sat down carefully. And not for the first time that afternoon, she thought about her valuable little plasma gun. She didn't know if her assailants had grabbed it from her, or if Lizard had it, and she preferred not to ask. Losing the gun was a genuine annoyance, and getting another one would be quite costly and problematic, but she decided to leave those concerns for the next day. The apartment was maintained at a very comfortable temperature, while on the other side of the windows, in the fading light of the late afternoon, the snowstorm was intensifying. It was absurd, but the android felt almost happy.

Lizard came back to her side carrying a pillow, a thermal blanket, and a bottle of cask-fermented Guitian wine.

"Weren't you the one who liked white wine?"

"No, it was the other rep," Bruna replied jokingly, pointing at the photo of a techno that occupied the apartment's main screen.

Paul glanced quickly at the image above his shoulder and then silently continued to spread out the blanket. The detective was afraid she'd said something inappropriate.

"Mmmm...Yes, I think I could do with a glass."

"I'll prepare something to eat," said the inspector.

And when he got up, on the way to the kitchen, he whispered something at the computer and the image on the main screen changed to a scenic view of Titan.

While the man rummaged about in the oven dispenser, the android sat looking outside. The snow was making the air look solid and covering the windows with a grayish veil. Under the weight of the storm, the afternoon light was dying early, and the electric light switched on automatically. Bruna knew she shouldn't ask but she couldn't stop herself.

"That rep on the screen, was she one of the victims?"

Lizard didn't answer, which didn't surprise Bruna. She was more surprised to hear herself rudely insisting, "Or maybe one of the suspects?" And after a minute's silence, to her own consternation, she even added, "Why don't you answer? Are you keeping details of the investigation from me?"

Lizard returned, carrying a tray with a couple of enormous bowls full to the brim with miso soup.

"I was going to make some reconstituted tuna sandwiches, but then I remembered your recent tooth implant. Make room for me."

He sat on the edge of the sofa and put an insulation band around the bottle to keep it cold. Then he uncorked the Guitian unhurriedly and poured out two glasses. He had a few sips from his own glass and looked out in the direction of the street. Outside, night had already fallen and the light from the apartment was reflected in the curtain of snow as if it were a painting.

"If you really want to know who it is, why don't you just ask directly?"

"What do you mean?"

"Dare to ask the question and I'll answer you."

Bruna was silent for a moment, ashamed.

"Fine. I assume it has nothing to do with the case. And I also assume I shouldn't poke my nose where it doesn't belong. But I'd like to know why you have that picture of an android."

Paul slowly stirred his soup, filled his spoon, blew on the liquid, sampled a little appreciatively and then swallowed the rest, while the rep waited impatiently for him to finish the pantomime and continue speaking.

"It's Maitena."

And he put another spoonful of soup into his mouth.

"And who's Maitena?"

Another round of stirring, blowing, and swallowing. Was he making fun of her, or was it hard for him to talk about it?

"It's actually a very simple story. When I was little, my parents disappeared. So my neighbor Maitena adopted me. An exploration rep."

"What happened?"

"She died. What do you expect happened? She reached her TTT."

"I mean, with your parents."

Paul raised the bowl and started to drink from it. He made a slurping noise as he sipped and, from time to time, he would stop to chew the miso. He took a very long time to finish it.

"They put them in jail. They'd kidnapped a guy. They were criminals. Or rather they *are*, because I think they're still alive."

"Your parents are criminals?"

"Does that surprise you? The world is full of them. You ought to know. It's part of your work," commented the inspector sarcastically.

He carefully wiped his lips with his napkin and, for the first time since he had sat down on the sofa, he lifted his head and looked into her eyes.

"I was eight when I was left on my own. Maitena raised me. She died when I was fifteen. You could say it was a happy childhood—thanks to her. I already told you that I have nothing against reps."

He stood up and threw the disposable bowl into the recycle bin. Bruna followed him with her eyes, not daring to say a word. Paul returned and sat down again. His thigh was brushing against the rep's hip.

"Do you know who owned the loft you went to this morning?"

The question disconcerted her. She was too submerged in the smell of him, in the heat of his closeness, in the dizzying intimacy of the moment, and it was an effort to emerge from it.

"The murdered memorist, I presume."

Lizard shook his head. He had a curious expression on his face, somewhere between mocking and belligerent.

"No. It belongs to Nopal. It's one of your friend Nopal's properties."

Bruna gave a start.

"Are you sure?"

"He didn't say anything to you, did he? I've already warned you: he's not to be trusted."

It was ridiculous, but Bruna wasn't at all pleased by the news. The assailants' use of the hidden door and the second staircase—didn't that suggest a sound knowledge of the place? She sensed a profound weariness sweeping over her and with it, a return of all her aches.

"I'm exhausted," she groaned.

"I'm not surprised. Here, have your injection. I think it's due."

Lizard handed her the injector tube, and the rep shot the paramorphine into her arm. Slowly, fresh waves of well-being began to wash over her body.

"Better?" asked Lizard, leaning toward her and placing a hand on her back.

Again, it was a totally natural gesture, a half-embrace, intoxicatingly affectionate.

"Muuuch better," mumbled Bruna.

She wanted Lizard with her entire body, with her mind and her heart, with her hands, with her all-consuming sex and with her mouth, capable of murmuring sweet nothings. She would have thrown herself on top of him were it not for the sudden drowsiness irresistibly closing her eyes. But hold on a minute. Hold on. Maybe it was too sudden. She made an effort to arouse herself.

"Why am I so sleepy?" she asked in a fuzzy voice.

"I gave you a sleeping pill together with the paramorphine. It will do you good to rest."

In the warm apartment, under the thermal blanket, wrapped in the inspector's embrace, Bruna felt cold. *I don't want to fall asleep*, she thought. Lizard the Reptile had turned up by her side after the beating. *What a coincidence*, as Nopal would say. And now Lizard had brought her to his apartment. And he'd put a photo of a rep on the screen so that she'd see it, and he'd told her an absurd story about a melodramatic childhood. She inhaled deeply, trying to stay awake, but the drowsiness was like the lid of a coffin closing, shutting her in. The small death of sleep. Or eternal, everlasting death. She felt a stab of fear. Lizard the attractive Caiman had drugged her. She was engulfed by the darkness of sleep before she could determine whether Paul was her lover or her assassin.

**Central Archive, the United States of the Earth.
Modifiable version**

ACCESS STRICTLY LIMITED
AUTHORIZED EDITORS ONLY

Madrid, January 29, 2109, 15:27
Good afternoon, Yiannis

IF YOU ARE NOT YIANNIS
LIBEROPOULOS,
CENTRAL ARCHIVIST FT711, QUIT
THESE PAGES IMMEDIATELY

ACCESS STRICTLY LIMITED
AUTHORIZED EDITORS ONLY

UNAUTHORIZED ACCESS IS A CRIMINAL
OFFENSE
PUNISHABLE BY IMPRISONMENT UP TO
A MAXIMUM OF TWENTY YEARS

Robot Wars
Keywords: Human Peace, Tenth Geneva Convention,
coltan mines, the Congo Crisis, ~~Replicant Conspiracy~~, ~~Lumbre
Ras~~.
#6B-138
Entry being edited

The Robot Wars, which began in 2079 and ended with the signing of **Human Peace** in 2090, are, together with the Plagues, the most serious armed conflicts suffered by Earth. The scale of violence that swept the planet in the second half of the last century led to the signing of the **Tenth Geneva Convention** in 2079, which was ratified by almost all of the independent states (153 of the 159 then in existence). They agreed to the substitution of traditional armed conflict with robot battles. Armies would be replaced by mobile, fully automated fighting forces that would engage each other in combat, like a gigantic, real-life version of a computer game. The architects of the treaty thought that in this way the carnage would end, or at least be reduced, and that wars could be converted into a type of strategic pastime, in the same way that ancient medieval tournaments were a milder version of genuine battles.

However, the consequences of this measure could not have been worse. In the first place, within hours of the agreement having been signed, war broke out throughout almost the entire world, as if some nations had been waiting on hold, robots at the ready, to commence battle. (Some political commentators, such as the renowned Carmen Carlavilla in her book *Slippery Words*, argue that the Tenth Geneva Convention was merely a commercial maneuver by the manufacturers of war robots.) As the wealthiest countries possessed a vastly greater number of robots than the poor countries, they had no intention of respecting the treaty despite having signed it, and they attacked the automatons with conventional troops, who destroyed large numbers of them because, based on the Geneva specifications, the robots were hamstrung by a chip that prevented them from harming humans. This chip, needless to say, was illegally and surreptitiously removed within a few weeks, the result being that the vast fields of smoldering scrap iron were instantly covered again in blood.

The counterattack by the automatons proved so devastating and out of control that more deaths were documented in six months than there had been in all the world wars that had gone before. The **Congo Crisis** belongs to this era. As is well known, 80 percent of the reserves of **coltan**, a mineral essential for the manufacture of all sorts of electronics, are to be found in the former Democratic Republic of Congo. The exploitation of the coltan mines had been the source of numerous conventional armed conflicts for a century, but the Robot Wars exceeded previously known levels of violence by far: the entire population of Congo was exterminated, with the sole exception of the president, Ngé Bgé, and the two hundred members of his family, who were out of the country when the massacre occurred and who continue to be the coproprietors of the coltan mines to this day. together with a shelf company that is in reality secretly controlled by technohumans.

****(*Note the totally unjustified and erroneous alterations to the text! I insist on the urgent need for an internal investigation. Central archivist FT711)*****

The so-called Congo Crisis was not the only extermination of an entire nation to occur during the Robot Wars, but it was probably the most important and the best known. The major world powers rapidly toughened their positions regarding this crisis and, in the end, the Geneva terms appeared to be adhered to down to the last detail: in the isolation of the devastated Congolese territory, among rusting metal and yellowing bones, robots spent more than a year destroying one another. Finally, the day came when the countries involved tacitly buried the Tenth Geneva Convention and went back to sending human troops to the front. As of that moment, until the Robot Wars ended, they were fought with both human soldiers and automatons, a fatal combination that resulted in a horrific mortality rate. ~~A carnage which, interestingly, the replicants escaped since, adhering to their customary practice of civil disobedience (all the rights, none of the obligations), they refused to participate in battle. Eminent authors, such as Professor Lumbre Ras, Nobel Laureate in Physics, have talked of an android conspiracy to decimate humans. They maintain—with abundant documentary evidence—that behind the extermination of the Congolese and the return to traditional warfare can be seen the backroom dealings of these artificial creatures, who, intimately linked through a secret lodge, constitute a genuine power on the sidelines whose sole aim is to subjugate humans.~~

****Crisis memorandum****
For the attention of the overall supervisor of Zone PPK

In light of the serious irregularities I have observed in the archives in the past few days, and given that my previous—and frequent—reports have produced no response from my immediate superiors, I have decided to resort to emergency protocol CC/1 of the General Law Governing Archives and submit a crisis memorandum to the person responsible for the zone.

I have been making note of a growing number of erroneous altera-tions to the texts of several archives (see attached documents). The alterations lack an EID (electronic identification; in other words, is it unclear who is responsible—a fact that is, in itself, already highly irregular). They are totally false, and all constitute blatant defamation of technohumans.

The aforementioned alterations are increasing rapidly both in number and in the brutality of the tone and the lies. The present document is a good example of what I am referring to. In reality, and in contrast to what is being maintained by the anonymous author, it was primarily combat technohumans that were killed in the Robot Wars—as in all the wars, unfortunately. This is why they were created. No techno refused to fight, as far as we know, and it goes without saying that the coltan mines do not belong to any android but rather to the Ngé family and to a very human arms consortium that produces war robots. Moreover, the supposedly eminent Professor Lumbre Ras does not exist; no amount of checking in Wikipedia and the annals of the Nobel Prizes produces any result. This shows how crudely the articles have been falsified.

Given all of the above, it seems reasonable to assume that the alterations follow a plan and have a concrete aim. It is not up to me to analyze what this purpose is, and to what extent it could be a question of a conspiracy, given the critical period of interspecies violence we are currently experiencing in the region (and not just in the region: it would appear that similar disturbances are happening in Kiev, New Naples, and Cape Town), but the alterations should undoubtedly be investigated with the utmost urgency by the appropriate person. I am so convinced of the extreme seriousness of the situation that, in light of my fear of a possible delay in response, I am going to do something that I have never done in my forty years as an archivist: I am going to keep the article in my inbox instead of returning it to the editing section and, in addition, I will send a copy of said article—and of this memorandum—to my personal computer.

I await your rapid response, and remain yours sincerely, Yiannis Liberopoulos, central archivist FT711

CHAPTER TWENTY-SIX

A delicious aroma of coffee and toast awoke Bruna. She opened her eyes and had to close them again immediately, blinded by the brilliant whiteness of the snow. But that briefest of glances was enough for her to put her world back in place. She was in Lizard's apartment. She'd spent the night there. The inspector had sedated her. But he didn't appear to have killed her. Bruna smiled at the nonsense that had just crossed her mind and cautiously opened her eyelids again.

"You've been sleeping for twelve hours. I was beginning to get worried."

Lizard was rushing back and forth, displaying an exhausting energy.

"I have to go down to the police precinct. Stay as long as you like. I've authorized the computer to recognize you. You can go in and out of the apartment and ask the screen for whatever you need."

"I assume I can only ask for *certain* things, though," she mumbled with her furry tongue.

"Obviously...To have a shower, eat something. I've given you basic domestic access. You wouldn't want me to open up my entire life from one day to the next."

Paul was speaking in a lighthearted tone, but Bruna blushed.

"I don't want anything," she grunted.

On the other side of the windows, the world was enveloped in a quiet, squeaky, white blanket.

"You drugged me last night."

"What?"

"You gave me a sleeping pill without my knowledge."

"It strikes me that it did you good."

"Don't do it again."

Lizard shrugged his shoulders, somewhat annoyed.

"Don't worry, I won't. And you're welcome. Hey—you're *welcome*. There's no need to overwhelm me with your gratitude," he added sarcastically.

He stuffed himself into an enormous winter coat with a hood and opened the door to leave.

"Lizard!"

The inspector paused in the doorway.

"That…that story about Maitena and your childhood, is it true?"

"Why would I lie to you?" Paul replied without turning around.

Then he glanced at her over his right shoulder.

"Incidentally, speaking of lies…last night and this morning they've been calling you insistently on your other mobile. You know which one I'm talking about: the illegal one."

And with that, he left.

The Caiman always managed to unsettle her.

When they'd reached the hospital, Bruna had managed surreptitiously to remove Annie's mobile—which she usually wore taped to her stomach—and after rolling up the thin, translucent sheet, had hidden it in the inside pocket of her backpack. Now, however, the mobile was lying unfolded on the table next to her. She grabbed it. Sure enough, there were six missed calls from Serra, Hericio's deputy. She made an effort to concentrate and assume the role of Annie Heart, and then hit the supremacist's number. The man's unpleasant face filled the screen. He looked irritated and suspicious.

"Where have you been?" he barked.

"It's none of your business."

"Of course it is. You're too mysterious, sweetheart. You appear suddenly out of nowhere, you disappear just as suddenly, and besides, I'm sick of not being able to see you. All that nonsense about the mobile being untraceable, about there being no picture when we speak. I'm beginning to think you're hiding something. And if that's true, I assure you, you'll be sorry."

Bruna took a deep breath.

"Let's clarify a few things: One, that's not how to treat a prospective donor. Two, I'm still not sure I want to give you my money. Three, don't ever threaten me or you'll never hear from me again. Call me when you know where and when I'll be meeting Hericio," she said in an icy tone.

She cut communication. She waited for two long minutes with her eyes glued to the screen. Finally, blue letters lit up: "16:00 at the bar in your hotel." Perfect! *The funding permit clearly hasn't provided the anticipated results*, the rep said to herself. *They still seem keen to fill their coffers*. They would undoubtedly pick her up at the bar and take her somewhere. Perfect. It wasn't yet 10:00. She had more than enough time.

Bruna felt her ribs. They were still hurting but not as much. The bone regenerator they had injected at the hospital seemed to be working. She took off the blanket and stood up carefully. Despite her recent beating, she in fact felt reasonably good. A check in the large mirror on the wall confirmed that she was still wearing yesterday's clothing—torn, stained with blood, and far too lightweight for the cold weather outside. She undid the fasteners and let her clothes fall to the ground. Her entire body bore the marks of the blows; it was a multi-colored map of the beating. The bruises climbed up her body to her face like a vine, and she also had a medicated bandage on her wrist. If she was going to see Hericio, she might have to hide all that with makeup.

Still naked, she walked to the kitchen area. She was as hungry as an ox, and the smell of toast and coffee Lizard had left floating in the air made her mouth water in anticipation.

"Screen, I'm Bruna," she instructed.

"I have authorization for two Brunas. Please give me your second name," replied the soft female computer voice.

The rep got annoyed. How come two Brunas? So that reptile Lizard spent his life bringing women to his apartment?

"I'm Bruna Husky," she growled.

"Welcome, Bruna Husky. What can I do for you?"

The rep ordered a gigantic breakfast and devoured it as she continued to mull over her bad mood. Then she had a vapor shower and ransacked Lizard's wardrobe in search of warm clothes, vaguely relishing the thought that something would finally be too big for her: she was used to always having to wear trousers that were too short and left her shins exposed. She had opened the door and was already leaving the apart-ment when she suddenly turned and went back inside.

"Screen, I'm Ingrid," she said, forcing her voice to sound higher-pitched.

It was a name that had become fashionable a few decades earlier, and the streets were teeming with a ridiculous num-ber of Ingrids; maybe Lizard had authorized one of them. In reality, she was using the name just to see how readily the man granted his domestic privileges.

"You are not Ingrid. You are Bruna Husky. How can I help you?" replied the electronic voice with an unshakable amiability.

The most recent computers were hopelessly tricky beasts to fool.

She walked out into a frozen Madrid that seemed to be wrapped in white lace. There was barely any traffic on the roads and half the travelators weren't working, despite teams of machine operators trying to unfreeze them with steam guns. The ground was crunchy and slippery even for her genetically enhanced sense of balance and motor coordination. Here and there, humans lacking these improvements were taking horrendous tumbles. *That could well be another reason for hating reps,* the android said to herself acidly. Bulky thermal clothing and big hoods had the advantage of making everyone look the same, even more so if, like her, they were wearing sunglasses to shield them from the glare. It was virtually impossible to recognize what sort of being each person was, which was a relief because the public screens continued to spew hatred despite the cold. They were all talking about an imminent crisis within the regional government. The subway was running normally, but it was bound to be packed, and Bruna didn't fancy being confined in a small space with a horde of furious humans, so she decided to walk to the Majestic. The thermometers were showing minus ten degrees Fahrenheit. It wasn't surprising that there were so few people walking, or that the travelator operators seemed to be moving with the unreal slowness of astronauts at zero gravity, slowed down as they were by layers and layers of cheap thermal fabric. The sky was the deep blue shade of Chinese lacquer and contrasted perfectly with the as yet untainted white of the recently fallen snow. There was no wind and the cold was amazingly quiet. Bruna began to enjoy her walk.

Why hadn't the murderers of the mem pirate killed her? There was no question they had had the opportunity to do so. And if they didn't want to kill her, why had they assaulted her? They could have left without any difficulty and without being seen, so why take a risk by attacking her? Did they want to give her a fright? Did they intend to injure her just seriously enough to remove her from the scene? Or maybe they did it to steal her plasma gun. That possibility was disturbing. She'd have to pluck up the courage to ask Lizard if he had found it.

On another tack, who knew that she was going to see the murdered memorist? Pablo Nopal, naturally. But it seemed unnecessarily complex and absurd for Nopal to arrange a meeting with the mem pirate, lend him his own house, kill the man while Bruna was there and then give her a beating as well. It didn't seem logical that Nopal would think up such a complicated script when he could surely have carried out his plan at other times and in a much simpler way. Or maybe not. What if the pirate hadn't trusted her? What if Nopal had made the mem pirate come to the house by using her as bait? What if the subsequent attack on her was nothing more than a smokescreen to obscure the murder? And after all, wasn't Nopal an expert in writing complex scripts? Apart from also being an expert killer, according to Lizard.

But Lizard wasn't out of the woods yet either—that unsettling man who always appeared and disappeared at the most opportune moments. That impenetrable giant who had already twice saved her from enigmatic assailants. Twice in less than a week. Too much of a coincidence, the memorist would have said. Not to mention his strange kindness, the offers of collaboration, and the unsought friendship. And why had he drugged her the previous evening? What had he been doing during the hours she was sleeping? Going through her belongings, no doubt; that was how he must have found Annie's mobile. Had he gone over to look through her apartment as well? Did that nosy Lizard know of the existence of Annie Heart, of Bruna's work as a dual personality, of the rooms she'd rented at the Majestic? The police had also been infiltrated, according to Myriam Chi. They must have been; this was a massive operation.

Four years, three months, and thirteen days. Thinking about the possible—or even probable—betrayal by the inspector made her ill. It would leave her entirely on her own again, so alone with her limited time and her death sentence; as abandoned as the wild bears before they became extinct, as Virginio Nissen had explained to her in their last session. Bruna recalled the psych-guide because she was passing close by the Health Arcade where Nissen had his consulting rooms. Moved by a sudden impulse, the rep changed direction and headed for the arcade. A few feet from the entrance, she crossed paths with a young woman who was crying and who brushed past her with the warm breath of her pain. *Each of us carries a personal burden*, as Yiannis used to say.

There weren't many people in the galleries of the arcade, and at least a third of the stores were shut. The managers probably hadn't been able to get there because of the snow. Nevertheless, the rep noticed at least two changes since her last visit. The first was that they'd opened a Memofree store, the popular franchise for erasing memories. Although memory manipulation technology had been around for almost a hundred years, Memofree used modern, revolutionary technology invented by Gay Ximen. Ximen's great discovery had reduced costs to such an extent that the procedure was now within the reach of ordinary people. "Selective memory erasure from 300 gaias," proclaimed the neon sign in the window, although Bruna knew that it could cost six or seven thousand Gs to get rid of the long, complex memories that affected various parts of the brain. "Quick, permanent, safe and painless: forget your suffering without suffering. Fully compatible with technohumans. It works. 100 percent guaranteed." The Ximen33 had been sweeping people's heads clean for decades already, and there were people addicted to the machine who, pathologically incapable of putting up with even the tiniest unpleasantness, would go once a month to have tiny prickles removed from their memories—an unpleasant argument, a fleeting lover they wished they'd never had, a party at which they hadn't sparkled. But there were also people who refused to use the machine even though they were carrying a stone in their hearts. Like Yiannis. Or like Bruna herself. She wanted to go on remembering Merlín no matter how much it might hurt. The human who had come out of the arcade crying might have been someone who had pulled out at the last minute, preferring to go on clinging to her pain. *We are also our pain*, thought Bruna.

The other change was an art exhibition on the ground floor of the arcade. It was alien art, of the Gnés to be precise, perhaps sponsored by the Gnés doctor who had his rooms on the first floor. The pictures, magnificent superrealistic holographs, floated halfway up the central hall. They were enormous works, twelve feet by twelve feet or bigger, totally and perfectly black. Rectangles of a continuous and deep darkness that, at first glance, all looked the same but which, when you stopped to look at them closely, showed themselves to be distinct, dizzying, and swirling in their blackness. They were a darkness full of movement and light, images that were hauntingly strange. The artist's name was Sulagnés and, if you looked closely, the black sparks that seemed to move within the pictures formed, and incessantly repeated, the one phrase

Agg'ié nagné 'eggins anyg g nein'yié

Bruna pointed the lens of her mobile at the letters, and the curved screen hugging her wrist instantly translated the sentence:

What I do shows me what I am seeking.

Beautiful, she thought, impressed by the alien's reflection. That was how it was; that was exactly how it was. That was her work as a detective, and that was life. It was dramatic to discover that the mind of a *bicho* could be so similar to hers. Vast interstellar abysses pulverized by the magic power of one small shared thought.

Bruna dragged herself away from her contemplation of the pictures with a degree of sorrow and made her way to the shop with the essentialist tattoos. She had, in fact, originally decided to visit the arcade because of Natvel. Fortunately, the store was open, and as she went in she recognized the smell of oranges, the amber half-light, the quiet, soothing atmosphere. Everything was so like it had been on her first visit that she seemed to have jumped back in time. Again, the beaded curtain stirred with a murmur like running water as the diminutive but strong body of the tattooist—male or female?—passed through it.

"I knew you'd come back," rumbled Natvel with his deep baritone voice.

And a very feminine smile appeared on his beautiful, oriental-idol face.

"Oh, yes?"

Bruna really liked the essentialist, but his shamanic airs made her nervous. Just then she had detected a certain tone of triumphant solemnity in Natvel's voice that didn't augur well.

"I knew you'd finally want to know your essential form."

"Oh. Great, but..."

"I know who you are, I know what you are."

"I'm delighted, but I don't want to know. That's not why I've come."

Natvel sighed and crossed his hands over his belly. He was the picture of patience. A small, imperturbable Buddha.

"I just wanted to ask you something: Those Labaric power tattoos, are they done with a laser?"

The question shook the tattooist sufficiently to stir him— *no, her*—out of her impassivity.

"By the universal breath, of course not! No energy tattoo can be done with that amateurish instrument."

"Energy tattoo?"

"One that's capable of transforming or disturbing the person who bears it...living signs that alter your life. There are positive energies, like essentialist tattoos, and negative ones, like the Labaric script of power; but in either case, it has been proven that the laser interrupts the flow of energy."

"I see. So then if someone does a tattoo with a laser using the Labaric script of power—"

"It would be an obvious and crude imitation. A forgery. And the tattoo would have no effect."

"And who might do something like that?"

Natvel frowned as she distractedly but energetically poked around inside her ear with her index finger. Then she examined the end of her finger, squinting a little, and wiped the wax on her tunic.

"Well, not a lot of people. In the first place, the Labaric writing of power isn't well known. It's a well-guarded secret. I've only ever seen two words written with that script. One was years ago, and I couldn't copy it. And the other was Jonathan's name, which I showed you the other day. So, although everyone has heard of that evil writing, virtually no one really knows what it's like. But you recognized the signs, didn't you?"

Bruna thought for a second: *yes, indeed. The* n *in* revenge *was exactly like the* n *in* Jonathan.

"Yes."

"So it's someone who knows the alphabet, and I can assure you, that knowledge is possessed by only a few. On the other hand, nobody in their right mind would devote themselves to forging a Labaric script. It's fierce and powerful writing and something pretty awful could happen to you if you went down that path..."

"So I assume that means that whoever did it is not a believer in that..." Bruna was going to say *nonsense*, but she contained herself. "...In those esoteric things."

"Oh, no, it makes no difference if you believe or not. I've already told you that the script of power is a well-guarded secret. If you do something unacceptable with it, you run the risk of an unpleasant visit from the Labarians, who are already unpleasant enough in their own right even at the best of times.

Why do you think I haven't displayed Jonathan's tattoo on the public screens? Why do you think I haven't sent it to the archive? As you've seen, I don't make a mystery of it, I don't mind showing you the word. But from that to publishing it, to officially revealing it…Let's just say that I look out for myself."

It seemed a sensible observation. So it had to be someone who was either totally unaware of the risks—unlikely, given the scale of the operation—or else sufficiently powerful not to be scared off by reprisals from the mafia sect otherwise known as the Ones. And who on Earth could feel safe from them? The entire planet was infested with a heaving mass of henchmen and spies from Cosmos and the Kingdom of Labari. Double and triple agents who took advantage of the weakness of the Earthling state, still too unstructured post-Unification and full of security holes, like any democratic system.

"You really don't want to know?" asked Natvel.

"What?"

"You don't want to know who you are?"

"I know perfectly well who I am."

"I doubt it."

And Bruna, mortified, had to acknowledge that deep down she was in effect far from being sure about this. But she would never admit it.

"Natvel, thanks for your help. You've again been most kind and very helpful, but I'd rather you didn't tell me what you see in me."

"Your essential design. Your form. What you are."

"Yes, that. It's all the same to me. I don't want to know."

"If it really made no difference to you, you wouldn't mind my telling you. There's a part of you that believes. That's why you're scared."

Stop bothering me, thought Bruna, irritated. *Stop pestering me.* "I have to go. Thanks again."

She smiled a tight little smile, and quickly left the store. Behind her she could still hear the essentialist's words: "That line which cuts your body! Not only does it divide you, it's also a rope that binds you."

The door to the store, with its old hinges, slammed too forcefully against the frame as it shut behind Bruna. Natvel was a good sort, but visionaries got on the detective's nerves.

She left the Health Arcade and strode off toward the Majestic, despite occasionally feeling a stab in her damaged ribs. The air was so dense and cold that it almost seemed to have a physical consistency; her body opened a path through the air like an icebreaker through a frozen sea. She was walking along looking at the ground, concentrating on where she was stepping, when her ears caught a phrase that shocked her: "And it was about time this government, which was leading us into a catastrophe, fell..."

She looked up. It was a message on a public screen. All the screens were heaping rabid personal allegations on Inmaculada Cruz, the eternal regional president. Bruna activated the latest news on her mobile and learned that the government crisis that had been brewing for the past few days had finally exploded in the middle of the cold snap. President Cruz had resigned and an obscure politician called Chem Conés had provisionally assumed power. The detective wikied the name Conés and looked at his biography: extremist, racist, a disciple of Hericio. His first resolution as acting president had been to remove all reps in government from their positions. "It's a temporary measure to protect them and to protect us; we're investigating the existence of a possible technohuman conspiracy and we still don't know if any of our government colleagues are implicated. If they haven't done anything wrong, they have no cause for concern, but for those who are trying to deceive us, I have to tell you that we will follow this through to the bitter end," thundered the man in front of a swarm of journalists. Other screens showed Hericio waving triumphantly to a crowd. "The leader of the HSP is the only one who can save us in these dangerous times," declared María Lucrecia Wang, the famous author of interactive novels. "I trust only Hericio," said Lolo Baño, the soccer player. The android shuddered. By all the martyred reps, what the devil was going on? The supremacist leader had gone from being an outrageous, marginal player to the Great White Hope. She anxiously inhaled a mouthful of freezing cold air because she was feeling choked. She had a worrying, almost physical sense that reality was closing in on her bit by bit, like a cage.

She entered the hotel, went up to Annie's room and, before applying her makeup, spoke to Lizard and explained to him what Natvel had told her about the Labaric script. The inspector was serious and taciturn. When she'd finished telling him about her visit to the essentialist, a long, uncomfortable silence descended over them.

"And nothing else?" Paul finally asked.

"That's all Natvel told me."

"But you, you've got nothing else to tell me?"

"What do you want me to tell you?"

"I have no idea…that's for you to say…about the illegal mobile, about what you're up to. What are doing in the Majestic Hotel right now, for example?"

Bruna lost her temper.

"I'm sick of you tracking me."

Paul looked at her severely.

"Bruna, things are really bad. I'm not sure you realize this. They're very bad in general, and they're bad for you. We've found Dani dead."

"Dani? So, who's Dani? Another rep victim?"

The face of a human appeared on the screen.

"You don't know who this is, Bruna?"

Yes, she knew...or she should know. That face rang a bell. The android put her hands over her eyes and made an effort to remember. She reconstructed the woman's features deep inside her mind and imagined them moving and alive. And then she recognized her. She uncovered her face and looked at Paul.

"She's one of the people who attacked me the other night when I was going home. It's the woman who seemed to be the leader of the group."

Paul nodded his head slowly.

"Dani Kohn. A racist activist. And a well-to-do young woman. The daughter of Phi Kohn Reyes, the director-general of Clean Water. A multimillionaire businesswoman. A bigwig. They're hassling us over her death."

They were silent again for a moment.

"When was the last time you saw her, Bruna?"

The rep put up her guard. A mix of fear and anger rose in her throat.

"When she tried to split open my head that night. That was the first and only time I saw her. What sort of question is that? What are you trying to insinuate? What are you after, Lizard?"

"They killed her with a small plasma gun—with *your* gun, Bruna. It's covered with your fingerprints and DNA."

Bruna expelled the air that she hadn't even realized she was holding in. A cold sweat spread across her back.

"Ah, the gun. It's true. I did have a plasma gun. An illegal weapon, yes. I admit it. But they took it from me. Yesterday, when the killers of the memorist attacked me. And I now think they probably attacked me for that reason: to take my weapon so they could incriminate me."

Paul nodded, tight lipped. An intense emotion hardened his features. Pent-up anger, maybe. Or sadness, perhaps.

"I shouldn't have told you all this. You're a suspect. I know you didn't shoot Dani, because she died early this morning and at that hour, you were in my apartment, sleeping, sedated, with me."

That *with me* gave the rep a strange feeling in her stomach.

"But you're hiding things from me, Bruna. I shouldn't trust you. Maybe it's true that a techno conspiracy is underway, who knows? I distrust humans and reps equally. We can all be sons of bitches. So it may well be that you want to kill me."

"Or maybe what's happening is that someone is trying to set a trap for me."

Yes. That would be the most satisfactory hypothesis. The trouble is that I don't trust satisfactory hypotheses. We tend to believe them no matter what logic might tell us."

"Maybe. Maybe it's simpler than that. When they attacked me, I remember firing a shot. Maybe Dani was one of the assailants; maybe I wounded her at that point and she died hours later."

"She was executed, Bruna. A shot to the back of her head next to her ear, point-blank range. Instant death. And it happened at around five o'clock this morning."

"So?"

"So stop lying to me and tell me everything."

How could she explain that she didn't trust him—that, in a certain way, she was afraid of him? And yet Bruna breathed in deeply and told Lizard everything he didn't yet know. She told him about Annie Heart and her appointment with Hericio. She felt like someone allowing herself to fall down a slippery, icy path, putting up with the vertigo and the fear of crashing at the bottom.

"Who knew about your meeting with the mem pirate?"

"I've been thinking about that already. Nopal, of course. And Habib, but he didn't know the time or the place. And my friend Yiannis, but he's above suspicion."

And you, she thought. *You knew about it, too, Lizard.*

"No one's above suspicion," grunted the man.

It was the last thing he said before he cut off, and the sentence left the rep with a sense of unease. Suddenly she remembered Maio. The alien was capable of reading her mind and so might have picked up on her meeting with the memorist. He was, moreover, from an extragalactic civilization, a remote world to which he could retreat without any fear of reprisals from Labaric thugs. Yes, of course, Maio was supposedly a political exile and would be in danger if he returned to his planet, but to what extent could she believe him? Even more to the point, what did Earthlings know about *bichos*? And what if the aliens were trying to stir up violence between the species in order to destabilize Earth and in this way be able to colonize it, as xenophobic groups maintained? Bruna was ashamed of her thoughts and pushed down her irrational fear until it was buried deep within her. It was unlikely that the immense distance that separated the two worlds would encourage a colonialist adventure.

But the possibility remained that Maio might be implicated in some conspiracy. For money, perhaps. Now that she thought about it, wasn't it surprising that the Omaá had suddenly appeared in her bed? And what should she make of his insistence at standing guard at her front entrance? *By the great Morlay, what a paranoid world!* Bruna said to herself with sudden disgust. Not only was she suspicious of everyone individually, but to make matters worse, it was also enough for someone to treat her with affection for them to be deemed even more suspicious.

She missed her huge, half-finished jigsaw puzzle; she needed to relax and the puzzle was the best way for her to switch off quickly. But there wasn't much time, so she carefully put on her makeup and pulled on her Annie Heart wig. Wrapped in the hotel's bathrobe, she used her mobile to log in to an Express store and bought a thermal wardrobe for her character. While she was waiting for the robot to arrive, she spoke with Yiannis and sent Habib a message. Both of them were worried about the political situation. The clothes took barely twenty minutes to arrive—Express stores were expensive but efficient. She dressed herself in a pink jumpsuit that matched a padded jacket she thought was hideous but which blonde Annie would undoubtedly adore, and then—the perfectionist's touch—she took two necklaces she'd brought along for the occasion out of the safe in the room. Nothing like a piece of jewelry to finish off her disguise as a conventional, intense young woman. She immediately rejected the light pectoral, which didn't go with her thermal clothes, and picked the other piece, her favorite: an ancient ivory *netsuke*, a smiling little man with a sack over his shoulder who hung from a string of rubies and little gold beads. The necklace was part of her packet of fake mementos; her mother had supposedly given it to her before she died. The *netsuke* was an unusual object, as the package of technohuman souvenirs always consisted of simple, ordinary objects: children's toys, holographs, cheap rings. However, Bruna had taken the *netsuke* to a specialist, who had certified that it was a genuine seventeenth-century Japanese piece from the Edo era. An extremely extravagant piece. Yet it wasn't the *netsuke*'s financial value that Bruna appreciated but its unique grace and even the emotion it awoke in her. Despite knowing that her mother had never existed, she couldn't help loving the *netsuke* with an affection that seemed to come from the depths of her impossible childhood. Whenever she wore the little man with his sack, she felt protected. And she needed to be protected when she confronted Hericio, whose status had so recently grown. She put on the necklace, checking that the clasp was well secured, and after a final glance in the mirror, went downstairs to the hotel bar, swaying her hips with the help of the high nonslip heels on her feminine snow boots, which were also pink and revolting.

When she sat down at the bar stool, it was 15:40. The bar was empty and the waiter darted solicitously toward her. Bruna ordered a vodka and lemon and a pile of cold sandwiches that she quickly proceeded to devour—she didn't want to be caught fainting with hunger during her interview with Hericio. When Serra arrived, she still had one left on her plate.

"The enigmatic Annie Heart," said the supremacist by way of a greeting.

He didn't look very happy.

"You're not playing dirty tricks on me, are you, Annie? I really wouldn't like that."

"And what makes you think I would be? Would you like a sandwich?"

Serra shook his head. He wasn't taking his eyes off her.

"Good," said the rep, wolfing down the sandwich with delight. It had cheese and nuts. *Bartolo would have loved it*, Bruna thought ludicrously.

"What happened to you?"

"When?" she mumbled with her mouth full.

"There. And there. You're covered with bruises."

The detective took her time chewing and swallowing. Then she answered dryly: "An accident."

"What sort of accident?"

"Traffic."

"You were knocked over by a car?"

"I was knocked over by the fists of two technos."

Serra looked at her attentively, doubtful but impressed.

"Really?"

"Well, if truth be told, I had told them they should get out of my way, that they should get off the travelator."

"And?"

"They didn't."

"That's why you weren't answering your calls."

"I was at the hospital."

Have you reported them?"

"No. What for? Those replicking judges would never do anything to them. That's where we're at, as you know. Total impunity for the monsters."

"Do you know who they are? Point them out to me and you'll see where their impunity gets them," bragged Serra, thrusting out his chest.

"No, you can do something better than that for me. You can provide me with a plasma gun."

"A gun? That's a big word."

"But I'm sure that if anyone can get hold of a weapon, it's you," cooed Bruna, flattering him.

The man swaggered visibly in appreciation of the praise. "Well, I don't know. It's not easy."

"I need it. I need that gun, don't you understand? A small plasma one; I don't need anything more than that. And of course I'm prepared to pay what it's worth. Are you going to allow them to hit me again without punishment when you could prevent it? Life is becoming too violent, and the immediate future looks set to be worse. All good humans should be carrying weapons."

Serra nodded.

"Yes. Absolutely. It's part of our agenda. We're reclaiming our right to defend ourselves. Well, I'll see what I can do. And now, let's go. Hericio's expecting you."

Bruna stood up. She was a head taller than the supremacist deputy. She placed her hand on the man's inflated chest.

"But you have to get it for me now. I'm leaving for New Barcelona tomorrow."

And to add weight to her request, Bruna-Annie briefly rested her head on the man's shoulder, although she had to bend down to do it.

"You are going to help, aren't you?" she asked affectionately.

Serra displayed a fatuous smile of superiority for all the world to see.

"Yes, woman. Relax. You can be sure that you'll have your little gun."

And grabbing Bruna by the elbow with the air of a happy proprietor, he led her out of the bar.

The things you had to do to get your hands on a weapon.

CHAPTER TWENTY-SEVEN

Bruna thought that the meeting would take place in some quiet, isolated place, but they headed for the HSP headquarters. It wasn't exactly the most discreet place in the city right now. A crowd was swirling around in front of the main entrance despite the prevailing cold: journalists, police, and supporters of every shape, color, and class. The supporters seemed suddenly to have multiplied exponentially. On the opposite sidewalk, some twenty Apocalyptics were banging their drums and announcing the end of the world with uncharacteristic joy. Serra shoved his way through the crowd and the android followed in his wake. They crossed the police cordon without any difficulty and then the party's security line, which was composed of very nervous young men. As they went through, the deputy arrogantly told them to remain alert; the order was unnecessary, but he was enjoying the ease with which doors forbidden to others were being opened for him, the crowds of people looking at him, and being in the leadership of a party that had turned itself into a star product overnight. He was walking so tall, with his shoulders back and his head held high, that he seemed to have grown several inches. Above them, one of the public screens was showing them as they went in. Someone in attendance was sending through the images. Serra swelled with pride and wrinkled his brow a little more, playing the role of important-politician-very-concerned-about-the-situation to the hilt.

"Things have reached boiling point," he commented once inside the lobby.

And he couldn't hold back a happy, toothy little grin.

It was a squalid office building, and the HSP was on the fourth floor in a large, ramshackle space with winding corridors and narrow cubicles everywhere. The door on the landing was permanently open, and hordes of people were going in and out. An air of chaotic, frenetic activity prevailed.

"Follow me."

They went through a maze of cheap, sliding partitions and windowless inner spaces lit by faint residual light.

"This is a labyrinth. It's served us well until now and it was cheap, too. But given how big this has become, we'll have to move to a more appropriate location."

They reached an office that was better furnished, and stopped in front of a desk manned by a youth whose chest was crisscrossed with straps and who had two plasma guns under his armpits. *What a nerve*, thought Bruna. *How powerful they think they are.*

"He's expecting us," Serra growled at the guard.

The youth nodded without saying a word and tapped the screen on his mobile. A reinforced door behind him opened with a click.

"Go in by yourself. When you leave, ask for me," said the deputy.

There was a short corridor on the other side of the door, and at the end of it, another reinforced door that unlocked when Bruna got to it. She opened it. Hericio's office was large and rectangular, with two more doors on the right and a big picture-window. Hericio was standing next to it, gazing out pensively, and the android had the feeling that this was a scene prepared especially for her—that, like Serra, Hericio was playing the role of leader-calmly-contemplating-his-historic-responsibility. Bruna crossed the room, ostentatiously swaying her hips, fully in the role of Annie the Destroyer. *If there are going to be performances, everyone should perform,* she said to herself.

"Annie, Annie Heart. Finally, I get to meet you," said the man, shaking her hand. "Come, let's sit over here; we'll be more comfortable."

They arranged themselves on the synthetic leather arm-chairs. The picture window, Bruna observed, wasn't real. It was nothing more than a projection of a street on a constant loop, similar to the images in the mem pirate's house—or, rather, Pablo Nopal's house. In reality, the office was like a strong room, with all the doors armor-plated and no access from the outside. The pretend window, the artificial leather, and the fake leader.

"I understand you want to make a donation to the party. I apologize for getting right down to business, but as you can see I'm very busy. Things are moving very quickly and I don't have any time to lose," he said pompously.

Then, as he listened to himself speaking, he thought he might have been too impolite.

"Or rather, in your case, no time to enjoy, to relax, to converse. I haven't much time to talk to you, something I regret."

"That's fine, Hericio, I understand. And I'm grateful to you for seeing me during these difficult times. But you also have to understand that I want to be sure that my money is going to end up in the right place."

"Rest assured. With an FP, you'll know what your money has been spent on down to the last G. Everything will be used for the party, of course. Speaking of which, our permit is on the point of expiring. We'd have to process your contribution within the next ten days."

"That's not a problem and that's not what concerns me. I'm even prepared to invest funds outside the law. What I need to know is whether the HSP is deserving of it—whether *you* are worthy of it."

Hericio lifted his chin with an angry, nervous twitch.

"Have you seen all those people downstairs? Out on the street? All those people asking us to intervene and save the situation? Look, Annie Heart, years ago during our period in the wilderness, we might have been desperate for your support, but today...You're the one who's asked to see me. If you want to participate in this transformational project, if you want to collaborate in the rebirth of humanity, then do it. And if you don't, you can happily leave by that door."

The tone in the man's voice had become increasingly pompous, and he ended his speech as if he were at a rally. That was why he'd received her today—and here—at party headquarters: to impress her with his success. He was a salesman and he was selling his party, which was on the rise. The rep fluffed up her hair with her hand and smiled, unperturbed.

"Well, all I can say is that it's in your best interest to convince me."

Bruna's aplomb disconcerted the politician. He leaned back in his chair, put his fingertips together in the manner of a preacher and scrutinized her with distrust.

"May I ask how much money we're talking about?"

"Ten million Gs."

Hericio gave a start.

"You don't have that much money, Annie."

"It's not just mine. I didn't tell Serra, because it's information that shouldn't be out there and it's none of his business, but there's a group of top-level professionals and business-people from New Barcelona backing me—quite well-known people. We've formed a supremacist lobby group, a clandestine group, because we support direct action. We're fed up with the traditional parties, who've led us into this despicable situation. But we've been thinking that the HSP might perhaps be different. We've followed you, we've listened to what you have to say, and we've liked what we've seen. And when we saw you were asking for an FP, we thought it was a good opportunity, and that it might be an indication that you were planning something. Although I have to tell you that we're still not convinced that you really are our man."

Hericio's face was a catalog of contradictory emotions: vanity, greed, distrust, excitement, fear, indecision. Greed won out.

"And what would I have to do to convince you?"

"Better to ask what *should you* have done. We believe in action, not words. So tell me what you really dedicate your-selves to here in the HSP."

The man looked stunned.

"I don't understand."

Bruna stared at him.

"Well then, let's speak frankly. In New Barcelona, some of us thought that the HSP had something to do with the recent replicant deaths—Chi and the others."

Now distrust won out. Hericio became so nervous that his voice sounded half a tone higher.

"Are you accusing us of murder?"

"We simply believed it was a marvelously thought-out campaign to incite resentment and awaken the sleeping conscience of the people. A stroke of genius in social agitation, really."

"Who do you think you are, suddenly appearing out of nowhere and accusing us of something like that?"

"I haven't come out of nowhere. I'm sure you've checked me out thoroughly. You know everything about me. I now see you even know how much money I have in the bank. I'm a competent and well-known academic. So now it's my turn to say to you what you said to me earlier. Trust me and show me that we can trust you, and the ten million is yours. But if you don't want to, I'll quite happily leave by that door."

Hericio swallowed.

"I'm not sure what you're proposing. I don't even know if you really have all that money."

"And I'm not clear that we're on the same wavelength or if we're after the same thing."

There was a short, heavy silence.

"You're covered with bruises," said Hericio, pointing at her with his finger.

"They're birthmarks," the rep replied with caustic sarcasm.

The man looked at her with incredulity and then got back to their earlier topic.

"So what do you want me to tell you, Annie? I've celebrated every one of the rep murders—and the disgraceful end of that freak Chi, in particular. I was even delighted—and I'll deny this if you repeat it in public—with the murder of the humans caused by that techno who blew herself up, that Nabokov. Every death is a tragedy, even more so if the victims are children, as in that case. But that slaughter has been fundamental to raising people's awareness, and it's well known that you can't have revolutions without victims. If truth be told, it seems a fairly small price to pay if we can thereby save society from degenerating. But neither I nor my party has had anything to do with all that."

"I see. And from this point on, what are you intending to do?"

"Lead this change, of course. We are in touch with other supremacist groups on various parts of the planet. There have been quite a few protest movements throughout the world this past week—nothing comparable to ours, but it's obvious that there's a global reaction brewing against all these disgraceful acts."

"That's all very well, but I'm talking about the here and now—about deeds, not words. What, specifically, is your next step going to be? Because right now, what's needed is something really dramatic, a final incitement. For example, now would be the perfect moment for a rep to assassinate…Chem Conés, for example. Chem is one of your disciples, a known supremacist, and right now, as acting president of the region, he's the main focus of attention. Imagine what a magnificent incentive that death would be for the cause."

A flash of emotion lit up Hericio's face. Bruna leaned forward and whispered, "We could help you with that. Professional help, efficient, secure."

But the light had already gone out. The man stood up and began to walk around in circles.

"I'm not saying you're not right. A death like that would be most advantageous. A martyr. Yes, that's it, our cause needs a martyr," he babbled.

He came to a halt in the middle of the office and looked at her.

"But it can't happen. It can't happen. I'll never take part in something like that, nor will I allow the HSP to participate. And do you know why, Annie Heart? Do you know why? Not for lack of courage or decisiveness, nor because of any moralistic prudishness, because I'm well aware that the greater good far outweighs one small act of evil. But when you do something like that, you run the risk of being found out. It possibly won't happen in your lifetime, because probably while you're alive, you'll be able to arrange things so that everything remains hidden. But after you've gone? Then the historians and archivists arrive on the scene like vultures and poke around in everything. And I have to look after my reputation—you understand, Annie Heart? I'm destined to be one of the great figures of history. I'm the restorer of the human race. The savior. Future generations will speak of me with veneration and gratitude. And I have to look after that legacy! I mustn't give the enemy any excuses, because I won't be there to defend myself, to explain myself. To date, I haven't had to get my hands dirty, and I'm not going to start doing that now when I'm at the gateway to posterity."

He's serious, Bruna said to herself, astonished. So astonished in fact that she realized her mouth was open, and closed it. Of course, she had never expected that the racist leader would openly confess his part in the plot; she had only wanted to air the topic to see how he would take it. *Throw a line in the murky waters*, as Merlín used to say. But she wasn't expecting a reaction like this. The guy really believed what he was saying. He was an idiot. She had a feeling—she was almost certain—that Hericio had had nothing to do with the deaths of Chi and the other reps. Either that or he was a consummate actor. Suddenly, she felt a ring of fire squeezing her temples. It was the price she paid for the stress of pretending to be someone she wasn't and for humoring this repulsive supremacist. For appearing to hate reps and even believing it a little in order to be more convincing. All the dissembling had given her a splitting headache. *Four years, three months, and thirteen days.*

"Fine. I think I'm clear on your position," said the android, getting up from her chair.

"And what...what's going to happen with the money?"

"I'll talk it over with the others" was Bruna's ambiguous answer.

Hericio's face crumpled ruefully, as he mentally waved good-bye to the ten million.

"We could do many things together," he pointed out accommodatingly when they were already at the door.

"We could. If you change your mind about what I've said, leave a message under my name at the Majestic Hotel. I'll call there daily for the next month to check."

The door closed behind her, and Bruna gave a small sigh of relief. She walked down the short corridor to the office. The youth with the straps and guns was still there, but what was worse, so was Serra. *By the great Morlay*, the migraine was drilling through her skull. The deputy approached her, cocky and smarmy.

"A robot will bring what you wanted to your hotel in two hours' time. You'll have to pay him in cash. Five big ones. Friend's price."

Five hundred Gs for a plasma gun. Not a bad price at all. If it worked.

"So I thought we could go to your room to wait for the robot," murmured Serra, moving closer to her.

Bruna put a hand on his shoulder and pushed him away. She intended to do it gently, but she was tired, and it must have ended up being too hard, because the deputy became angry.

"Hey, what's going on! You've gotten all you wanted from me and now you're trying to dump me? You think I'm the sort of person a blonde like you can laugh at?"

Uh-oh, the usual fireworks. Chest thumping like a gorilla to scare her. Bruna breathed in and tried to contain herself and concentrate in between the lashes of pain whipping across her forehead.

"It wouldn't even occur to me to laugh at you, Serra. What's happening is that I'm not feeling well. I have a horrendous headache. Now, you have two options: you can either believe what I'm saying and let me have a rest and, if you like, we can see each other tomorrow afternoon, or you can assume it's the typical excuse and kick up a fuss and we ruin our fun. You choose."

"You were leaving tomorrow."

"In the evening."

Serra thought for a moment, sulking.

"It's true that you don't look well."

"It's true that I don't feel well."

The guy stepped back and let her past.

"What time tomorrow?"

"Four o'clock."

"I'll cancel the robot. I'll tell it to make the delivery tomorrow afternoon," he grumbled, pointing his finger at her.

"It's up to you," growled Bruna as she left.

Nobody saw her out and she became lost in the rambling corridors. It took her forever to find the main exit, and another eternity to make her way through the tight and ever-growing crowd packing the street. When she managed to reach the opposite sidewalk, she leaned against the wall and vomited.

"Repent, sister! The world will end in four days," trilled an Apocalyptic next to her.

She threw up again. That damn migraine was killing her.

CHAPTER TWENTY-EIGHT

Hericio, somewhat disconsolate, stood gazing at the door through which the explosive Annie Heart had disappeared. It was tough to renounce ten million Gs, especially now that they needed to move to better headquarters and acquire the level of representation that their new leadership role demanded. *But principles are principles*, he told himself emphatically, and the fact that he had been capable of choosing glory over despicable money made him feel lofty. His eyes suddenly became moist, an emotional tearfulness brought on by his own greatness.

Then he heard a very soft sound behind him, a rustle of clothing or a footstep, and he knew that Ainhó was there, that she'd come into his office through the back door. Her inopportune entry irritated him, and he cursed himself for having given her the access code; what was he thinking at the time? He blinked a few times in an attempt to rid his eyes quickly of tears, repressed his bad humor and turned around. Ainhó, arms folded, was smiling at him.

"This mania of yours for coming and going like a ghost is beginning to annoy me," said the politician, without being able to avoid a touch of acrimony.

"You used to welcome my coming to see you," Ainhó replied, without losing her smile.

"Did I? Perhaps. But now I'm too busy. I don't know if you've noticed, but the situation has changed. Now I'm the solution, the renaissance, the future. People expect great things from me, and I'm going to deliver."

And as he was saying *people*, he swept his hand through the air in a broad, majestic gesture that seemed to take in the fake window, the virtual city visible through it, and even the whole world. Ainhó laughed.

"Have I noticed? My dear Hericio, I'm the one who's put you there!"

"*You*? I've been in politics for thirty years!" replied the man indignantly.

"Thirty years of exclusion from parliament."

"That's a—"

"Okay, fine, I withdraw it. And I ask your forgiveness. I don't want to argue with you. Let's enjoy some peace and quiet. Friends?"

Ainhó extended her hand, but Hericio was still too irritated.

"Friends?" she had to repeat.

There are few things as awkward as ignoring a person with an outstretched hand, so the politician relented and shook it, though reluctantly and with a wry face. Then he went and sat behind his desk. The desk was imposing, and the chair very tall; they made him feel powerful, and he wanted to overwhelm his visitor.

"So, I've already told you I'm very busy. Why have you come here? What do you want?" he grunted.

Ainhó delayed her response until she had sat down in a chair opposite the politician. Then she crossed her legs in a matter-of-fact manner and smiled again.

"Let's just say it's a courtesy visit. I've come to congratulate you on how well things are going for you, and to see how you are. How are you, Hericio?" she asked with what appeared to be genuine interest.

"Fantastic...ahem...although I seem to be...I'm losing my voice."

And now this, thought the supremacist, lifting his hand to his throat. He was becoming increasingly irritated.

"Aha! Losing your voice—so I hear. Returning to what we were saying. Don't you recall that I told you I'd make you famous? That I'd take you to the center of the political stage? That I'd turn you into the man of the moment?"

"I...don't..."

"You do, Hericio, you do. Back then you really were interested in what I had to say. We agreed that I'd mount an operation, a campaign to boost your image out there, and that of your party. You didn't want to know what the campaign would involve, and that was the right decision. In any event, I wouldn't have told you."

"I—"

"Wait a minute. Forgive me for interrupting you. If you don't mind, I'm going to take this off."

Ainhó pulled back the right sleeve of her jacket a little and, grabbing hold of a bit of skin at her wrist, pulled downward and peeled the skin off her hand. It looked as if she was removing the skin, but in reality, she was taking off a very fine transparent dermosilicon glove. She carefully put the object into an airtight bag and sealed it.

"Phew, that's a relief. No matter what they might say, you end up being allergic to these things. Getting back to what we were discussing, I want you to know that you form part of a vast operation. You thought you were hiring me, you thought that ridiculous amount of money you gave me was paying for a publicity campaign...You poor devil. I wasn't working for you; rather, *you* were working for *me*. You're my work, I've created you. And you're nothing more than a pawn within a grandiose master plan. So grandiose that it would never fit inside your pea brain. Nothing to say?"

"..."

"I see. I'd like to think that you're silent because you're embarrassed by your own stupidity, but I fear it's the result of the neuromuscular block I transmitted to you earlier through the glove when we shook hands. Contact poisons are incredibly ancient; they were used during imperial Roman times, the Middle Ages, the Renaissance. In these hypertechnological times of plasma guns and penetrating shots of nitrogen, I thought it elegant to resort to something classical—with a touch of modernity, of course. It's tetrapancuronium, a stronger, synthetic version of curare. An instant and devastating toxin. You become paralyzed within seconds, as you've been able to verify. You're unable to move. But you are able to see, hear, and feel. Within twenty minutes, the toxin paralyzes the respiratory muscles and the victim dies of suffocation. But don't worry, we won't get to that point. Everything clear so far? Any questions?"

"..."

"Ha-ha, forgive the tasteless joke. And forgive me as well for spying on you before when you were talking to Bruna. Well, you think she's Annie Heart, but in reality her name is Bruna Husky and she's a replicant! I'm sure that would make you shudder if you weren't paralyzed. Don't you find it repugnant that you received her here, in your own office?

That you conversed with her so amiably? That you lusted after her? Because I'm sure you desired her...so blonde, so hot, so voluptuous. Well, you and that rep said something very interesting, that the cause needs a martyr. And it's true. You're both right."

Ainhó calmly stood up and removed a sizable imitation leather sheath from the inside pocket of her jacket. It contained a large butcher's knife. She walked around the desk with the knife in her hand and approached the paralyzed Hericio.

"It's nothing personal. And I'm not one of those people who enjoy doing this sort of thing. No. But it's what has to be done, and I'm going to do it. Because I'm absolutely clear how far we have to go. And I'm also clear which path to take. As you can see, I'm going to use the knife now. Again, a traditional weapon. Much less elegant than poison, of course. But even older. Basic. Look, you've had the misfortune of landing in the middle of history's stampede, and that's why you're going to be trampled. I'm sorry, but you're the ideal martyr. Moreover, your martyrdom has to be outrageous. Spectacular. That's why I'm doing this...and this...hmmm, I'm trying to be quick, but it's not that easy, believe me. And on top of everything else, the wound stinks...yuck. Nearly there. I think I might make another cut here...Aha! And now, I'm removing the intestines with the tip of the knife...That's it, good, it looks terrific. It looks quite a lot like the threatening hologram Myriam Chi received. Remember what you were saying a short time ago? That business of the greater good far outweighing one small act of evil? Well, you've been my small act of evil for today, my poor Hericio. But wait, it can't be, are you moving an eye? Oh, no. No need for concern. It's only a tear."

CHAPTER TWENTY-NINE

He ought to have been pleased, because it was the reply he'd been looking for when he sent his memorandum, but he was in fact feeling nervous and intimidated. Yiannis had always been an orderly person, a meticulous and legalistic type, so breaking not one but two major administrative regulations was something that made him feel quite uneasy, despite the fact that he'd broken them knowingly. Moreover, the response had been much more immediate than he had expected, and that also heightened his anxiety. Less than an hour after he'd sent the memorandum, his supervisor's secretary had already summoned him to an urgent meeting. And it wasn't a holograph meeting but a meeting in person, something truly inconceivable. And on a Saturday to boot! So now here was Yiannis, sitting on an extremely modern sofa in the supervisor's antechamber, waiting to be received. He'd been waiting almost an hour, despite the secretary having told him to get there quickly. Of course, it could be premeditated, a tactic designed to wear him down and make him more nervous. And if that was what they were trying to do with this long wait, he had to admit that it was working. Yiannis stirred in his seat, and the sofa rocked gently in the air like a cot. Damned designer furniture.

"Yiannis Liberopoulos? Mrs. Yuliá will see you now."

Finally. The archivist followed the young woman who had come for him. She had a line of hair running down her long neck like a brush, in the Balabí style. Alien hairdos were very fashionable among young Earthlings, so now they all looked like horses with cropped manes.

"Come in, come in, Yiannis, my friend. Please sit down."

Yiannis, my friend? It was the first time in his life that he'd seen the woman. He hesitated momentarily, not really knowing where to seat himself, as the room was decorated in the latest minimalist style, with ethereal furniture that was barely visible. He finally opted for a line of bluish light and sat down on it with some trepidation. The line adapted itself to his body and provided support for his back. The supervisor was sitting in a similar chair behind a semitransparent table that merged with an enormous round screen. The decor must have cost a fortune. The Central Archive, one of the most powerful of the USE institutions, was owned by PPK, a huge private corporation, although the Central Planetary State had full voting rights on its board of management. And there was no question the archive was a fantastic business, since all the citizens on Earth had to pay a fee each time they accessed its resources.

"I have read your memorandum and in the first instance, I want to thank you for your interest and professional zeal. Because I'm sure you were motivated by the best of intentions. But you'll understand, in the whole time I've been in this position, no one has resorted to emergency protocol CC/1. I don't know if you're aware that when this protocol is activated, a copy of your message is automatically sent to the state's central administration. And to be honest, we all find that very tiresome. Government officials will now turn up, and they'll carry out an investigation."

"But that's fine, that's perfect. We need the USE security services to investigate the irregularities as a matter of urgency."

The supervisor turned her head to one side like a bird and fixed her eyes on Yiannis. She was a skinny, wiry woman with small, hard eyes that rarely blinked.

"Oh, Yiannis, Yiannis. Either I'm not explaining myself well or you're not understanding what I'm saying. Your memorandum was a mistake. An error. A case of overzealousness, to be precise." She was speaking gently, as if she felt sorry for the archivist, but there was a sharp edge to her voice.

"Overzealousness? But how? Have you actually read my memorandum? And the other documents? It's undeniable that someone is manipulating the entries."

"I have read everything, I have studied everything, and my experts have studied everything as well. There's nothing. You're imagining things. There's nothing more than a few small insignificant mistakes here and there. The usual errata."

"But—"

"The usual errata! Your behavior is much more serious than those trivial mistakes. You've removed an article from the editing process, interrupting the flow of information, and what's even worse, you've made an illegal, personal copy of a text that has not as yet been authorized. It's unacceptable behavior."

Yiannis noted that he was blushing. He couldn't avoid feeling that he was a criminal; it seemed unacceptable to him, too. The standard phrases of regret and apology began to form in his mouth.

"According to the General Law Governing Archives, removing an illegal copy can be deemed an act of espionage. You could go to jail for it," continued the woman.

The threat was so excessive and so obvious that Yiannis instantly swallowed the excuses he had been on the verge of offering. He snorted indignantly.

"I doubt that anyone would consider me to be a spy. I informed you instantly of my actions. I merely wished to alert you as soon as possible to the gravity of the situation."

"But what problem are you talking about? You're old, Yiannis, you're tired. You're imagining things. Didn't you say that Professor Ras didn't exist? Look."

The woman touched the computer and a cascade of images inundated the big screen: Lumbre Ras at home in New Delhi; Lumbre Ras at an interplanetary holograph conference; Lumbre Ras receiving his Nobel Prize—if that little olive-colored man really was Professor Ras, as the documentary entries Yiannis was looking at suggested. He was stunned; this very morning, barely a few hours ago, there was no one of that name on the Internet. Nothing. Lumbre Ras hadn't existed. And now information about him was inundating the screen. Yiannis felt dizzy for a moment. Could it be true that he had been mistaken, then?

"You see? There is no problem, Yiannis. *You* are the problem."

No. It wasn't a mistake. It was a conspiracy. Someone had falsified all those images and loaded them into the system in a few short hours. He felt his dizziness growing. He felt he was floating over an abyss.

"If you don't take my report seriously, I'll speak to the management committee," he said weakly.

"You're not going to speak to anyone, Yiannis Liberopoulos. You're fired. And, by the way, we've impounded your main screen."

"What? My computer? You've gone into my house? But how dare you," he stammered.

"Article 7C/7 of the Law Governing Archives—recovery of stolen material. We went with the police. All perfectly legal. And don't bother checking your mobile, because it no longer has the copy you made this morning. We've erased it remotely from your console. So you have nothing. And no job, either. And you can be grateful that we won't be pressing charges. And now, if you don't mind…"

Yiannis got up meekly and left the office and then the building like an automaton, barely aware of where he was going. They had fired him. The archive was his life and they had fired him. And on top of that, they had entered his house and removed his computer. And in addition, something terrible was happening—a coup d'état against the regional state or maybe the planet. His head was spinning and he was covered in cold sweat. He was so dazed that he didn't notice the car slowly coming toward him along the snow-covered street. A dark vehicle with tinted windows. In fact, he didn't see it until it was right on top of him. Until the car roared and rushed at him like a black cloud. Yiannis shrieked, jumped backward and twisted his ankle; the car skidded, skated over the ice and grazed him as it went past— Yiannis saved himself by a matter of inches. The archivist, barely breathing, was struck by a terrifying suspicion. *They've tried to kill me*, he thought. *They want to kill me.*

Just then, the vehicle managed to right itself. The tinted window on the driver's side was lowered and a man poked his head out and looked at him, enraged.

"Immmbeciiiiiile!" he yelled as he drove off.

Yiannis stood there, taken aback. And then he looked around. He was in the middle of the street. He made an effort to mentally reconstruct his last movements. He was so beside himself that he must have stepped off the sidewalk without paying attention to the traffic. The driver hadn't tried to run him over; Yiannis had thrown himself under the car's wheels without looking. His old heart was pounding in his chest and the ankle he'd just twisted was aching. Yes, he really was an imbecile.

CHAPTER THIRTY

Should it prove necessary, Nopal could disappear in under an hour. He had half a dozen secret apartments scattered throughout the world and a handful of fake identities at his disposal. In other words, Pablo Nopal wasn't always Pablo Nopal. In fact, half of the memorist's existence remained submerged in the dark waters of the invisible, like the artificial icebergs in the Bear Pavilion. Year after year, with persistence and a notable talent for the clandestine, the writer had been constructing himself a parallel life. Dummy companies, front men who had no idea for whom they were working, ID tags so perfectly forged that they were impossible to detect. (They were, in reality, genuine IDs produced by corrupt officials.) And a secret network of informers, because there's no power without knowledge. It might be true that money didn't provide happiness, thought the memorist, but it bought security, which was more important and less volatile than happiness. What more could a sensible man aspire to than to be reasonably protected from pain? Even if one had to resort to socially condemned means and prohibited behavior to achieve it.

Nopal had not chosen to be like this. He had not voluntarily chosen the path of illegality, in the same way that the socially marginalized do not choose to be marginalized but instead find themselves banished to the other side of the line of what is deemed normal. Destiny had been unfair to the memorist, destiny had treated the memorist brutally, and he had been forced to learn to defend himself and to respond to violence with violence. The true survivor is the one who doesn't hesitate to do whatever is necessary to survive, and Nopal was not the sort to hesitate. He often admired himself, observed his own behavior with a somewhat surprised curiosity, because he was unable to understand how it was possible for someone like him, who loved life so little, to be capable of hanging onto it so tenaciously, so fiercely. Maybe he did it out of pride, out of a firm decision never ever again to allow himself to be humiliated. Or maybe it was a question of cells behaving naturally, as they should, of the determination of the body to continue existing, of that feverish yearning to live that made many terminally ill people fight to their last breath to extend their existence despite their pain and deterioration. *Yes, the metaphor of the sick man isn't bad*, thought the memorist. Nopal had always felt that there was something pathological about him, something that suffered. Life was an accursed illness that ended up killing you.

CHAPTER THIRTY-ONE

B runa entered her hotel room almost blindly; visual distortion was one of the devastating side effects of her migraine. She lunged at her backpack and took out a paramorphine injection. She still had three left of the eight doses the hospital had given her. She injected one into her arm with trembling hands and fell onto the bed totally exhausted, waiting for it to take effect. She immediately felt the drug begin to course lightly through her body, putting an end to the throbs of pain, reaching past the back of her throat with the freshness of snow, sweeping away the maelstrom of bright corpuscles that were preventing her from seeing. What an indescribable relief!

She opened her eyes with a small start. So, she'd fallen asleep. She looked at her watch: she'd lost an hour but felt extraordinarily well. Rested and like new. She was in the room she'd hired as Bruna, although she was still wearing her human disguise. When she'd reached the hotel, she could only think of laying her hands on the paramorphine and had disregarded her usual work practices. She hoped that no one had seen her going into the room and that no one had checked the security tapes. It had been a mistake, but in any case she was going to leave the hotel right away. She jumped up and quickly began to rid herself of Annie Heart. When Husky reappeared in the mirror with the tattoo line scoring her body (dividing her, tying her down, as the essentialist put it), she felt strangely happy. It was like recovering an old friend.

She packed her bag and moved on to Annie's room to pick up her belongings in there as well. She had almost finished when someone knocked on the door.

"Damn."

She checked the screen and saw the image of a robot. She smiled, suddenly cheerful: she had just remembered the plasma gun. Maybe that cretinous Serra hadn't canceled the deal. When she opened the door, she saw that the robot was an old, battered courier. It probably didn't have visual verification capacity, which suited her. When the machine sensed Bruna's presence, it began to produce sentences on its display screen.

Package for Annie Heart

Delivery subject to personal verification

ID please

The detective took out the fake ID tag provided by Mirari and held it up to the robot's eye. The antiquated pile of metal gave a beep of confirmation.

ID accepted

Delivery requires prepayment

500 gaias in bills

Bruna went out into the corridor and walked to the automated teller machine that was on every floor next to the elevator. She paid for the two rooms, Annie's and her own, and then withdrew five hundred Gs from her account. She returned to the robot and put the money through the opening. The cover on the safety box opened and a pretty, electronic Thai massage kit appeared.

"Hey, what the devil?"

The robot was already disappearing down the corridor, squeaking as it went. Bruna was on the verge of making it come back and demanding the return of her money, but then she thought better of it. She went inside the room, cleared the top of the small table and opened the package. Inside was a strange, egg-shaped, silicon object with wheels and suction cups—presumably the Thai massage kit—capable of automatically massaging, sucking, and applying soothing oils as it traveled over your body. The contraption had a central opening through which to insert the various liquids, and when Bruna opened it, she found the plasma gun inside. An ingenious hiding spot: the shape of the weapon had been adapted to that of the massage machine. The gun looked homemade and ugly; it looked as if it had been made from recycled, mismatched parts. That explained why the gun was so cheap. She set the weapon to minimal charge and microimpact, pointed it to one side of the bed and fired. There was a slight, silent throb of light, then Bruna bent down and confirmed that there was a minuscule hole in the bedspread, something like the hole left by a moth. It looked like the ugly, junky machine did in fact work. Better than nothing. Things were becoming too dangerous to go around unarmed.

When she left the Majestic, night had already closed in but the air felt slightly warmer; the polar crisis was beginning to relax its grip. Although she was burdened by the weight of her bags, she didn't even try to catch a cab: it was a given that at that hour, with the fear that prevailed, no one would stop for a rep. The travelators were working again, and Bruna walked quickly to combat the cold and to escape from the barrage coming from the public screens, which continued to show pictures of violent technohumans, supremacist declarations, interviews with Chem Conés and Hericio, and news of other, similar disturbances happening in various corners of the USE. The screens were burning with racial hatred. Bruna wondered if the beginnings of the Rep War had been like this. Would the androids have felt just as persecuted, just as plague-ridden, in that fateful year of 2060? Would the Jews have felt the same in the twentieth century? Would they have sensed the beginning of their end in the same way that she now sensed the political and legal escalation in the campaign against technohumans? *Four years, three months, and thirteen days.* The way things were going, what tragedies could happen in the four years she had left? She didn't even know if she'd manage to live until her TTT. The future was crushing black rock, the roar of an avalanche.

**Central Archive, the United States of the Earth.
Modifiable version**

ACCESS STRICTLY LIMITED
AUTHORIZED EDITORS ONLY

Madrid, January 30, 2109, 10:30
Good morning, Yiannis

> ACESS DENIED
> YIANNIS LIBEROPOULOS IS AN
> UNAUTHORIZED EDITOR
> IF YOU DO NOT HAVE A VALID CODE
> QUIT THESE PAGES IMMEDIATELY

ACCESS STRICTLY LIMITED
AUTHORIZED EDITORS ONLY

> UNAUTHORIZED ACCESS IS A
> CRIMINAL OFFENSE
> PUNISHABLE BY IMPRISONMENT UP
> TO
> A MAXIMUM OF TWENTY YEARS

YIANNIS LIBEROPOULOS, YOU ARE ADVISED
TO QUIT THESE PAGES IMMEDIATELY.
ANY ATTEMPT TO PERSIST IN FORCING THE
SYSTEM WILL GENERATE AN ALERT TO THE
POLICE IN THIRTY SECONDS.

COUNTDOWN TO POLICE ALERT

29

28

27

26

25

24

23

22

21

CHAPTER THIRTY-TWO

B runa opened her eyes and confronted Yiannis's face an inch from her own, shouting and gesticulating anxiously.

"For heaven's sake!" she exclaimed, sitting upright.

A wave of unsteadiness rocked her world. The room shook, her head ached, her stomach turned somersaults. Her body reminded her—before her mind did—that once again she had had too much to drink the night before. The archivist's shape was flapping frantically around the room like a trapped sparrow. It was a damned holo-call.

"Yiannis, that's it. I'm canceling your holograph authorization right now," groaned the rep, steadying her head with her hands.

"They've fired me! It's a conspiracy! And I can't get into the archive! I tried to let you know last night but you weren't answering."

True enough. She had a clear recollection of refusing calls. She'd arrived home, tired and depressed, and started to drink. At other times she drank because she was happy and relaxed. Or then again, because she was distressed. She was always finding reasons to get drunk. Looking back, her short life was composed of a succession of nights she could scarcely

remember and countless mornings whose unpleasant beginnings she remembered all too well.

"Let me see...calm down and explain it to me again.
Slowly. As if I were a *bicho* and didn't understand your lan-
guage very well."

Yiannis began to rush through the story of his conversation with the supervisor.

"Okay, okay, I see. Look, it would be better if I came over
to your place. I'll be there in under an hour," said Bruna.

And she switched off, cutting the old man off midsentence.

Four years, three months, and twelve days.

She breathed in and stood up.

Nausea and dizziness.

She decided to give herself another paramorphine injection.
It wasn't the best way to get rid of a hangover; it was like killing flies with a plasma gun or cutting off a hand because of a
sore finger. But she knew she would feel better instantly if she
did, and these times were so unsettled that it seemed wiser to
go outside with all her wits about her. Anyway, her ribs were
still hurting a bit, she rationalized, in an attempt to exonerate herself as she injected the dose. One more to go. A pity.

She looked at herself in the mirror. She had slept in her
clothes again and they were all wrinkled and crumpled. She
was still wearing the genuine *netsuke* from her fake mother
around her neck. She decided to leave it on; she felt she needed
its company. Or its protection.

The outside thermometer was showing fifty-seven degrees;
the polar crisis was over. She had a brief shower with water,
chose a metallic green outfit from her closet and got dressed,
now feeling really well, rested and alert. And hungry, too. She
headed for the kitchen area to prepare herself something and

then she saw it—the puzzle was finished! Solved. She looked at it in amazement, and in among the shreds of fog that were blotting out the previous evening, she seemed to see herself placing the pieces. She must have been working on the jigsaw puzzle until all hours, and with extraordinary luck or superhuman determination. The image of the cosmos was complete and in the center, in the critical section that had previously been missing and had resisted her efforts for months, could now be seen the Helix planetary nebula, that spectacular gaseous object located in the constellation Aquarius that astronomers referred to as the "Eye of God." *The Helix, of course*, thought Bruna, almost disappointed at how obvious it was. How had she managed not to guess? The Helix was the most famous cosmic accident and there were even a couple of crazy sects that believed it was sacred. The final piece of the puzzle had triggered a small 3-D effect and the image seemed to vibrate and pulse with the vastness of space. A beautiful eye trimmed with filmy, reddish eyelashes and with an intensely blue iris; a giant eye looking at her. *What I do shows me what I am seeking.* She was seeking the Helix nebula; she was seeking something obvious, and she hadn't realized it. And she had had to get drunk and lose consciousness—she had had to allow herself to be guided by sheer intuition—in order to finish the jigsaw puzzle. The Eye of God. The lovely, cold, and indifferent eye that observes us.

After quickly eating some turkey-flavored protein burgers, she put the junky plasma gun in her backpack, convinced that the outside world was going to be somewhat more unpleasant than it had been the previous day, and headed out. And the good weather indeed seemed to have added fuel to the fire of hatred. Groups of demonstrators surrounded by police cordons were yelling out slogans that Bruna couldn't catch, while the public screens above her head were spewing forth torrents of violence. There were overturned cars, broken store windows, burning recycling containers. As she passed through the lung-park, she saw that several of the delicate artificial trees had been shredded and uprooted. Street intersections had been taken over by the army, and Bruna had to show her ID at two security control stations. She was worried she'd be frisked and they'd find her gun, but luckily that didn't happen. She was really on edge by the time she reached Yiannis's house.

The archivist's apartment was as old-fashioned as he was. It was a beautiful building, about three centuries old, which had survived various wars without excessive damage but was badly in need of refurbishment. The apartment had dark little corridors, useless rooms, and an incomprehensible number of bathrooms. Yiannis lived his entire life within the two main rooms, one converted into a living room and the other a bedroom, but he used the rest of the apartment to store the incredible amount of junk he kept, including an astonishing quantity of old, valuable paper books. Bruna had lived in one of those book-lined rooms for some months after Merlín's death. Yiannis the human had taken care of her in the same way that the techno Maitena had looked after Lizard. But now relations between the species were decaying.

No sooner had she gone through the door than Bruna noticed something new: the little table in the entrance hall that was normally a mess had been cleared and the sole object on display was a blue jug with three yellow tulips. Natural flowers! The rep was stunned.

"Look at that. You've tidied the table."

"Hmmm…" replied the old man ambiguously, making a vague gesture with his hand.

They walked down the hall and into the lounge, and there she was, smiling demurely. Bruna had trouble recognizing her initially, as she wasn't wrapped up inside her billboard-lady panels.

"Hi, Bruna. I'm so pleased to see you," said RoyRoy enthusiastically.

"Me too," replied the rep automatically. "Although I'm a bit surprised to see you here. Have you left Texaco-Repsol?"

The woman looked at Yiannis with a slightly embarrassed expression.

"Well, I've…I've helped her to free herself of that slave labor. Let's just say I've bought her her freedom!" replied the archivist on her behalf.

And then he laughed nervously at his own words.

"I mean, I've lent her money until she can find something better, and till then, she's…she's living here with me."

"Oh, good. Right. Terrific," said Bruna.

"Yiannis is very generous. But you already know that," added RoyRoy.

Yes, the android knew it. The archivist wasn't doing any more for the billboard-lady than he had done for her. Moreover, Yiannis looked…excited about RoyRoy. And she looked different too. Younger. More sure of herself. It was enough to make the rep happy for her friend. Bruna dropped down into the old, green armchair. Yiannis sat down on the sofa next to the woman. They made a sweet little couple.

"Not at all. RoyRoy is the generous one. You wouldn't believe what a support she's been in all this. Lucky she was here last night. As I'm sure you'll understand, I came back from the interview with the supervisor totally devastated."

"Yes, of course."

The woman couldn't have been in Yiannis's home more than two or three days, but there were traces of her everywhere. The furniture was arranged differently and the bookshelves were tidy. The screen showed successive images of Yiannis's child and of an adolescent whom Bruna took to be RoyRoy's son. *Oh yes, the perfect couple, and intimately united by the worship of their dead.* She bit her lip, recognizing that her thoughts were unkind.

"So tell me exactly what that woman said to you yesterday, then," she muttered.

Why was she so irritated? Why wasn't she pleased that the old man had fallen in love? Hadn't she felt that Yiannis was pushing her to hold on too tightly to the pain of Merlín's loss? And wasn't it better that he had found another, closer sorrow with which he could identify? The archivist was telling his tale, but Bruna was unable to concentrate on what he was saying. She saw Yiannis and RoyRoy sitting there, sitting together, humans, similar, much older than her, but even then probably longer-living. She saw them together while she was alone, hopelessly strange even among the strange.

The screen switched on automatically with a breaking news bulletin. An image appeared of Helen Six, the journalist currently in vogue, with such a tragic expression on her face that Yiannis stopped talking and the three of them started to listen to the news. And that was when they discovered that Hericio was dead.

He had been assassinated the day before. Not only had he been killed, but he had also been tortured. Someone had slit his stomach from top to bottom and then removed his intestines while he was still alive. It had been a horrific crime.

Just like Chi's hologram, Bruna thought immediately, despite being sunk in a sort of stupor. Yiannis looked at her.

"But didn't you tell me yesterday that you were going to see him?"

RoyRoy gave a start, opened her eyes wide and covered her cheeks with her hands.

"Bruna! What have you done?" she wailed.

"Meee?!" the rep spat out, outraged.

Then something very odd happened. The archivist raised his hand in the air as if he were going to say something, then brought it to his throat and slowly collapsed on his side.

"Yiannis!" gasped RoyRoy, leaning toward him and then also toppling over.

Bruna leaped from her chair and rushed to the two inert bodies. Small yellow bubbles were coming out of RoyRoy's mouth. Then Bruna noticed the smell, a subtle smell of danger. There was something in the air, a chemical threat. She held her breath but it was already too late. She noticed that her legs were getting heavy, and her body was no longer holding her upright. She fell to the floor, but she wouldn't give in. With an enormous effort, and assisted by her extraordinary strength, she painfully dragged herself on all fours toward the window. She had to get there; she had to open it. She focused mentally on the distance she needed to cover. But she was moving very slowly and she wouldn't be able to go on holding her breath much longer. She was only halfway there when a reflex reaction made her swallow a mouthful of air. She felt it filling her lungs deliciously, liberating her from the agonizing suffocation, and she also noted how it was poisoning her. It was like a sudden misting over her eyes. And then darkness and nothingness.

CHAPTER THIRTY-THREE

Bruna opened her eyes. The house was buzzing and shaking. Liquid shadows looked as if they were chasing one another across the ceiling. It took her a few moments to understand that the noise was being caused by the sky-trams passing right in front of the window. Of *her* window. Another one went by. Again the noise and the fluttering of the shadows. Bruna breathed deeply as anguish overwhelmed her. She knew what she had to do, and it was terrible.

She looked at the clock: Monday January 31, 2109, 09:30. She had to get a move on. *Four years, three months, and eleven days. Four years, three months, and eleven days?* What did that mean? Why had that temporal computation suddenly popped into her head? She got out of bed with a deep sense of unease. She was dressed. Better: more time saved. She felt dizzy, confused. A patina of unreality seemed to cover everything, as if life were skimming over every surface. She didn't recognize her house, for example. She knew it was her house but she couldn't quite remember it. That, however, was unimportant. What was important, urgent, frightening, was the mission she had to carry out in order to save little Gummy from his terrible fate. That was all too clear. Her mission and the child's predicament stood out above the general unreality of her surroundings, which were like the fixed, detailed image of a horse running across a hazy background. Those were the only things she needed to do. Those were the only things she needed to know.

The belt was on the table, unfolded and displayed as if it were a jewel. And next to it, a small hologram of Gummy. The child was roaring with laughter, his little screwed-up eyes sparkling, his chubby cheeks smooth. He was two and a half. Bruna remembered herself kissing that new skin—that sweet, delicious flesh—and hot tears of fear and pain began to run down her cheeks. She swatted them away with her hand, as if she were killing an insect and then, with an enormous act of self-control, put on the belt. She was aware of how it worked: first, she had to deactivate the safety switch, and then she had to press the touch-sensitive membrane for at least twenty seconds. When she lifted her fingers, the tiny ampoules would open, allowing the lethal gas to escape. At least it would be a quick death: less than a minute before she suffocated. Nothing like what they had promised to do to Gummy if she didn't keep her side of the bargain. An interminable, sadistic death. Bruna suppressed her retching. *Stay calm*, she implored herself. She had to concentrate. The deafening clamor of another tram spurred her to action. She was to release the content of the ampoules in the main sky-tram interchange to take advantage of the large number of people and the enclosed space. It was located four blocks away. She switched off the holograph ball and put it in her pocket. She was heading out when she realized she wasn't wearing her mobile. How strange. She glanced around but couldn't see it. She searched for it more carefully: among the wrinkled sheets, in the bathroom, on the floor. Her mobile wasn't anywhere.

"Screen, locate my mobile."

There was no response. She looked at the screen; it was a very old model. She tried switching to manual and tapped a number. The computer wouldn't make the call. How odd. The feeling of unreality grew, an unreality buzzing around her like a swarm of flies. Then Gummy's face lit up inside her head again with icy clarity. What did it matter whether or not she had her mobile? She was going to die in a few minutes.

And yet...

Four years, three months, and eleven days. Again, that absurd mantra flashed through her mind. The elevator had an "Out of Order" sign on it, so Bruna walked down the filthy stairs, feeling she was carrying a stone in her heart, an ever heavier weight that was slowing down her steps. The number she'd tried to call with her computer was Paul Lizard's. So who was Paul Lizard? An acquaintance, maybe a friend. Lizard's name emerged from all the confusion like a secure harbor in a stormy sea. A corner of light in the icy shadows. Someone who might possibly help her? With each step down, Bruna felt more torn between the need to accomplish her mission and the horror that the killing inspired in her. But she couldn't avoid it. She had to do it.

And yet...

She reached the ground floor and noticed that the building was a sort of apartment-hotel. How strange that she didn't remember. In the damp, dark lobby there was a small counter and an electronic screen that displayed the prices. The light was on, but there was no one there. Suddenly, Bruna's feet propelled her to the counter. She looked at the small screen and saw that it was active. She keyed in Lizard's number before she realized what she was doing. The policeman's face appeared instantly. Because he *was* a policeman. Bruna gave a start as she remembered this and, at the same time, the mere sight of the man's features made her want to cry with relief.

"Bruna! Where the devil are you?" shouted Lizard.

"I'm…at home," she stammered.

"You're not at home because *I'm* at your place! Bruna, what's going on? You're disconnected. What's wrong with your mobile? I know about Yiannis and RoyRoy."

Yiannis and RoyRoy. The names generated concentric waves in her clouded mind, like stones falling into muddy water. She began to hear a muffled buzzing in her ears.

"I have to go. I have to do something terrible," she moaned.

"Wait! Bruna, what are you saying? What's happening?"

"I have to kill. I have to kill a lot of people."

"What!? But why?"

"If I don't do it, they'll torture Gummy," she wailed.

"Gummy? Who's Gummy?"

"My son! My son!" she yelled.

Lizard looked at her, stunned, as if someone had just hit him on the head.

"You don't have any children, Bruna," he whispered.

The buzzing was becoming deafening.

"I have to go."

"No, wait! Where are you? Listen carefully to what I'm saying. You can't have children. You're a rep!"

Four years, three months, and eleven days.

"What does *four years, three months, and eleven days* mean, Lizard? You must know."

The inspector looked at her, bewildered.

"I have absolutely no idea. Please tell me where you are, Bruna. I'll come and get you."

She shook her head.

"I'm sorry. If I don't do it, they'll torture Gummy."

"Wait—please. How do you know? How do you know they won't hurt him anyway? Maybe you'll kill those people you have to kill and then they'll hurt him anyway."

Bruna thought that over for a few moments. No. They wouldn't do that to him. She knew that with absolute clarity and certainty. If she did her part, the child would be saved.

"You're in Montera Street! I've located you. Don't move; I'll be there in five minutes!" he shouted.

"I can't. I'm off."

"Where?!" asked Lizard, in agony.

"To the sky-tram interchange," Bruna replied.

And turning around, she headed outside, dizzy, nauseous, deaf to her surroundings.

She walked quickly, enclosed within the bubble of her nightmare, oblivious to the preaching of the Apocalyptics, the racket from the public screens, the looks of fear or revulsion that she was stirring up in her path. She walked like an automaton, totally focused on what she had to do. But when she reached the enormous star-shaped interchange, her feet stopped. The buzzing inside her skull became more intense, a noise that was beginning to be painful. She visualized the circular, jagged blade of a saw cutting her brain in two and she shuddered. Then, from who knows where, the image of a woman with a black line drawn around her body—a woman split by her tattoo—came back to her. *Four years, three months, and eleven days.* For a few seconds, she couldn't move and she could barely breathe. Then Gummy's face burst into her head, and everything went into motion again. She checked that the belt was ready and decided to take the elevated walkway so as to enter through the side door of the building. Just then, a car screeched to a halt on the sidewalk next to her and a man leaped out. It was Lizard. Bruna stepped back a few paces, on guard, ready to fight him if he tried to stop her. But he remained standing a few feet away.

"Bruna…relax…"

"Don't come any closer."

"I won't. I just want to talk to you. Tell me, whom do you have to kill? How are you going to do it?"

"Let me past. You can't stop me."

"Listen, Bruna, your brain has been manipulated. I think they've injected you with an induced-behavior implant. They've made you believe you have a son, but it's not true. We have to remove that implant before it kills you."

The buzzing intensified. Maybe Lizard was right. Maybe the implant business was true. But her son was still in the hands of those monsters. Small, terrified, and defenseless. The terror she imagined the child must be experiencing almost made her scream. She deactivated the safety catch on the belt and moved her hand toward the touch-sensitive membrane.

"They told me what they'll do to Gummy if I don't obey," she said, her voice breaking. "I can't stop myself. I have to release the gas before noon. If I can't do it in the interchange, I'll do it right here."

"Wait. Hold on, by all the damned species! Please! Don't do it. If it's gas, it won't have the same effect here in the open air as it would in the interchange, right? They wouldn't want you to release it here."

"Perhaps. But it's a very effective neurotoxin. I know it kills in under a minute and it's very potent. It will work here, too."

Paul looked around. A few feet away there was a trave-lator loaded with people. And then there was the overhead walkway, cars, buildings.

"Shit, Bruna, I'm begging you; wait a minute, please. Please! I've called a friend of yours. He must be just about here. Wait, please."

The rep panicked. She touched the membrane with two fingers. She left them there, pressing on the belt.

"If you've called for reinforcements...if you're thinking of shooting me...I've already deactivated the safety catch. If I take my fingers away from this membrane, the ampoules will open and the gas will escape."

Lizard blanched.

"No, please. I've only alerted a friend of yours, honestly. Give me ten minutes—no, twenty. That's all I'm asking you. It's not 12:00 yet. I'm only asking you for twenty minutes. If you still want to go into the interchange at 11:30, I'll let you go. I'm begging you. Twenty minutes, and in return for that I'll take care of your child. After you're dead. Someone will have to look after him."

Bruna felt a dizzy abyss opening up in front of her. It was true; she hadn't thought of that. Someone would have to take care of Gummy. *Four years, three months, and eleven days.* She gasped in anguish and pressed her fingers a little more firmly against the membrane.

"Okay. Till 11:30. And you'll take care of my boy. But don't call anyone, and don't move."

"I won't do anything. Calm down."

They were the longest twelve minutes of Paul Lizard's life. As far as the rep was concerned, they passed like a night-mare, like a feverish delirium. Like a slow fog perforated by sudden horrendous images that flashed across her mind like knife strokes.

Pablo Nopal arrived at the thirteenth minute.

"Hi, Bruna."

The android studied him anxiously. She knew him. And he disquieted her in some way, though she didn't know why.

"What a beautiful necklace. What a lovely *netsuke*. It was your mother's, do you remember? When you were little and your parents were going out for dinner, your mother would come into your room before she left. You pretended to be asleep but you could see her bending over you, slim, and making a rustling noise in her elegant clothes, perfumed, outlined by the light from the corridor. And this little man would be dangling from her neck. Then your mother would put a hand over the *netsuke*, and like that, while she was holding it, she would brush your cheek or your forehead with her lips. No doubt she would hold on to the necklace so it wouldn't hurt you as she bent over, but that scene crystallized those ingredients inside you forever: the promising night; the glow of the corridor; your mother's kiss as she grabbed the little man as if he were a talisman; the secret key that would allow her to teleport herself to that mysterious, happy life that awaited your parents somewhere."

That's what Nopal said with his serious, calm voice, and suddenly Bruna saw herself there, inside that sleepy body and that bed, inside the warm cocoon of the sheets and her mother's fragrance, which wrapped around her like a protective ring. The burning memory cut through her sharply, leaving her breathless, and it was just the first of many. Nopal unraveled memories from the tangled ball inside her mind and little by little, the hazy outline of everything began to recover its definition. Half an hour later, Bruna had gone through her dance of the phantoms again; she had cried again as the deception was revealed, and she understood that she was a rep. That she couldn't have children. But Gummy was still crying deafeningly within her. Her child continued to call her and need her. The rep moaned. Tears burned her eyes. With her left hand, she reactivated the safety catch and then withdrew her numb fingers from the membrane. Lizard moved as if he were going to approach her, but Bruna halted him with a fierce yell.

"Don't move!"

The inspector stopped in his tracks.

"Now I'm the one asking you for five minutes."

No one said a word.

The rep bowed her head and closed her eyes. And she set about killing Gummy. She remembered the weight of the child in her arms, his warm animal smell, his sticky little hand touching her face, and then she told herself, *It's not true, he doesn't exist. He doesn't exist!* She repeated the words with a silent shout until she had managed to erase the image bit by bit, like the pixels of a defective graphic. Then she moved on to her next memory of the little boy, and the next. His first wobbly steps. That quiet, blue summer afternoon when Gummy ate an ant. The way he said "candy" in his funny baby-speak—*dandy*; the little bubbles of saliva at the corners of his mouth. And how he used to put his hand inside hers when something frightened him. None of that existed! It didn't exist! The memories were disappearing, bursting like soap bubbles, and the pain became ever more unbearable, more searing. It was like burning yourself and then scraping the blister. But Bruna kept going, agonizing, suicidal, scratching around in living flesh until she reached the final memory and burst it. And right down there, in the depths, after she'd completed Gummy's imaginary death, Merlín's real death was poised, waiting for her. Bruna Husky was back, whole.

Slowly, she opened her eyes, exhausted and aching. She looked at the expectant Lizard and Nopal.

"So, is the implant still going to kill me, like it did the others? Will my brain explode? Will I gouge out my eyes?" she asked in a hoarse whisper.

And just at that moment she lifted her head and saw herself. Suddenly, her image was swamping the public screens: Bruna as she actually was, and as Annie Heart; Bruna entering the Majestic Hotel; Annie entering the HSP headquarters. And she saw the big, red 3-D flashes signaling breaking news: "Techno Bruna Husky Guilty of Torture and Murder of Hericio." It was just on twelve o'clock.

CHAPTER THIRTY-FOUR

It was Bruna's idea. She needed to have the implant removed, but if she went to a hospital, she'd be arrested. Then she thought of Gándara.

"The medical examiner?" asked a surprised Lizard.

"He knows how to remove artificial mems, even if it is from cadavers."

"Yes, but are you sure about him? He's a strange character. Won't he turn you in?"

Bruna shook her head, and that was enough for the world to start spinning. She was feeling increasingly dizzy.

"No, he'll do the right thing; he's a friend. And if we give him some money, he'll be even friendlier," she murmured weakly.

She was convinced she was going to die and her only hope was that Lizard would prevent her from gouging out her eyes. The inspector called Gándara. The medical examiner worked nights and wasn't at the Forensic Anatomy Institute, but Paul gave him some vague excuse and managed to make it sound official and urgent enough for Gándara to promise he'd be there quickly.

"I'll make sure he keeps his mouth shut," grunted Nopal.

"What do you mean by that?" asked the inspector, somewhat concerned.

"I'm talking about money. I'll give him some Gs."

The three of them were in the policeman's car. They'd ordered the vehicle to darken the windows in order to hide Bruna; the public screens were showing images of her incessantly, and unfortunately she was too easy to recognize. Lizard and the memorist seemed to have signed a truce, a temporary alliance the rep would have found very odd if she had been in a state to think about it. But she was feeling so awful that ideas didn't seem to register in her brain. In fact, she hadn't noticed something even stranger: instead of arresting her, the inspector was helping her escape.

By the time they reached the Forensic Institute, Bruna's heart was beating abnormally fast and she was experiencing cold sweats. Lizard stopped in a discreet corner of the parking lot, left Bruna in the car with Nopal and went in search of the medical examiner. He returned with the doctor in tow after what seemed an exasperatingly long time to Bruna and Nopal.

"You look terrible, Bruna. You look like my usual customers," said the medical examiner by way of a greeting.

They had brought a robot-cart with a capsule.

"We'll have to remove her clothes," said Gándara.

They took off her clothes and the *netsuke* necklace, laid her down inside the capsule and lowered the transparent lid. The clearly visible bruise marks made her role as a corpse more credible. They entered the building and passed through security control quickly and almost without any checks, no doubt thanks to the caustic and somewhat imposing presence of the medical examiner. Then they rolled down the corridor until they reached one of the dissection rooms.

"I've indicated it's a secret official matter and given the order that no one is to come in," Gándara informed them.

He told the robot-cart to park itself in the middle of the room underneath the instrument module and open its lid. The room was icy cold. Lizard looked at the rep's naked body, so pale and defenseless inside the capsule, and felt cold for her. And devastation and fear, too, and something akin to a distressing weakness that might have been tenderness.

Gándara put on his lab coat and gloves and switched on the powerful antibacterial light above them.

"Well, now...how are you feeling, Bruna?"

"Bad."

Concerned, Gándara looked at her.

"Do you know what day it is?"

"Monday...January 31."

Her voice sounded fuzzy.

The medical examiner checked all her vital signs with a body meter.

"Tachycardia, slight hypothermia...Right. We can't waste any time. If you've got a mem, it has to be removed now."

With quick, precise movements the doctor pulled down a frightening machine hanging above his head and switched it on. It began to emit a menacing hum.

"You have to keep very still. Is that clear? Imagine you're a corpse."

The rep opened her eyes wide in acquiescence. Gándara placed the metal tip of the machine in the android's nose and pressed a button.

"There goes the probe."

Bruna whimpered and her hands contorted painfully.

"By all the damn species, Gándara! Can't you make it more bearable for her?" growled the inspector.

"What do you want, Lizard? We don't have anesthetics here. I don't know if you realize it, but we don't need them. Keep very still, Bruna; it will be quick. And it isn't really such a big deal. Hey! Nobody's ever complained, ha-ha."

The progress of the nanoprobe through her brain could be seen on the screen, a probe so tiny that it had to emit a fluorescent flicker in order to be visible. The trail of light moved back and forth in the gray matter like a comet gone mad in an enclosed universe. Gándara frowned.

"It's not possible."

Bruna was panting hoarsely. Her fists were clenched and her body was so tense that her toes were curled like claws. That beautiful, suffering body, that battered flesh that the antibacterial light tinged with an unreal, purplish color.

"Shit! What's happening? Wasn't it going to be quick?" the inspector exploded.

The luminous worm ran around the screen one last time and then switched itself off. The probe hissed as it retracted. Gándara removed the implement from the rep's nose and turned to Nopal and Lizard.

"There's nothing there."

"What?"

"There's no implant. No artificial mem apart from the regular technohuman memory, which is still sealed and intact."

"That can't be. I'm a memorist, I spoke with Bruna, and I know she's the victim of an implant with fake memories. I know that for an absolute fact," said Nopal.

"Well, there's nothing there I'm telling you. Nothing. And I'm absolutely certain, too," said the medical examiner, somewhat annoyed.

But then he looked at the rep and scratched his right earlobe, as he tended to do when he was nervous.

"Though maybe…"

He lifted the rep's hands, which were still tense.

"Hmmm. Bruna, have you noticed if you have more saliva than usual?"

The detective nodded.

"Now I've got it. Rigidity, excessive salivation. I'm sorry, but I have to reinsert the probe. This time it really will be quick."

The implement unfolded itself again with the buzz of a drill, the fluorescent worm reappeared on the screen, and the android moaned. But Gándara had spoken the truth. Within a few seconds, the probe was done and back out. He switched off the machine and pushed it back up to the ceiling. He was excited.

"I think I know what's happening. It's fantastic! I've heard rumors about it, but I've never seen it."

"What? What?" asked Nopal and Lizard in unison.

"Sodium chloride crystals. You can program them like a chip, but they dissolve in the body after a few hours without leaving any trace. In other words, they implanted an artificial mem made of salt, and what's happened is that it has dissolved. But I could still find traces of a higher than normal salinity. Nothing serious."

"So she's not going to die?"

"No, absolutely not. The salt has created a slight electrolytic imbalance in her brain that is responsible for the dizziness, rigidity, and the other symptoms. Luckily, I have some ultra-hydration capsules that I use when the bodies they send me are too mummified. I'll insert one of them subcutaneously and, with a bit of rest, she'll be like new in twenty-four hours."

"They didn't want to leave any trace of the memory manipulation. That's why they chose gas as the means of death. That way, Bruna's body would have been intact when they brought her to the medical examiner, and when they did the autopsy, they wouldn't have found anything. I mean, it would look as if Husky had committed all those horrors consciously and of her own free will. A perverse, avenging techno versus the human race," mused Lizard.

"The perfect enemy," murmured the rep weakly.

"Right, this small jab is to insert the hydration capsule... done. In a few weeks' time, if you feel like it, stop by and I'll take it out. As it's a product intended for dead meat, it won't be absorbed. It's totally harmless, so you can carry it all your life if it doesn't bother you. Now you should go as soon as you can. Having you here puts me in an awkward position," said Gándara.

"An awkward position that we appreciate and want to thank you for," said Nopal.

And he shook hands with the medical examiner, leaving a few bills in the doctor's hand. Gándara smiled and put away the money as if it were the natural thing to do.

"I'd have done it anyway, but with this I feel much more loved and content. You can leave by the back door, where the robots take out the bodies. It will look better if she's dressed."

Lizard took Bruna in his arms and lifted her out of the capsule. The coarse material of his clothing scratched her naked skin. The rep would have stayed curled up against the inspector's chest forever—she would have slept in that bodily refuge until her TTT arrived—but she felt better and knew she had no choice but to move. So she dressed, and even walked unstably of her own accord to the outside door, helped by Nopal. The back door opened onto a cargo dock attended by robots. A few empty capsules were stacked up next to the wall. Lizard, who had gone to fetch the car, appeared right away and picked them up.

"We have to find a safe place to hide you until you recover, and until we manage to clear up all of this."

"She can stay at my place," said Nopal.

"No. Not in your house," Lizard replied categorically.

The memorist looked at him with a mocking smile.

"And why not, if you don't mind telling me?"

The inspector was silent.

"Are you afraid I'm implicated in the plot? Or are you scared she'd prefer to be with me?"

They're fighting over me, thought Bruna. *How quaint.*

"I've had you under surveillance for over a year. If she goes to your place, my men will find her immediately," said Lizard, scowling balefully.

Oh. So after all that, Paul wasn't fighting for her. It was nothing more than a simple question of strategy. Bruna tasted something salty in her mouth. Too much saliva and too much bitterness.

Nopal turned white with rage. An incandescent, quiet fury.

"Oh, fine. I'm delighted you've finally admitted that you're spying on me. That's police harassment. I'm going to file a complaint against you."

"Do whatever you like."

"Stop here!" ordered the memorist.

Lizard stopped the vehicle and the man got out.

"Nopal—" said the rep.

The memorist raised his finger.

"You, be quiet. As for you, Lizard, I'm going to finish you. Believe me."

Lizard looked at him phlegmatically, his eyes half-closed.

"I believe you. Or rather, I believe you'll try. That's why I'm having you watched. Because I think you're capable of doing those sorts of things."

Nopal gave a brief, sardonic guffaw.

"I'll finish you off in court. I'll report you, and it will be the end of your career. Enjoy your brief moment of power while you can."

And turning around, he strode off up the street.

Bruna and Lizard watched in silence as he walked off.

"You called him," Bruna said finally.

"Hmmm."

"But you hate him."

"When you spoke to me about your son, I realized it would be very difficult to get you out of the delirium they'd implanted in you. Then I remembered him and thought he might be able to help you."

"How, um…How did you know Nopal had been my memorist?"

"I didn't."

"And how do you know I didn't kill Hericio?"

"I don't."

"So why are you helping me?"

"I don't know that either."

Bruna was silent for a few minutes while she tried to digest the information and finally decided to leave it for later. She was exhausted and very confused. Although she was feeling a little better, she urgently needed sleep. She needed a safe place where she could rest.

"Do you know what happened to my mobile?" she asked.

I found it in your apartment. Here, take it. I've altered your data in the central police computer so they can't trace you. I assume they'll take a couple of days to realize that."

The rep strapped the flexible, transparent little machine on to her wrist and called Yiannis. Lizard had told her that both the archivist and the billboard-lady were alive, and that the gas was nothing more than a narcotic substance from which they'd both recovered without any problems. They were the ones who had alerted the police to the detective's disappearance. Yiannis's anxious face filled the screen.

"Ah, Bruna, by all the sentients, how good to see you! Where are you? How are you? What happened? They do nothing else but display images of you everywhere, saying dreadful things about you. And then there are those pictures of you going into the HSP in disguise. Unfortunately, it all sounds quite believable."

Bruna gave Yiannis a brief, if weary, summary of the situation and then brought up the need to find a place to hide. Clearly, Yiannis's house wasn't an option: she'd already been attacked there once. But she couldn't think of anywhere else. Especially keeping in mind that everyone thought she was an assassin.

The old man's face lit up.

"Wait. Maybe the *bicho* who was so taken with you, the Omaá...Didn't you tell me you took him to the circus with the violinist? Couldn't you stay there for a few days?"

"But I hardly know Maio and Mirari. Why would they trust me? They'll be thinking I killed..."

And then it dawned on her. No, they wouldn't think that, because Maio would know she was innocent. It was worth a try.

"Good idea, Yiannis. I'll try."

So, while Lizard drove toward the circus, Bruna relaxed and allowed herself to fall into a troubled sleep.

CHAPTER THIRTY-FIVE

She was lying face up on the bed and the darkness was squeezing in around her, as heavy as a wet blanket. Bruna had just woken up and she was afraid. But what was frightening her wasn't that they wanted to kill her, or that they'd put a salt mem in her brain, or that someone had chosen her as the scapegoat in a sinister plot. After all, those were genuine dangers, concrete threats against which she could try to defend herself. In those sorts of situations, your heart pounded and your brain filled with adrenaline. There was something very exciting about real danger. An exuberant reaffirmation of life.

No. The fear Bruna was experiencing right now was different. It was a dark, childhood terror. A deadly pain. It was the same fear she'd suffered at night as a child, when her fear of things had crawled through the shadows like a slimy monster at the foot her bed. *By all the damn species*, thought the rep despairingly; she'd never been little; none of that had ever existed! It was nothing more than a false memory, someone else's memory. Suddenly, a blindingly obvious idea flashed into her head: Pablo Nopal probably really had lived through all of that. That was the explanation for the incredibly expensive *netsuke*: it was his mother's necklace. That was the reason for the genuine way in which Nopal had described the scenes when he dragged the android from her delirium. In one dizzying instant, Bruna understood that the memorist was inside her, transformed into a frightened child, and she felt disgust and yet at the same time an unspeakable tenderness. She didn't want to see Pablo Nopal ever again. Not true. She *did* want to. Even more than that, she needed to see him; she needed to ask him about his mother, about his father, about his childhood. She wanted to know more things, more details; she was hungry for more life. What fascination, and what a nightmare!

Four years, three months, and eleven days. Actually, ten days, because it's already forty-one minutes after midnight. The dawning of February 1.

Life was a story that always ended badly.

She breathed deliberately for a few minutes, trying to relieve the pressure of her anguish. She thought about Merlín and sheltered in his memory—this one indeed a genuine memory, a precious and unique memory, the lived and shared memory of his wisdom and his courage. *There is a time for everything under the sun: a time to be born and a time to die; a time to cry and a time to laugh; a time to embrace and a time to be apart,* her lover had said to her a few days before he died, already very weak, but in a clear, calm voice. Merlín had always liked that fragment from Ecclesiastes. Beautiful words to organize the shadows and soothe the raging storm of pain, even if only for a moment. Now, as she relived that scene, Bruna again felt some small comfort, as if her pain were obediently going back to where it belonged.

The detective was in Mirari's dressing room, on the bed behind the screen. Maio usually slept there, together with Bartolo, but they'd allowed her to use the bed. The door was locked with a key and there were no windows in the room; the rep felt as if she were inside a safe. The Omaá and the violinist had reacted extraordinarily well, offering their support without asking any questions. Of course Maio didn't have to ask her anything. She checked the time again: 00:48. The last show would be over in about twenty minutes and then Maio and Mirari would come back to the dressing room. Bruna felt better and she was hungry. But she didn't want to turn on the light and activate the food dispenser; she didn't want to make a racket and betray her presence. She would wait till they returned.

The beep from her mobile sounded thunderous in the silence of the night, and the rep moved her hand quickly to stop it. It was Habib.

"By the great Morlay, Husky!" sighed the rep. "Thank goodness I've found you."

"Habib, I haven't done any of the things they're saying I did."

"Of course not. I've always been certain you're not guilty, but I thought they might have inserted one of those killer mem*s*, like they did with Chi. Did they implant one, Husky? Are you okay?"

Bruna briefly explained the situation to him, adding, "But I feel much better already."

"Well, you don't look good. Although I can barely see you...You're in a really dark place."

"I'm in—"

Habib looked scared and interrupted her.

"Don't tell me where! Don't tell me where! I don't want to know where you're hiding! It's safer for everyone. Imagine if they were to catch me and do the same thing to me that they did to Hericio! I'd tell them everything!"

Bruna looked at him, a little taken aback. Habib appeared to be at the end of his tether.

"Okay. Fine. You're right."

Habib made an effort to compose himself.

"I'm sorry. Everything is so awful that...I'm a nervous wreck. I have an appointment tomorrow with Chem Conés and three hours after that, with the delegation from the Government of Earth. I'm going to explain to them how we see things. I'll tell them why we think we're dealing with an antirep conspiracy, and I'll ask them to put an end to this madness. I'll also talk to them about your situation. Can I tell them everything you've told me?"

"Everything except the involvement of Lizard, Nopal, and Gándara."

"Of course. Naturally. Well, wish me luck. I'll call you later."

He cut off, and the little bluish gleam of the screen disappeared like a will-o'-the-wisp among the shadows. Immediately afterward, Bruna heard something. A barely perceptible sound. A very slight vibration of the air. Alarmed, she sat up. And then everything seemed to stop: time, Earth's rotation, her heart. She uncoiled herself like a spring and threw herself head first onto the floor before she even knew why she was doing it, and as she rolled across the floor she watched a noiseless, blinding thread of light split the rickety old bed. Black plasma. Led by instinct, she crawled from one corner of the room to the other, pursued by shots from the silent death machine that was creating a trail of holes behind her. Her rep-enhanced eyes could make out the silhouette of the assailant, despite the dark. He was by the door, the lock of which he had undoubtedly forced with remarkable stealth. He was of average height and was wearing a thermal sensor helmet that enabled him to see his target better in the darkness of the night and through solid objects, like the screen. Bruna took in all of this in a flash while she slithered and scrambled across the floor like a cockroach in the shadows, absolutely convinced that the assailant would kill her with his next shot or the one after that. There was no way to get close to him without exposing herself, and there was no other way out except through the door the assailant was blocking.

Suddenly, she saw something appear behind him—huge, touching the lintel with its head. It was Maio. The *bicho* raised his colossal arm and drove his fist down onto the assailant's skull, sending him crashing to the floor. But the helmet must have protected him, because he rolled himself onto his back like some vermin, aiming at the alien with his gun. Bruna imagined Maio's broad, translucid chest and multihued entrails exploding as a result of the impact: a black plasma shot would kill him. So she launched herself at the assailant like a feline—pure intuition, genetic coding, and training. She dived ferociously, efficiently, and savagely and, grabbing the man by the back of his neck, she twisted it. It was a crisp, deadly movement executed without thought or emotion, the perfect stroke of an assassin. His neck cracked and the man slumped between her hands. He was dead.

"Bruna."

Maio turned on the light and spoke in his babbling voice.

"Bruna…I sensed you; I realized you were in danger, and that's why I came."

The rep was still kneeling on the floor, the crumpled body of the assailant between her legs. She removed the helmet. He was a young man, unknown to her. His head was leaning grotesquely to one side, and his face looked relaxed but sad. Less than a minute ago, he had been alive, and now he was a corpse. A flood of images washed over Bruna. Bloody knife cuts pierced her memory, and this time the images were from her real memory, of her real past—nothing to do with the imaginary fear of her fake childhood. It wasn't the first time Husky had killed; her years in the military had been tough. But killing wasn't something you became used to.

"Bruna, Bruna, I sensed you before, and I sense you now," whispered Maio.

He approached the android and gently placed one of his huge, too-many-fingered hands on top of her shaved head. Warmth, gentleness, shelter. The flurry of sharp knives died down a little. The corridor had filled with people: Mirari, with the bubi in her arms; other circus performers; members of the audience craning their necks to see better. The Omaá's departure from the stage in the middle of the show, in full flight, must have aroused considerable attention. Never mind the commotion caused by the fight, the dressing room had been destroyed. And now all those humans were staring at her, wide-eyed and terrified. Bruna pictured herself kneeling with the lifeless body of her victim resting on her lap. It was like an image of the *Pietà*—the *Pietà* of the godless. She wasn't sorry for the man, who was a killer; she was sorry for herself, for her lethal automatism. She didn't have to kill him, but she hadn't even had time to think before doing it. A woman opened a path through the crowd and aimed a regulation plasma gun at her.

"Police. Bruna Husky, you're under arrest."

CHAPTER THIRTY-SIX

The policewoman who arrested Bruna was as excited and pleased as if she'd won the Planetary Lottery, but her immediate superior quickly arrived and, also feeling exultant and happy, took charge. But his happiness was equally short-lived, as the rep's detention was wrested from him by his boss. And in this manner, over the course of a few hours, the rep was passed from one person to the next up the hierarchical police ranks in an unstoppable manner, as if she were rich booty being fought over by pirates. And after the forces of law and order, it was the turn of the politicians, who, like sharks caught up in a feeding frenzy, also tried to hang onto a mouthful of her capture, until finally, at four o'clock in the morning, it was decided to lock her up in one of the high-security cells inside the Law Courts to await the arrival of a more reasonable hour to stage a grandiose media event. They wanted to squeeze every last benefit out of her arrest. Bruna spent two minutes talking to a public defender, an apathetic human whom she told she was innocent of course, and whom she requested to contact the lawyers of the Radical Replicant Movement. After that, she was left alone in a state-of-the art prison cell, a space that was permanently lit and constantly monitored. She tried to control her anguish and catch up on some rest. She still didn't feel all that well physically.

But much to her surprise, at five thirty in the morning, the policewoman who had first detained her, accompanied by one of her colleagues, came to fetch her. This time, the woman was bad tempered and taciturn, perhaps as a result of her bitterness at discovering how little personal triumphs counted when one had too many superiors farther up the chain. She curtly ordered Husky to stand, and altered the program on her electronic shackles to enable the techno to walk. They'd nobbled Bruna with every conceivable means of restraint: manacles on her feet, paralysis cuffs, and even a knockout collar around her neck capable of remotely inducing heart failure. It was clear the humans were frightened of her. Extremely frightened. And finding her with someone lying in her arms whose neck she had just broken hadn't exactly helped the situation.

The taciturn policewoman threw a big, dark gray cape over the rep's shoulders to cover all the convict hardware and pulled a black mesh cap over her head all the way down to her eyebrows. *Given my height, the sweeping cape, and the cap pulled down so low, I must be an extraordinary sight*, thought Bruna. If this was how they hoped she'd pass unnoticed, their attempt would undoubtedly be a complete failure.

Thus attired, the android was led through the quiet, empty corridors of the Law Courts by the two officers. When they took the back stairs down to the storage and equipment levels, Bruna began to worry. Given that she was tied up, electronically blocked, and defenseless, any idiot would be able to do as he pleased with her. She asked where they were going, but neither of the officers bothered to answer. It wasn't light yet and that part of the building was illuminated only by emergency lighting. The atmosphere was unreal and nerve-wracking.

They walked through an unexpected gym on the second level of the basement, came out into an underground parking lot and got into a car similar in make and color to the one Lizard had—clearly a police vehicle, although it had none of the official markings. The woman darkened the windows and tapped in their destination manually, so the rep continued to be none the wiser as to where they were headed. Twenty minutes later they stopped at the back entrance to another enormous building. But by this stage the rep already knew where they were: the Reina Sofía University Hospital. The police officers knocked and identified themselves, and the door opened. A security guard led them through a maze of corridors until they reached the psychiatric services area. Or at least that's what was written in big letters on the wall. Then the guard unlocked the door to one of the rooms and nodded at the rep to go in. Bruna did so, and the door was locked behind her. She looked around. She was alone. It was a very large space, more like a conference room, illuminated by the weak, soulless light of a few ecolight tubes. Along one side there was a work table with two or three chairs in front of it; on the other side were about twenty chairs arranged in two semicircular rows. The best feature was the huge windows that looked out onto the hospital's inner courtyard, which was large and resembled a medieval cloister. The building was very old. Bruna knew that it had originally been a hospital and then an important art museum for more than a century. The building had been destroyed during the Robot Wars, and when it was restored, it regained its former status as a hospital. The rep went up to the windows to have a look at the dark outdoors and noticed that they had incorporated a grid of electromagnetic wires. Bars. She was still in a cell, although a much bigger one.

"Hi, Husky."

Bruna turned around. Paul Lizard was standing at the door. He grimaced in a way that could have meant anything from a smile to disdain, came into the room and walked up to her. He was carrying two cups of coffee.

"Want some?"

"No."

"Fine."

He calmly drank one of the coffees, followed by the other. Then he stood looking at her with a concerned expression on his face.

"It wasn't easy to arrange to have you brought here. I eventually managed to convince the delegate from the Government of Earth. I told her that, given the current state of play, we couldn't guarantee the safety of your life if people knew where you were. And that's true."

Bruna didn't say a word.

"She authorized me to transfer you, because I told her I'd be able to lock you up here; she's obsessed with ensuring you don't escape. This hospital has a high-security psychiatric wing. They're looking for a room to put you in. It's assumed that only half a dozen of us know where you are. We'll see. I'm convinced the police have been infiltrated."

"Right," replied the rep despondently.

"How are you feeling?"

"Very tired."

"Well, try to grab some sleep. We have some tough days ahead of us."

The rep appreciated that plural *we*; it made her feel slightly less alone. She looked at Lizard: he, too, appeared pale and exhausted.

"Thank you for everything, Paul."

"Don't thank me. It's frustrating not to have solved this case. We're trying to identify the guy who attacked you yesterday. How did he find out you were at the circus? I even got to the point of thinking that they might have implanted you with an intramuscular locator chip, but the thorough search they gave you last night before they put you in the cell didn't come up with anything."

Lizard stopped talking for a few seconds and then gave the rep a sidelong glance.

"Too bad you killed that man. It would have been very helpful if we'd been able to interrogate him."

The detective stiffened.

"He was going to shoot Maio."

"I'm not accusing you, Bruna."

"I'm not defending myself, Lizard."

Something sharp and bitter had suddenly come between them. The inspector grunted and rubbed his face.

"Okay. I'm off to see if there's anything new. I'll be back later."

He went to the door and rapped on it with his knuckles, and it was opened for him. He was already on the way out when Bruna shouted at him from the other side of the room: "Hey! You people have made me what I am."

"What?"

"I'm a combat techno. You're the ones who made me so quick and so lethal."

Lizard frowned at her.

"I'm not the one who made you like this. And anyway, I like you the way you are."

CHAPTER THIRTY-SEVEN

Taking Lizard's advice, Bruna installed herself in a couple of chairs next to the window and spent the next hour trying to take a nap. But each time sleep loosened her muscles and her consciousness began to cloud over, she would experience an abrupt, dreadful sense that she was falling and suddenly wake up. The cuffs and control collar were heavy and uncomfortable, and the electromagnetic bars were humming softly in the silence like mosquitoes. She looked out in the direction of the courtyard. Dawn was breaking. The air was a dense, bluish color that was becoming lighter by the minute, as if it were fading. She stood up, and after making her way clumsily on her hobbled legs to the light switch, she turned off the ecolight tubes. The new day instantly entered through the windows with devastating force. *Four years, three months, and ten days.* And this new day promised to be calamitous, too.

She shuffled her way back to the same seat by the window. She could have had her choice of twenty chairs, but humans and technos are creatures of habit: they always try to turn any chair into a nest. It was 07:10. Would they give her something to eat if she asked them? *Four years, three months, and ten days.*

The door opened hesitantly and Habib's head appeared. The rep leader came in, closed the door behind him and smiled with embarrassment.

"Habib!" Bruna exclaimed with relief.

She had never imagined that seeing another android would give her so much pleasure.

"Did the public defender let you know I was here? I wasn't sure if he'd do so."

Habib walked over to her and patted her awkwardly on the shoulder in a friendly way.

"I'm really sorry," he said sympathetically.

And in the same moment, still smiling, he quickly and expertly took out a plasma gun and held the barrel up to the detective's temple. Bruna looked at him in amazement.

"I'm sorry, Husky. I like you. But if you had any idea what's at stake…It was a deal I just couldn't turn down."

The man's hand trembled lightly, a negligible, involuntary movement that, as the detective was well aware, preceded a shot by a tenth of a second, and she knew it was the end. *Heroes die young*, she thought absurdly in that final moment. But suddenly the world collapsed. A tremendous explosion, a shower of broken glass; Habib slumped on the floor. It all happened at once. Bruna stood up and a pile of glass fragments fell off her and landed, tinkling, on the floor. She bent over the body lying on the ground. He was dead. He had a round, black hole in the middle of his forehead and an opening at the back of his skull. She fixed her gaze on his weapon: the junky, badly made gun Habib was carrying was the one Hericio's deputy had sold to her.

"By the great Morlay!"

Blood and brains stained the brilliant shards of glass scattered everywhere. The rep looked toward the large window. Someone had fired from outside and the glass was broken, although the electromagnetic grid was still working, still buzzing.

The door crashed into the wall as it was violently thrown open, and Lizard rushed in with the force of a battering ram, weapon drawn.

"It's Habib! He's dead!" babbled the android.

The inspector threw a quick glance at the body.

"Who fired?"

"I don't know. It came from outside."

Lizard walked up to the windows. The courtyard was beginning to fill with people drawn by the noise.

"Paul, Habib came to kill me."

The inspector turned around and looked at her.

"That gun—do you see the plasma gun in his hand? That gun was mine. They took it from me the day before yesterday when they kidnapped me."

"By all the sentients, Bruna, how many more weapons have you got hidden away out there for them to steal from you? Anyway, I assume they manipulated Habib's brain as well so that he'd do this."

Bruna slowly shook her head. She was certain the techno had been in full possession of his faculties.

"How did I look under the influence of the salt mem? How did I behave?"

"As if you'd gone mad."

Just like Cata Caín, the rep neighbor who had gouged out her own eye. Tense, feverish, delirious.

"Habib behaved perfectly normally. He told me he was sorry, but they'd made him an offer he couldn't refuse. I'm sure he was involved in the plot. But why? And who killed him?"

Lizard tapped his mobile.

"I'm calling for reinforcements. I don't dare leave you on your own."

Just then the policewoman and her colleague appeared at the door.

"Where did you get to? Your orders were to guard this room at all times," thundered the inspector.

The officers stood there opening and closing their mouths, looking embarrassed.

"I...I felt dizzy and...we went to..." stammered the woman.

Lizard pointed his sleek, regulation plasma gun at them.

"Hand over your weapons right now. You're under arrest."

The pair of them, distraught and with hands trembling, meekly complied, and then Lizard handcuffed both of them to an old radiator out in the corridor. The inspector came back into the room and closed the door behind him, dejected.

"What do you think, Bruna? Are they just incompetent or corrupt? You can't trust anyone one in this damn case."

The man walked over to Habib, trying not to step on the brains strewn everywhere, and scrutinized the body.

"And you say it's your gun?"

"Yes, he held it to my temple. I think he wanted it to look like suicide. I'm sure he's wearing a dermosilicon glove so as not to leave any fingerprints."

Lizard nodded in agreement.

"Probably. But how did he find out where you were?"

"I told the public defender to let him know."

The inspector snorted angrily.

"Right. Well, I've called in a couple of reliable colleagues to come and protect you. They'll be here any minute. Naturally, the examining magistrate and forensics will arrive too, and someone charged with taking away that pair of imbeciles I've left handcuffed out there. And undoubtedly some police bigwig or politician will also appear to protest. That's a given. I'm going to see if I can find somewhere else to put you."

Bruna looked at him transfixed, her expression totally transformed.

"Paul."

"What's up?"

"I'm wondering…why all this effort to kill me? They've already gotten what they wanted from me. Well, I didn't release the gas, but they have made it look as if I'm guilty of Hericio's murder. What do they gain by removing me from the scene now?"

"You can't prove your innocence."

"Yes, but why the rush to finish me off? Right now I can provide them with a lot of airtime and be very useful to them. I'll appear everywhere as the rep assassin. But it looks like they're desperate to liquidate me. Yesterday they sent that guy, and today it's Habib himself, who I don't think is a minor player in the game. They're risking a lot to kill me. Why?"

Lizard rubbed his fleshy forehead.

"What do you think?"

"My son. The memory of my son. It was so real! And all that love and that pain."

Bruna shivered.

"It still smarts inside. Listen, what if they used real memories as a model? Some memorists do that. I know mine did. That would certainly have been easier for them than inventing something sufficiently intense and believable. What if that child really existed? What if they're afraid I can still remember something? I mean, what if they're scared I can remember them?"

"And could you?" asked Lizard with interest. "The salt crystal has already dissolved."

"But there are bits still left...tiny fragments of feeling, although they're rapidly erasing themselves. Just as the memory of a dream is wiped out as the day progresses."

"Well then, give it a go right now. Try. What do you need?"

"Quiet. Concentration. Maybe darkness would help."

Luckily, the windows had venetian blinds, which Lizard lowered. The room was plunged into a cold semidarkness. They sat down at the work table, as far from the body as they could. With her back to Habib, Bruna leaned her elbows on the table, buried her face in her hands and tried to remember.

It was like descending into a cellar in the shadows. A chubby little hand. That was the first thing she saw. A plump baby hand with little dimples on the knuckles.

A sudden pain constricted her throat. Oh, that touching, uniquely beautiful hand of her son! That child for whom she was prepared to die and to kill!

The memories—broken, fragmented—kept arriving like the flotsam from a shipwreck that waves deposit on the shore. A crash of the sea, and the image of a child appeared, running after a ball, sweaty and happy, bubbles of foam. And now she was seeing Gummy in the hollow of his cot, waking up, his lips still puffy from sleep.

That child for whom she was prepared to die and to kill.

Pain was circling around the bottom of her brain like a shark.

Gummy singing, Gummy whimpering, not really wanting to cry. Houses and stairs, tree-lined avenues dappled with sunlight, the sound of the wind. The child smiling from someone's arms. That smiling child was very still. And the person holding him in her lap was still as well. It was a photo. And the person holding the child was a woman. To kill and to die. Bruna knew that woman. She was young and she was dressed in a different style, but she knew her without a shadow of doubt. The rep opened her eyes.

"It's RoyRoy."

CHAPTER THIRTY-EIGHT

After Habib's death, the revelations succeeded one another with devilish speed. *It's like the final stages of a jigsaw puzzle*, thought Bruna, when the few remaining pieces began to fit in place at a dizzying pace as if they were attracting one another, until the gap that was left, the final unknown piece, was closed, finally revealing the entire design.

In Habib's office they found a second computer that, although protected by a sophisticated security system, was easily accessed by the experts and revealed a mine of essential information, including the material used to create the threatening holograph sent to Chi, and an encoded list of contacts that they were meticulously analyzing. The anatomical-recognition program proved that the eye reflected in the butcher's knife belonged to Habib himself. That it was his eye, as apparent as the eye of the Helix nebula, was an obvious conclusion that had, however, never occurred to Bruna. It was no doubt Habib who had provided Chi with the information about the first dead replicants and who had left the threatening ball in her office. It was Habib who suggested they should infiltrate the HSP, and who sent the chip to Nabokov so she'd go mad. That data chip was what he must have been looking for so desperately when the two of them were searching Chi's apartment. He was always around, that damn Habib, but the detective didn't see him.

One of the first names they were able to decode from the list of contacts turned out to be that of a second-rate racist bully who'd already had problems with the law over assaults and public indecency. The man was arrested at his house like a rat in a trap, and an hour later, he was confessing all that he knew—which wasn't a lot, apart from the fact that the Democratic State of Cosmos also seemed to be connected somehow to the whole business. The police actually already knew about this, since their experts had been able to break into Habib's computer only because his sophisticated security system came from Cosmos, and it had already been broken earlier by Earthling spies.

And as for RoyRoy, Lizard himself led the operation that went to retrieve her from Yiannis's house, but when they arrived, she wasn't there. She had disappeared, leaving behind all her belongings, including the stunned and desolate archivist. Perhaps the billboard-lady had arranged it so that Habib would give her a coded call when he'd accomplished his mission and had decided to flee when the call didn't come through. The central ID database spent hours analyzing some pictures Yiannis had taken of RoyRoy, and in the end it found that her real name was Olga Ainhó and she was a famous biochemist who had disappeared fifteen years earlier. An apartment in the Salamanca district had been rented using Ainhó's ID tag, and in the apartment they found a small lab with the capacity to synthesize neurotoxins, as well as documents with various images, the majority of them recordings of scientific experiments. But there was also a close-up of Hericio's evisceration with a spine-chilling audio of Ainhó explaining to her paralyzed victim why she was doing it to him.

Bruna had spent all the previous day, Tuesday, and that night in detention, but the avalanche of evidence ended up exonerating her. The duty magistrate had released her at 10:00 on Wednesday morning, and it was now 10:38 and she was having breakfast with Lizard in a café near the courts. The inspector had been waiting for her at the door of the courts when she walked out.

"When I recall the fuss Habib made about me not telling him where I was—ha! By that stage he already knew that I was at the circus. It was Yiannis who suggested I go there, and Yiannis was with RoyRoy. What a despicable fraud," mumbled Bruna with her mouth full of a sticky bun.

"Lately we've been recording all the RRM communications. A security measure. I guess Habib was establishing an alibi when he called you," Paul commented.

"Not just that! He also called me so that his henchman would be able to locate me inside the circus. The sound and light from the mobile led that character straight to me. What I can't understand is why Habib was open to doing all this."

"Money or power. Which ends up being the same thing. Those are always the basic reasons."

"Do you think so? In this case, I'm not so sure. A rep activist collaborating in a supremacist plot targeting reps? And working for Cosmos, a power on whose territory technos are banned? I don't see why he'd take part in a plan that might lead to his own extermination."

Ever since the plot had begun to unravel, there had been a storm raging inside Bruna's head. A flood of facts, churning and clashing and pairing up with one another in search of meaning. The rep needed to reinterpret and untangle what had happened. Now she realized, for example, that if the enemy always seemed to know of her movements, it was because the archivist was telling RoyRoy everything. Ainhó, that is. She felt a prick of resentment toward her garrulous friend, but it was immediately diluted with compassion. Poor Yiannis. He must be devastated. To discover that the woman with whom he had fallen in love was a monster capable of coldly disemboweling someone must be terrifying. Moreover, everyone knew that emotions inevitably affected the brain cells. That was why she didn't want to fall in love again. She threw a discreet glance in Lizard's direction, and he seemed stronger to her than ever. A wall of flesh and bones. A man so big that he was blocking out her light. The inspector had cut everything on his plate—the fried eggs and the entire slice of ham-flavored soy—into small uniform pieces, and now he was rhythmically eating the little squares, leaving the egg yolks till last. He was like a child, an enormous child. A moist warmth flooded Bruna's chest. The gooey softness of affection.

"Thanks for coming to get me this morning. It was very thoughtful."

"Actually, I came to make you a semiofficial proposition," grunted Paul.

Bruna choked on her bun. She leaned back in her chair feeling ridiculous. Whenever she let her emotions go, she ended up burned. *Four years, three months, and nine days.* She hastened to compose her features into a serious, professional, somewhat disdainful expression.

"Oh, a proposal. Excellent. What is it?"

"We've just found out that Olga Ainhó is a member of the diplomatic corps of the Embassy of Cosmos. Unbelievable, isn't it? She's never appeared publically in anything connected with the delegation, but she is accredited. And we think that's where she's taken refuge. I got the ambassador out of his bed, and he didn't take it at all well. He denies that the woman has committed any crime, he talks of fake evidence and an orchestrated campaign, and says that Ainhó has full diplomatic immunity."

"In other words, he's admitted that she's there."

"In reality, no. Officially, the Cosmics categorically refuse to collaborate and the matter is turning into a sort of international incident. In short, the ambassador is an idiot, but it would seem that behind the scenes they're trying to defuse the situation. They've called to tell us that the ministerial counselor has agreed to receive us. An informal meeting, they stressed. At his home. At 12:00 sharp."

"Receive *us?*"

"I thought you might like to come along," said Lizard.

His fleshy cheeks crowded together into an irresistible smile that lit up his entire face. Nothing remotely like his usual sarcastic, tight-lipped, disdainful sneer. The warmth of that radiant expression softened the rep again.

"You should smile more often," she said in an unexpectedly hoarse and intimate tone.

Lizard closed up like a Venus flytrap. He swallowed the last piece of his egg, gulped down his coffee and stood up.

"Shall we go?"

And Bruna again felt like a complete idiot.

The members of the Cosmos diplomatic delegation lived on the top floors of the embassy. The building was a huge, truncated, inverted pyramid, so the widest part was on top. However, while the first ten floors were glass and totally transparent, the top four floors were clad with huge blocks of stone and windowless. The result was disturbing. It looked as if, at any moment, the heavy stone mass was going to pulverize its glass base. Whereas the headquarters of the Labarians was a neo-Gothic and archaic building, this one was neofuturistic and subverted traditional values, perhaps to symbolize the social subversion the Cosmics espoused. Either way, both buildings were inhuman and oppressive. The section clad in stone was reserved as residences for the legation; the more powerful you were, the higher up the pyramid you lived. As the ministerial counselor was second in command, his residence, which he shared with two other high-ranking officials, was one floor from the top. The vast top floor, the biggest one, the one that was oppressively squashing all the other floors, housed the ambassador. *That relentless hierarchical architecture must also have a lot to do with life on Cosmos*, thought Bruna.

Inside, the embassy resembled a military barracks. Ultramodern and technological, of course, but like a barracks. Austere, monochromatic, and full of diligent soldiers who walked as if they had a metal rod instead of a spine. A female officer in an impeccable uniform accompanied them to the door of the minister's apartment. A robot opened the door and led them into the living room, a spacious room with no windows but with two walls totally covered by 3-D images of the Floating World. It really felt as if they were in space.

"Pretty, isn't it?" said the minister as he came into the room. "I'm Copa Square. Coffee, a soft drink, an energy drink?"

"No, thank you."

Square asked the robot for a ginseng concentrate and sat down in an armchair. He was a tall man with perfect features. So perfect that they could only be the product of a knife wielded by a good surgeon. Not a single catalog item here.

"You understand this is strictly off the record and, that said, also a sign of our goodwill. Despite the Earthling campaign of slander and deceit."

He was smiling as he said this, but it was a cold smile. He was one of those people who use courtesy as a veiled form of threat. A fairly common occurrence among diplomats.

"I thought the idea of an unofficial meeting meant we were going to be able to dispense with the usual clichés. You know Ainhó did it," Lizard said calmly.

Copa Square's smile became more pronounced. As did his coldness.

"Ainhó has already left Earth, protected by her diplomatic status. An embassy vehicle took her to the orbital elevator, and by now she will be arriving at Cosmos. It makes no difference whether she did it or not. You are never going to be able to put her on trial, and on Cosmos they will never know what happened here. In a way, it is as if everything that happened here was…nonexistent."

"Yes, I know that on Cosmos you have strict censorship, but I never thought you'd brag about it."

"And yet it is something to be proud of. In the first place, technologically. Creating technology capable of filtering and controlling the vigorous, multipronged flow of information is a scientific accomplishment. But on top of that, and even more importantly, it is an ethical and political achievement. The population does not need to know about anything that can be manipulated and misunderstood. Our people do not believe in gods. They do not believe in riches. On the Cosmos, as you know, private property and money do not exist. The state provides, and individuals receive according to their needs. But the human being has to believe in something in order to live.

425

And our citizens believe in the ultimate truth, in happiness and social justice. We are building paradise on our Floating World. I know reality is complex and contradictory, and it has to be managed from the shadows. But that ultimate truth has to remain pure and clean so that the people will not become disillusioned. In order to protect all those ordinary people who do not understand that the shadows exist."

"So I see…it's a curious paradise of believers run by cynics," interjected Bruna sarcastically.

"If you are saying that for my benefit, you're confused. You have no idea the extent to which I believe in that truth, which burns at the heart of everything I do."

Square was silent for a few seconds, looking at Bruna quizzically.

"You are the technohuman that Ainhó manipulated. I can understand that you would be outraged. But in reality, everything that happened to you is a consequence of what you are. You androids are so artificial."

"Is that why we are forbidden on Cosmos?" Bruna asked, trying to contain her rage.

"For that reason, and because you were conceived as slaves. You are too different. You do not fit into our egalitarian society."

"You say that what happened has to do with the artificiality of reps, and I assume you're referring to the mem implants and such," Lizard interrupted hurriedly before Bruna could reply. "But we know that before Unification, Ainhó was working on a secret EU plan to develop behavior-inducing implants for humans. So our brain is just as capable of being manipulated as theirs."

It had been a shot in the dark up to a point, but it landed.

"That EU plan you refer to is typical of Earthling hypocrisy: big, public condemnations of censorship, but at the same time, you are full of dirty secrets. That project was dismantled overnight, and all of Ainhó's work was confiscated. Almost twenty years of research. And since she refused to accept the situation, her career was destroyed. A heroic achievement on the part of the free world."

"Of course on Cosmos there are no individual professional careers. Just one unique and great career—of the political hierarchy," muttered Bruna.

"And you immediately offered her your protection," said Lizard, disregarding the rep's comment.

"Olga Ainhó is a great scientist and the DSC needs every conceivable assistance to advance its project."

"But she doesn't share your ideological passion, does she? She didn't strike me as a paradise enthusiast," said Bruna.

"Ainhó's is a privileged mind, but she's a wounded woman. Her sixteen-year-old son had the idea of surreptitiously breaking into the closed-down lab to retrieve his mother's files, and he was gunned down by the security guards—who, it must be said, were technos. Combat androids like yourself."

Which explains the sadism, that perverse detail of gouging out one's own, or other people's, eyes, reflected Bruna with a shiver. *What a sick woman.*

"Ainhó never overcame it," continued the Cosmic. "She is pathologically obsessed with her son's death. She lives solely for revenge, and that sometimes causes a person to commit grave errors. In fact, that could be a good explanation of what has happened. A hypothetical and totally unofficial explanation, naturally."

"Aha! You mean that a mentally unstable Ainhó conceived a megalomaniacal plan of revenge against Earth in general and technos in particular," said Lizard.

"Hypothetically, that could be the case."

"And Cosmos has now repatriated her and offered her shelter out of sheer generosity," added the rep.

"We have many enemies and we need every conceivable support, as I have already said. She may be unhinged, but she is a genius. We would not want to have to do without a scientist of her stature. Hypothetically."

"Why do you bother to receive us and offer us this absurd explanation? We are nothing more than a small regional investigative squad, but without doubt, all of Earth's secret services now know that you're stirring up social conflicts to destabilize the USE," said Lizard calmly.

Square gave him a withering, aristocratic look of disdain.

"The Democratic State of Cosmos is a neutral state and is totally respectful of existing legislation."

"Come on, Square, you know we're in a secret state of war. The Second Cold War. And cold wars sometimes become too heated. Between you and the Ones, you have all the terrorist groups on the planet on your payroll. You'll do anything so long as it debilitates the United States of the Earth and increases your power and influence. Speaking of which, that small detail of the fake tattoos struck me as exquisitely Machiavellian. You also managed, in passing, to compromise the Kingdom of Labari."

The diplomat raised his beautiful eyebrows a little.

"I have no interest in continuing to listen to your tired clichés and your insults, so I think this is the moment to put an end to our conversation."

"Just one more question: How did you persuade Habib?" asked the rep.

The minister looked at her with a strange expression of malevolent delight, like a snake contemplating its paralyzed prey before devouring it.

"I did not convince anyone. You continue to be wrong about me. But I will tell you something about Habib. He had lived *sixteen* years. What do you think about that? You believe that all you technos have to die at ten years of age, but that is not the case. We have scientific knowledge at our disposal that makes it possible for technos to live much longer—twenty years, even thirty. And if truth be told, that knowledge would also be available to Earthlings if they were genuinely interested in developing it. How do you feel now, Bruna Husky, knowing that there are other androids who do not die so early? Are you not revolted by this famously free world that cannot even be bothered to do research into TTT because it is not profitable? Would *you* not be prepared to offer your services to Cosmos in order to be able to live even one year longer? Would *you* not be prepared to do anything?"

Lizard almost had to drag her out of the embassy. He had her gripped firmly by the arm, and it was thanks to this that the rep was capable of walking along corridors, going down stairs and making it to the street, because otherwise she would have been paralyzed by the weight of her thoughts and by panic. By her fear of death, and her own anger, and her desperate desire to live.

They got into the car and Lizard took Bruna to her apartment and went in with her, because he felt she was still too upset. Once inside, the inspector—who seemed to be permanently hungry—suggested they make something to eat.

"Eating cheers you up. That's why they used to have that tradition of banquets at funerals."

So, to Bruna's amazement, the inspector prepared a rice dish into which he threw everything he could find in the food dispenser: peas, shrimp, green onions, eggs, cheese. And then they sat down and ate and drank in silence. When they were opening the second bottle of wine, the detective dared to extend a bridge over the abyss that had opened up in her mind.

"They don't all die, Paul. There are reps who don't die."

"They *do* die, like everyone else. Just a bit later. And I assure you that those extra years won't be enough for them. They're never enough. No matter how long you live, it's never enough."

"It's not fair."

Lizard nodded in agreement.

"Life is unfair, Bruna."

That was what Nopal was always saying: *Life hurts.* The rep remembered the memorist with a surprising stab of nostalgia. With the intuition that he would understand her.

Just then there was a knock at the door. It was a robot courier, sent by Mirari. It left a box in the middle of the lounge, a rather large box, covered profusely with "Fragile" stickers. Intrigued, Bruna opened the package. A furry ball shot out of the container and attached itself to the rep's neck with a shriek.

"Bartolo!"

"Bartolo good, Bartolo beautiful," whimpered the bubi.

By the great Morlay, said Bruna to herself, terrified at the thought of having him in her apartment again. But the creature was so upset that she couldn't prevent herself from stroking its back. She could feel the greedy-guts' agitated heart—or whatever it was those *bichos* had for a heart—beating against her shoulder.

Still holding Bartolo, she went over to her screen and called the circus. Maio's face appeared, more doglike than ever, bearing a knowing look.

"So, what's happened with the bubi?" the rep asked impatiently.

"Hi, Bruna. You know I like Bartolo, and we get on well, but he's eaten the trapeze artist's sequined costume. And she's told us, 'Either he goes or I go.'"

"Bartolo good," whispered the greedy-guts in Bruna's ear, his voice still choked.

Okay. Okay! The android resigned herself. She'd keep the bubi—for now. She'd find another place that would take him.

"That's okay, Maio. It doesn't matter. And by the way, thanks for saving my life. For everything."

The alien sparkled a little.

"It was nothing. You saved mine, too."

"Is Mirari around?"

Maio twisted around and pointed at Mirari lying behind him on a sofa at the back of the room.

"She's asleep. I'll wake her up shortly for the performance."

"I wanted to know how much it would cost to fix the dressing room. The black plasma left it in ruins."

"Don't worry about it. The circus is insured and the insurance will cover it."

Suddenly, the Omaá stretched his neck and tensed, raising his hand as if he were asking for a pause. A few seconds later, he relaxed and turned back to the detective.

"Mirari was dreaming they were amputating her arm. She has lots of nightmares over that arm. Sometimes they wake her up. But this one's over now."

Maio and Bruna looked at each other in silence for a few moments, and during that time the rep could see the *bicho* getting darker, until he had turned an intense reddish-brown color.

"Well, good-bye," said the alien in full chromatic flight.

"Bye, Maio. And thanks."

The image disappeared. Bruna became aware that she had a smile on her face. And that her spirits had lifted somewhat. She felt better.

"What's so funny?" asked Lizard.

"Nothing."

Nothing she could tell him about, of course.

They gave the bubi something to eat and then the animal, clearly exhausted, curled up on the couch and began to snore. Paul stood up and stretched. His fingers touched the ceiling.

"I'm delighted to see you're more relaxed, Bruna. I guess I should go."

The rep said nothing, stunned. The inspector's pronouncement had taken her by surprise. She had seen herself preparing Bartolo's food together with him, bustling around the apartment as if their being together would continue quite naturally. But now he was saying that he was going. She wasn't expecting it. It was absurd, but she hadn't anticipated that Lizard would leave. Nor had she anticipated that he would stay. She simply wanted to go on like this, next to him, in this tiny peace, in a time without time, without conflict. She just wanted this postlunch conviviality to last forever. *Four years, three months, and nine days.* But no, that counting didn't work anymore. There were reps who lived twenty years. Again the dizziness, the abyss.

The inspector cleared his throat.

"It's been good working with you. Maybe we'll get together aga⸀ for another case."

"Yes, of course."

Don't go, thought Bruna. *Don't go.*

What was the matter with her? The android had never had any problem asking a potential partner to stay. She'd never had many doubts about how to use her words, her hands, and her tongue in order to have the other person react in the way she wanted them to. Now she was feeling too many things. She wanted too much and she didn't know how to ask for it.

"Thanks for the meal," said Lizard.

"You're welcome. I mean, thank *you*. You prepared it."

Lizard opened the door, and the android's stomach contracted painfully until it was the size of a marble.

"Would you like a whisky?" she asked in desperation.

Paul looked at her, amazed.

"I'm going..."

"To drink to a successful conclusion! It will only take a minute."

"Well..."

The inspector came back inside, but stood beside the door. The android filled two glasses with ice and went in search of the bottle. A client had given it to her as a present, but the bottle was still unopened. After she'd poured out the drinks, she gave one glass to Lizard and held the other one in her hand. She hated whisky, so she didn't take a sip.

"By the way," said the inspector.

"Yes?"

She could hear herself sounding overly eager.

"What killed Habib was a 9mm metal bullet from an old-style gun, probably a Browning Hi-Power."

It wasn't what Bruna was hoping to hear. It wasn't what she *wanted* to hear, even though it was interesting information.

"Oh, the same sort of projectile used to kill Nopal's uncle, right?"

"More than that. Both bullets were fired from exactly the same weapon...I already told you Pablo Nopal couldn't be trusted."

"Well, if it really was him, this time he saved my life," she replied, too curtly.

Lizard looked at her thoughtfully, his head slightly askew. Then he put his glass down on the shelf next to the door. A final, definitive gesture.

"Absolutely true. Well, good-bye."

Okay, so he's going, thought Bruna, containing her anger. *Let him go then, right away.*

"Bye."

Lizard opened the door again. And then closed it again. He leaned back against it, picked up his glass again and, after draining it, chewed on a piece of ice thoughtfully.

"Just one thing, Bruna. This story is over."

"This story?"

"Yes, the investigation, our collaboration, the reason for our being able to go on calling each other. I mean, it's now or never...the tale is done. Either I stay with you tonight or we won't see each other again."

Maybe it wasn't a very romantic proposal, but it proved enough. The rep walked slowly toward him, noting that there was a silly smile on her face, and feeling that sort of wonderful amazement of the first moments of a long-awaited sexual encounter. *It's happening*, the android told herself. *Better yet, it's going to happen.* And so Bruna reached for Lizard and put her palms on his chest, feeling the warmth of that hard yet comfortable body, and, leaning against him, put her tongue inside his mouth. His tongue was cold and tasted of whisky. And the android, who liked only white wine, suddenly found the taste of that perfumed saliva—that strong, scented tongue—delicious.

Desire ignited inside the rep like a sudden fit of madness. Bruna wanted to devour Lizard, wanted to feel devoured, wanted to fuse with him and burst like a supernova. She tore off her clothes, breaking the fasteners and tried to do the same to the inspector, who resisted. They rolled around the floor, panting, biting each other's mouths, squeezing and groaning in a jumble of arms and legs, looking as if they were engaged in hand-to-hand combat rather than a sexual encounter, until he managed to straddle her, catch hold of her wrists and immobilize her.

"Wait...wait...my precious savage. Take your time," he whispered hoarsely.

And in that position, holding her trapped by his weight, Lizard calmly removed the last of his clothes while the rep trembled between his legs and watched him undressing for the first time, taking pleasure in that glorious, wonderful moment when a lover's body is revealed. Both of them were now naked, and slowly, while their bodies were connecting and their skin communicated of its own accord, Paul leaned over her and opened her lips with his own.

For Bruna, sex was a strange and incomprehensible thing. When it was a matter of an occasional lover, when she only wanted to warm her body, it was sharp, loud, and simple. But when her partner was also warming her heart, as was the case with Lizard, then sex became something deep and complex, and the mere act of kissing was like beginning to fall into each other.

They separated briefly to catch their breath; they moved apart to look at each other, to confirm the wonder of being together. Lizard's body was robust, not fat, the skin a little worn with age. How Bruna loved that mature skin, she who would never reach old age. In the middle of his chest, and stretching upward from his pubis, there were two handfuls of hair—surprising in an era when all men completely waxed their bodies. The rep buried her face in the tight curls of the man's sex, enjoying the scratchy feel of that soft undergrowth and the woody smell of his body. She needed to possess all of Paul, to become acquainted with every inch of his skin, kiss his small marks and scars, run her tongue over those hidden folds. That was what the rep was doing—smelling and licking and exploring that warm, marvelous territory—when Paul grabbed her by the arms and, lying on top her, slowly penetrated her. *We're blending our* kuammil, thought Bruna unexpectedly, feeling round, huge and complete, totally filled by Lizard. And she pulled herself tightly against him until she had succeeded in touching his heart and killing death.

CHAPTER THIRTY-NINE

When Bruna arrived at the Bear Pavilion, Nopal was already there. He was gazing at the glass wall of the tank in a melancholy fashion. Tons of shimmering blue water, still and empty, were pressing against the glass. Melba was nowhere to be seen.

"I don't have any luck with that wretched bear. I never manage to see her. Are you sure she exists?" asked Pablo by way of a greeting.

"Positive."

She sat down on the bench next to the memorist without really knowing how to behave. Nopal had called her that morning—after Lizard had gone, luckily. He supposedly wanted to give her back the *netsuke* that he had kept when they'd had to remove her clothes at the Forensic Anatomy Institute. Bruna was still in bed when he rang, protected by the smell of Paul, by the traces of Paul's fingers, and by the memory of the warmth of his body, and when Nopal suggested to her that they meet, the idea seemed like a good one to the rep. In fact, she was so receptive to the idea that she was the one who picked the pavilion as their meeting place.

Now that she was seeing the memorist face to face, however, the rep was feeling bewildered and uncomfortable. *What am I doing here?* she asked herself. And then, concerned, she thought she'd made a serious mistake in coming. There were too many unspoken issues between them, and now they were cramming the android's mouth and leaving her mute.

"Here. Your necklace."

Bruna took it. The little man with his sack. The image of a mother, the smell of her perfume, the rustle of her dress; the fleeting farewell kiss on party nights immediately switched on in her mind. She felt a mild unease.

"It belonged to your mother, didn't it? All that business of the kiss at night...It was your mother."

"Yes."

The unease grew. Not only was her memory a complete lie, but on top of that she was also now certain that it was another's memory: Nopal's. And the knowledge that her false memory was someone else's reality turned that falsehood into something much more harmful and grotesque, in the same way that knowing some reps might have more years to live intensified the anguish of dying.

"Keep your damned necklace. I don't want it," said Bruna, throwing the *netsuke* onto the bench.

Nopal didn't touch it.

"I gave you the best I had, Bruna," he said calmly.

"And also the worst. All that pain—for what? The death of my father—why? The evil and the suffering. None of that makes any sense."

"You have three times as many scenes as other technos. You're much more complex. You know about melancholy and longing. And the emotion that beautiful music or a word or a picture inspire. What I mean is that I gave you beauty, Bruna. And beauty is the only eternity possible."

They looked at the tank of water in silence for a few minutes. That blue, hypnotic wall. Then it was true that she was different. What she'd always felt was now being confirmed. And for some reason, that certainty reassured her. *Four years, three months, and eight days.* She bit her lip, annoyed by her instinctive counting. Now, each time that obsessive countdown fired off inside her head, Bruna recalled Copa Square's words with a sudden bitterness: *Wouldn't you be capable of doing anything in exchange for living even one year longer?* he'd asked. *No,* said the rep to herself. *Not anything.* Or that's what she hoped.

Everything had changed these past few days; everything was so confusing. Beginning with the unlikely fact that she was sitting next to her memorist. She sneaked a peek at him, amazed that she wasn't feeling more terrified. Bruna had always believed that she'd be horrified to meet her writer, that she'd hate him for having given her such a painful existence. And yet...The android was unable to define exactly what it was she felt for Nopal. There was resentment, but fascination, too. And something resembling love. And gratitude. But why gratitude? For having created an identity for her? For making her distinct and proud? For designing her to be like him? But on the other hand, if Pablo Nopal had made her in his image and likeness, then had she also inherited his killer instincts? All those times when she'd killed—weren't they just the result of her genetic conditioning? Thinking about all that made her hair stand on end.

"You killed Habib, but you saved my life. I suppose I ought to thank you."

"Your life is very important to me, because I gave it to you. But I didn't kill anyone."

"You're lying."

"How would I have known that you were in the Reina Sofía Hospital? Or that Habib was going to attack you?"

"True, those are good questions. How did you find out?"

Nopal smiled.

"Let me tell you something, Bruna. I'm innocent. *Innocent*. And so are you."

He picked up the necklace from the bench and stood up. Stepping up to her, he placed it around her neck. It was such a natural act that Bruna didn't object. She simply remained seated where she was, like an idiot, looking at him. The memorist bent over and kissed her on the cheek.

"Be good," he said.

And he walked away.

Seconds later, the bear appeared, swimming majestically in the intense blue, her spongy fur waving around her body like sea anemones. The last of her species, that oh-so-solitary Melba. Then Bruna did what she'd spent several days thinking about doing and punched a number into her mobile. Natvel's moon-face filled the screen. The tattooist looked at the android impassively and merely asked, "Now?"

"Now. Please."

"A bear. You're a bear, Bruna."

The words of the essentialist didn't surprise her at all. If the rep had come to the pavilion today, it was because she had intuited the tattooist's reply. *There is nothing magical about it at all*, Bruna told herself skeptically. It was nothing more than a consequence of the nexin, that experimental enzyme that boosted her ability to empathize. She had undoubtedly picked up Natvel's thoughts during their last encounter. But despite her intense dislike of the esoteric, the rep felt strangely moved. She got up from the bench and walked over to the glass.

Melba was looking at her from the other side, eyes like black buttons. Bruna pressed her palms up against the glass, sensing the weight and push of the water, the turbulent power of that other life. And for an instant, she saw herself next to the bear, the two of them floating in the blue of time, in the same way that Bruna had floated in the night and the rain nearly two years ago, next to the dying Merlín; floating on that bed like a piece of flotsam in the midst of a shipwreck. All of which was very painful but very beautiful, too. And beauty is eternity.

"You're Husky! Aren't you? You're Bruna Husky!"

Someone was tugging at her arm, dragging her out of the never-ending blue. She turned around. Three adolescent humans, two boys and a girl, seemed tremendously excited to see her.

"You're Husky. What luck! Can we make a rep-video of you?"

The young people pointed their mobiles at her, recording her from every angle.

"Hey, what are you doing? Cool it. Leave me alone!" she growled.

Bruna was accustomed to inspiring fear in humans even when she was smiling, and terror if she was angry. But now, despite her growls, the kids continued to leap around her without batting an eyelid. She literally had to run to escape from their enthusiasm, and when she had raced out through the main doors of the Bear Pavilion and reached the avenue, she could already see the recording the kids had just made playing on the public screen.

"By all the damned species!"

She started to walk up the street, paying attention to the screens and seeing herself on many of them. Some were images that had been displayed earlier, when they were looking for her as an assassin: Bruna as Annie Heart, and Bruna as herself, going into the Majestic or into the HSP headquarters. But there were many more. She even saw the data on her own ID tag. And now they weren't accusing her of anything—quite the opposite. Now the public screens were gushing with an exaggerated tale of heroism. At grave risk to her own life, Bruna Husky the technohuman had managed, on her own, to dismantle an extremely dangerous conspiracy. Technohumans were very good. Supremacists were very bad. And the Labarians and the Cosmics were extremely bad, always conspiring from on high to take control of Earth. Astonished, she connected to the news on her mobile, usually somewhat more reliable than the public screens, although only by a little. The conspiracy had collapsed like a house of cards. Various police officials, a horde of extremist heavies, several lawyers, a judge, and two people high up in the Central Archive, had been arrested. Chem Conés, the acting president of the region, was declaring emphatically that, with the invaluable assistance of technohumans—loyal colleagues in the government and on the planet—he would get to the very bottom of this repugnant supremacist plot. It made Bruna ill to listen to all that fake waffle, that lying tale of a happy world, being trumpeted aloud with such effrontery by one of the most vicious of racists. Conés was going to save his own neck and his position, like so many other fanatics. Of course, foiling the conspiracy wasn't going to put an end to supremacism, nor to the tension among the species, nor to the devious underground activities of Cosmos and Labari, always keen to destabilize the United States of the Earth and extend their power and influence over the planet. *But at least it's a battle that has been won*, sighed Bruna. A breathing space. A reprieve.

The news was so exciting that the rep felt an impulse to call Lizard to talk over what was happening, but she held back. He hadn't gotten in touch with her either. As she thought about the inspector, a small knot of unease lodged itself in her breast. Lizard had woken up very late; he'd had to leave in a hurry; they hadn't made any arrangements. She didn't even know for sure that they would see each other again. But then again, wasn't she a bear? A solitary animal, just as the psych-guide had said. The one that didn't live in a group or even with a partner.

"Better that way," she said out loud. "Less possibility of confusion and making a fool of yourself."

Four years, three months, and eight days.

Or maybe eight years, three months, and four days.

Bruna knew she was going to die, but perhaps she no longer knew the exact date.

She tried to contact Yiannis again. He still wasn't answering. She had tried to get in touch with him a few times since she'd been released from jail. He never answered. At first, she hadn't persisted. She assumed he was hiding, ashamed, and she herself was a bit annoyed with him for being such a bigmouth. But now the lack of any news of the archivist was starting to concern her. She decided to stop by his apartment.

She crossed Madrid with growing discomfort, because everyone was looking at her and pointing her out. She tried to take a cab, but because there was another sky-tram strike, all the cabs were taken. The world had gone back to being full of reps, as if they had emerged from under the rocks where they'd been hiding, and many of them greeted her like a long-lost friend as she went by. She began to feel really irritated.

Someone was moving out of Yiannis's building. A busy crew of robot-movers was transporting boxes and furniture into a truck. She went up in the elevator with one of the robots, and they stopped on the same floor. Bruna had a terrible feeling. She went out onto the landing with the squeaking, metallic machine behind her and did, indeed, find Yiannis's front door open and the apartment half-emptied. In the entry hall there was a blonde human wearing overalls, loading up the robots as they arrived. The one that had come up with the rep was given a small tower of stacked chairs.

"What's going on here?"

The blonde looked at her as if she were an idiot.

"What do you think? A moving company, transport robots. And the answer to today's mystery question is…" she said sarcastically, using the patter from a popular competition.

"What I mean is, I know the tenant, Yiannis Liberopoulos. I didn't know he was moving. Where is he?"

"No idea."

"Where's the furniture going?"

"Nowhere. It's not actually a move. It's a sale. He's sold the entire contents of his apartment. We're emptying it."

"What? But…that's not possible."

Her consternation was so obvious that the blonde softened and set about consulting the job information stored on her mobile. Four robots were lined up in front of her waiting to be loaded, making a slight tinkling sound as they idled.

"Here it is…Yes, Yiannis Liberopoulos. Just as I told you. Sale of entire contents. How odd…There's no address for him, no information about him. There is a contact person, a

Bruna Husky. She's the one who's to be paid the money for the contents."

"What?!"

The rep grabbed the woman's hand and, giving it a tug, checked the screen of the mobile for herself.

"Hey!" protested the blonde.

Yes indeed, there was her name. The sole beneficiary of the sale. Bruna turned around and raced off. She thought she knew where Yiannis would be.

"You're welcome, lady, you're welcome!" she heard the blonde complaining behind her.

By the great Morlay, let me get there in time, please; let me get there in time, the rep kept murmuring as she ran. She decided not to take the travelators because they were so congested that they'd slow her down, so she covered the distance as quickly as she could on foot. It was a punishing forty-minute run, and when she entered the Finis Building, she was out of breath. She headed for the reception desk in the middle of the lobby but spotted Yiannis before she reached it. He was sitting in one of the armchairs in the waiting room, gloomy and lost in thought. She went up to him and dropped down into the chair beside him.

"What are you doing here?" she panted.

The archivist jumped and gave her a startled look.

"Ah, Bruna…Well…I'm sorry…So…you see…"

And he gestured vaguely around him: the spacious, pretty waiting area done up in soft green colors, with intimate, indirect lighting, and peaceful music. A dozen other people—some on their own, some in couples—were scattered throughout the space, but apart from the background music, silence and an air of devotion reined, as if the waiting area were a church.

Finis was the biggest euthanasia company in the USE, and the only one operating in Madrid.

"Yes, I see. But the question is, what the hell are *you* doing here?"

"Well, that's obvious. I'm no use for anything. I don't like life. And I'm already very old."

"Rubbish. You're useful to me. I need you. Come on, let's go. We'll talk about it calmly, but outside. This place terrifies me."

"It's not true. I'm no use to you. They almost killed you because of me. I'm an old imbecile. I should have made this decision long ago."

"Do you know what Merlín would have given to be able to go on living, damn it?!" Bruna howled in outrage.

Her shout reverberated around the lobby, and everyone stared at her. Two security guards rapidly headed her way.

"You have to leave right now. You're disturbing the peace in this place."

They were two solid combat reps. Bruna stood up calmly, feeling a barbaric, self-destructive joy.

"This is going to be amusing," she muttered fiercely.

"No, no. Keep still. Calm down, please," begged Yiannis, grabbing her arm.

And then, turning toward the guards, he said, "We're going. We're on our way right now."

And so they were. They left Finis, walking side by side like two zombies, too agitated to talk. A few hundred feet farther along there was a tiny urban park, barely the size of a traffic circle. They headed toward it without thinking and sat down on a bench underneath a young birch tree. The tree was full of shoots. It was a lovely morning. February was one of the best months of the year; after that the heat started to become oppressive.

"See what a lovely day it is. It's bad taste to want to kill yourself on such a beautiful day," grumbled Bruna.

"I have nothing. I've given up my apartment. I've sold my furniture."

"I know."

"I've transferred all my money to you."

"I'll return it to you, don't worry."

They sat quietly for a short while.

"Everything's happened so quickly: adolescence, youth, the death of my son, the rest of my life. One day you wake up and you're an old man. And you can't understand what's happened. How quickly it's all gone by."

"If you don't carry out any more idiocies like the one today, you're still going to live longer than me. Don't make me angry."

"'*Non ignoravi me mortalem genuisse*—I've always known I was mortal,' Cicero used to say that."

"'*Neque turpis mors forti vito potest accedere*—death is not ignominious for those who are strong.' Also Cicero."

The archivist looked at her, delighted.

"You remember!"

"Of course, Yiannis. You've taught me many things. I've already told you that you're useful to me in all sorts of ways."

They were silent again, but it was a companionable silence. Suddenly, Bruna visualized the seat they were sitting on, the circular garden, the city of Madrid, the Iberian Peninsula, the greenish-blue globe of the Earth, the small solar system, the multiarmed galaxy, the vast cosmic darkness dotted with constellations, red dwarves, and white giants…the entire universe.

And in the middle of that indescribable immensity, she wanted to believe for just one moment in the consoling illusion that she wasn't alone. She thought about Yiannis. And Maio and Mirari. About Oli. Even about Nopal. And in particular, she remembered Lizard, to whom she dedicated a very light thought, a barely there thought, holding her breath. There was a time to laugh, a time to embrace. Although bears might only come together to mate, maybe she would be different in this, too.

"Well," sighed the old man. "Then I'll have to see if I can rent my apartment again, And I'll go to the archive to see if they'll rehire me now that everything's over. Although, you know—and I'm not saying that I want to kill myself, not anymore—but there's something marvelous about getting rid of oneself. That supreme liberty of ceasing to be who you are. Putting myself back in my old existence seems quite depressing to me."

"Then don't do it. Find yourself another apartment. And work with me. I'm suggesting that you become my business partner."

"Are you serious?"

"Absolutely. You know a lot about everything and you're very good at research, comparing information, and analyzing things logically. We'd make a formidable team."

Yiannis smiled.

"It would be fun."

"It will be fun."

The public screen closest to them started to broadcast some breaking news: "Parliament has declared that it is illegal to charge for clean air." Yiannis gave a small shout of joy.

"You see. I told you. We mustn't give up hope! We mustn't stop pushing for things to improve!"

Even Bruna was impressed, although the rep wasn't as convinced as the archivist. The owners of the clean air would undoubtedly find some loophole, and the Zero Air Zones would continue to be miserable, contaminated ghettos that poor people would have real difficulty leaving. But even so, the constitutional resolution was very important. Bruna had been able to experience a fundamental social change in her short rep life after all. With a bit of luck, perhaps even that child deported by the tax police would experience one, too.

"Congratulations, Yiannis. You're going to be very useful to me. So let's test your powers of deduction: Why me?"

"Why you?"

"Yes. Why did RoyRoy pick me?"

"I don't know. Let me see...Well, you're a combat rep; you look pretty terrifying with that line that divides you; you suited her purposes very well from a media point of view in terms of what she wanted to achieve; you're a detective, so it was likely you'd have weapons...And besides, it gave Habib an excuse to hire you. In fact, you had the perfect profile. It could be that they used a profile search program and your file came up."

Ah yes, the ubiquitous electronic affinity programs. People used them all the time to find employees, carpenters, lovers, friends. Yes, maybe Yiannis was right; maybe she had found herself caught up in this nightmare thanks to a stupid, blind machine. There was always a degree of banality in every tragedy.

"It's a good hypothesis. You see. You did really well. Shall we go to Oli's bar to celebrate?"

As she got up, Bruna noticed that there was something on the ground next to the bench. She moved it with the tip of her shoe. It was a torn, dirty 3-D poster: "Repent!—February 3—The End of the World." The words flashed faintly, almost out of power. It was one of the banners belonging to the Apocalyptics.

"Today is the third, isn't it?"

"Yes."

Bruna looked around her. The splendid morning, the peaceful garden.

"Well, it looks like the world isn't ending today after all," said the rep.

"I think not."

"Well, that's a relief."

A BRIEF NOTE

As more than one reader will no doubt have guessed, the beautiful quotation at the beginning of this book, "What I do shows me what I seek," is not from Sulagnés, the artist from the planet Gnío, but from the French abstract artist Pierre Soulages—creator, among other things, of a fascinating series of huge, completely black paintings.

ABOUT THE AUTHOR

Photograph by Violeta de Lama, 2011

Rosa Montero is an acclaimed novelist and an award-winning journalist for the Spanish newspaper *El País*. A native of Madrid and the daughter of a professional bullfighter, Montero published her first novel at age twenty-eight. She has won Spain's top book award, the Qué Leer Prize, twice—for *The Lunatic of the House* in 2003 and *Story of the Transparent King* in 2005. A prolific author of twenty-six books, her other titles include the short-story collection *Lovers and Enemies* and the novels *Beautiful and Dark*, *My Beloved Boss*, and *The Heart of the Tartar*.

ABOUT THE TRANSLATOR

Lilit Žekulin Thwaites is a Hispanist specializing in contemporary Spanish literature, translator, and former professor in the Spanish department of La Trobe University, Melbourne, Australia. She lives in Melbourne with her husband, Tim, and their three children.

14372660R00268

Made in the USA
Charleston, SC
07 September 2012